MUSCOVY

Russia through Foreign Eyes
1553–1900

MUSCOVY
RUSSIA THROUGH FOREIGN EYES
1553–1900

FRANCESCA WILSON

PRAEGER PUBLISHERS

New York · Washington

BOOKS THAT MATTER

Published in the United States of America in 1970 by
Praeger Publishers, Inc., 111 Fourth Avenue, New
York, N.Y. 10003

© 1970 in England, by George Allen & Unwin Ltd.,
London, England

Library of Congress Catalog Card Number: 70-109485

Printed in Great Britain

TO FRED

ACKNOWLEDGEMENTS

The rarity of most of the books used here would have made my task impossible without the traditional courtesy and help of the London Library and of the staff of the British Museum. The librarian of Friends' House, Ted Milligan, introduced me to the manuscript letters of George Edmondson and kindly permitted me to make many extracts to illustrate the difficulties of Daniel Wheeler. At a time of much acrimonious discussion about quotations from other people's books, Mr Montgomery Hyde generously permitted use, at my own discretion, of *The Russian Journals of Martha and Catherine Wilmot,* edited by himself and the late Lady Londonderry. Miss Mary Chamot very kindly found me exactly the picture I was looking for of a troika pursued by wolves, and advised me on other pictures. The Radio Times–Hulton Library and the Mansell collection, though commercial concerns, were painstaking and friendly beyond what they are paid for.

All these kind people took away much of the difficulty in writing this book and I am very grateful to them all. I am also grateful to my Muscovite factotum Fred Wolsey, who has taken a keen interest during the writing of this book, offering patient criticisms and wise suggestions (many of which I accepted) and carrying from end to end of London what he describes as 'far too many books written about Russia'.

SOURCES OF ILLUSTRATIONS

Plates Ia, IVa and b, VIIIb, Xa and XVIb: J. A. Atkinson and J. Walker, *A Picturesque Representation of the Manners, Customs & Amusements of the Russians*, London, 1804. Plates Ib, IIc and XIIa: Radio Times-Hulton Library. Plates IIa and IIIc: C. de Bruin, *Voyages de Corneille Le Brun*, Amsterdam, 1718. Plate IIb: J. Struys, *Voyagien door Moscovien*, Amsterdam, 1676. Plates IIIa, VIa, VIIb and line illustrations 6, 7, 9, 10 and 14; M. I. Pilnyaev, *Stary Peterbourg*, St Petersburg, 1887. Plates IIIb, Vb, VIb, XIIb, XVa and line illustrations 3, 5 and 13: Mansell Collection. Plates Va and XVIa: G. Kennan, *Siberia and the Exile System*, London, 1891. Plates VIIa, IXa and b, XIa and b, XIIIa, XIVa, XVb and line illustrations 2, 11 and 12: Dixon, Biancardi, etc. *La Russia*, Milan, 1880. Plates VIIIa and XIIIb: R. Johnston, *Travels through Part of the Russian Empire*, London, 1815. Plate Xa: A. A. Goncharov and P. V. Gordeyev, *The Kremlin of Moscow*, Moscow, 1958. Plate XIVb and line illustration 4 reproduced by kind permission of Miss Mary Chamot, from two reproductions of popular nineteenth-century prints in her possession. Line illustration 1: A. Ortelius, *Theatrum Orbis Terrarum*, Amsterdam, 1570. Line illustration 8: R. Ker Porter, *Travelling Sketches in Russia and Sweden*, London, 1813.

PREFACE

Is your journey really necessary, as they used to ask us in the Second World War? Not the journeys of the foreign visitors to Russia—they had their reasons for them—but our journey into the past to accompany them? I think it is. Many of the earlier travellers impart the excitement they felt in their discovery of an unknown country and their narratives can be read with the sort of pleasure that *Robinson Crusoe* and *Gulliver's Travels* still give. They saw Muscovy with the eyes of children to whom everything new and surprising is equally significant: black or white, repulsive or attractive. Every detail is concrete and sharp.

We have chosen to begin with, not the pioneer Herberstein, but the adventurous and lovable English sailor, Richard Chancellor who, thwarted in his search for Cathay stumbled, instead, into the court of Ivan the Terrible, all gold and jewels and barbaric pomp. (The Tudors, with English arrogance, claimed that Chancellor had discovered Muscovy as Columbus had discovered America.) Even a century later, the Dutch sailor Struys, penetrating to the Caspian, had no less a sense of wonder and discovery. His account of his imbroglios with Cossack brigands and fierce Tartars reads like a picaresque novel.

The visitors whose records are most valuable are those who lived longest in Russia, learned the language, made friends with the people: men like Captain John Perry, engineer to Peter the Great; Dr Cook, physician to Prince Galitzin; Martha Wilmot, the Irish girl who helped Princess Dashkov to write her memoirs; the Quaker Daniel Wheeler whom the Tsar Alexander I invited to drain the St Petersburg marshes; Herr Kohl who studied Russian life for six years. (Yet admittedly the French, whose visits were usually briefer, were amongst the most acute observers, as for instance Madame de Staël, whose whirlwind *tournée* lasted only two months.)

Here we must apologize for a gap; we have no Italians (except for Casanova). The Italians contributed more than any other nation to the arts and visual glories of Russia. It was Italians who from the fifteenth to the seventeenth centuries were building churches in Kiev and the walls, towers and churches of the Kremlin. In the eighteenth century it was to architects like Trezzini, Rastrelli and Quarenghi that St Petersburg owed its superb layout and many of its most splendid buildings. What did they think of the Muscovy to which they were giving so much? Unfortunately we have been unable to trace any personal account of their impressions and experiences. Yet it matters little, for their record in marble, stucco, in stone and gorgeous ornament are more lasting than the records of foreigners who have left us only words. Again it was Italians who, in the 1730s, brought opera to St Petersburg; it was Italians who, along with the French, taught Russians the ballet. On Scythian soil they sowed seed which bore strange fruit —something different and magical which the West still enjoys.

Each of our many travellers tells something about Russia which can be discovered in no other way. With their foreign eyes they saw, in startling colours, things that to the natives were so familiar that they never noticed them. Unfortunately, as all these travellers, except Macarius, Patriarch of Antioch, were Westerners they were convinced that they belonged to a superior culture, an attitude which scarcely changed until the myth of the Slav soul was propagated towards the end of the nineteenth century. In consequence most of them failed to see the virtues of a primitive people or values in institutions that were not on the Western pattern. There is a tiresome note of condescension in their writings.

There is another reason why the earlier foreign impressions of Russia are especially valuable. For various geographical and historical reasons, education in Russia developed so late that few Russians wrote about their country. When Karamzin wrote his *History of Russia* at the end of the eighteenth century, he made considerable use of foreign accounts of his country. The present collection, however, is not concerned except incidentally with Russian history. The documents chosen describe the Russian scene and the Russian people: how they lived in their cities and their villages, what they ate and drank, how they built their houses, tilled their fields, worshipped at home and in their churches, bore the tyranny under which they lived, celebrated birth, marriage and death— day-to-day things, not high politics or international relationships. For this reason, few ambassadors' reports are included.

Only foreign impressions of European Russia are given. Fitzroy Maclean, in *A Person from England*, has told the exciting stories of travellers in Asiatic Russia. George Kennan's great human document *Siberia and the Exile System* is no exception to this rule. His book deals with European Russians, not with Kalmucks, Kirghiz or Yakuts. The abbé Chappe D'Auteroche's *Journey into Siberia* is also only incidentally about Siberia. His rendezvous in Tobolsk was with Venus; his story about the Russians he met on his journey.

The richest period for foreign accounts, the nineteenth century, is the hardest from which to select and, after 1860, the least necessary. We can read the Russians on themselves. For one of the strangest phenomena in European literary history had occurred. The

Muscovites, with a pentecostal suddenness, realized the potency of the written word. In the words of a Russian writer:

> 'Little more than a century was allotted to our literature to epitomize—in a violent foreshortening—the millenia of European tradition, and to add a new domain to the old spiritual universe of the West. . . . This was something strikingly different from the long, slow, organic formation of other literatures. Russian literature did not arise as a tree—slow to grow, hard to decay, organic. No, it exploded like a rocket, displaying a short, sharp, transient radiance on the darkening horizon of Western civilization.'[1]

For the first time, we in the West could read the Russian view of the monotonies and beauties of their landscape, the joys and sorrows of their people, their passions, aspirations, superstitions and beliefs, their oppressions, follies and sufferings, in Gogol, Turgenev, Herzen, Tolstoy, Dostoievsky and Chekhov; even if great poets like Pushkin and Tyutchev were sealed from us by a language we had not mastered.

Readers will come to the narratives in this book with their own prejudices. Some will be most impressed by the contrast between the Soviet Russia of today and the Tsarist Russia of yesterday; they will point to the staggering feats of the cosmonauts and scientists whose forebears were serfs; to the women effective in every walk of life, whose granddams were tied to the soil, old hags at thirty, or doomed to cards, cosmetics and idleness.

Others will find in these descriptions of Tsarist times certain perennial features. They will mutter, '*Plus ça change . . .*' They will talk of the unchanging effect of climate on Russian character, that inexorable climate: autumn with its bitter rains that turn roads into swamps; winter that, for months, buries the whole world under snow, and breeds inertia; spring which, however lyrical with sudden blossom and Easter's joys, isolates villages and farms for weeks by disastrous floods; summer with its intolerable heat, dust, flies and drought. The Soviet with all its technological skill cannot change the climate. They will point, also, to the constant effect of history and geography on the Russian character: the influence of the Orient ('Scratch a Russian and you find a Tartar'), of the steppes, vast and lonely as the ocean, breeding melancholy and a fatalistic capacity for endurance. There will be among them many who maintain that absolutism is inherent in Russia, that Siberia has a more ominous sound now, in the days of Solzhenitsyn's *Ivan Dennisovitch*

---

[1] N. Bachtin, *Lectures and Essays* (Birmingham 1963).

and *The First Circle*, than it had in the days of Dostoievsky's *From the House of the Dead.*

It is perhaps inevitable that many in the West see Russia in these sombre terms (Siberian prisons, Dostoievskian gloom) but this is to ignore the immense forward drive of the Russian people, the long hopes that characterize their attitude to the universe (Gogol's dashing troika, horses with the whirlwind on their manes). It is on the foundation of this long view that, again and again, Russia has, with superhuman effort, pulled itself out of swamps that would have engulfed another nation. In early encounters our travellers were amazed to see Russians working not for themselves but for their grandchildren. Were they guided by a star they saw in the East? The star might be, as in our day, a sputnik heralding the dawn of technological achievement, or the birth of a new hope for man. Have we in the West, in our present pessimistic mood, lost this long view?

Russia is a country of violent contrasts. This book will be useful if the reader, startled as our travellers were by the juxtaposition of these contrasts, sees Russia as a whole: on the one hand, Ivan the Terrible, on the other, Ivan the beggar saint; on the one hand, oppression and cruelty, Turgenev's despair, Dostoievsky's suffering; on the other, colour, life, triumph—the Cossack choir, the Easter ritual, Borodin's *Prince Igor*, Diaghilev's ballet. Side by side there is the darkness and— the sudden glory.

CONTENTS

PLATES

ILLUSTRATIONS IN THE TEXT

PART 1
1553–1600

TUDOR DISCOVERERS OF MUSCOVY

INTRODUCTION

When Hakluyt attributed to the English seaman, Sir Richard Chancellor, 'the strange and wonderful discovery of Russia', he was characteristically insular and ignorant. Sigismund von Herberstein had visited Russia as Imperial ambassador in 1517 and 1526, had published a book on it in 1549, and become known on the Continent as the discoverer of Russia. He had given Westerners the first extensive description of Russian history, geography, government and customs, but it could not be fairly said of him, any more than of Chancellor, that he had discovered Russia. Kievan Russia had had close links, both dynastic and commercial, with the rest of Christendom. A daughter of King Harold had married the son of the Grand Prince of Kiev and there were English mercenaries there in the eleventh century.

This so-called Kievan period in Russian history started when Vladimir accepted Christianity (c. 988), not in the Latin but in the Greek Orthodox form. It witnessed the rise of a brilliant civilization, revealed not only in architecture, literature and the applied arts but also in the spirit of freedom, so alien to the Muscovite principle of the subject's complete subjection to the state.[1]

The Kievan period came to an end when, in 1224, the Tartars invaded Russia.

> 'Few catastrophes so great or so enduring in their effects have overwhelmed a young and struggling country. The Tatars were no undisciplined horde of feckless barbarians, but a force of some half a million trained light horsemen, representing an empire which in the lifetime of Jinghis Khan, its creator, had been extended from Manchuria to the Caucasus at a cost of more than eighteen million lives. . . . Every important Russian town, Novgorod excepted, was burned or put to the sack.'[2]

For nearly two hundred years Russian principalities and city republics survived only by utter and humiliating subservience to their Asiatic masters. All contacts with the West were severed. Russia virtually disappeared from the map of Europe. Only in the fifteenth century did she begin to re-emerge. By this time the power of the Golden Horde had been broken. The yoke of the Tartars had been shaken off but they had left a legacy; the Muscovite Grand Dukes had learned from the Great Khans the

[1] G. Vernadsky, *Kievan Russia* (London, 1948).
[2] H. A. L. Fisher, *History of Europe* (London, 1936), p. 379.

art of absolute rule, an art never forgotten in Russia and, in Tsarist times, reinforced by the Church, with its emphasis on submis-
sion and its doctrine of the divine right of the ruler.

Ivan III (1462–1505) received ambassadors from the Holy
Roman Empire, but none came from England. So it came about
that, when Herberstein's book was published in 1549, no one in
England took note of it. In the forty years after it was published
it went into eighteen editions in many different languages, but no
English edition came out until 1576. For us it was Richard Chancellor who had discovered Muscovy (as unknown to us as America
when Columbus accidentally bumped into it)—and not the German Herberstein.

For readers of English this is an advantage. We get a sense of
discovery from our Tudor sailors and merchants, who noted down
everything they saw with a freshness of vision and an excitement
which we do not find in the sober and scholarly Herberstein.
Moreover, we have it in their sonorous sixteenth-century prose.

Herberstein knew some Russian and went about his studies of
Muscovy conscientiously, even consulting Russian archives.
From him the Continent took its stock notions of Russia, which
lasted for hundreds of years: the excessive cold in winter so that
the spit from your mouth freezes before it reaches the ground and
you lose your nose unless you rub it with snow; the intolerable
heat in summer, which burns up whole corn-fields and forests;
the black wolves and white bears; and, above all, the tyranny of
the Grand Duke of Muscovy, who makes all his people, even the
greatest of his princes, slaves—and these Russians, Herberstein
adds, seem to prefer slavery to freedom. As for women, they are
kept in Oriental seclusion and beg their husbands to beat them,
else they think they do not love them. As a good Catholic, Herberstein was shocked by many things: that communion was in both
kinds and given to small children, that priests married, and so on.
A good part of his account concerns the indignities he suffered at
the hands of the Grand Duke's messengers, who seemed to think
that their lord was more important than the Holy Roman Emperor
whom Herberstein represented. His outrage at these 'misunder-
standings' is the most entertaining part of his book and make
Herberstein seem quite human. He describes how he managed not
to be the first to dismount from his horse, nor the first to uncover
his head, even how he did not get up and bow to all the princes at
each fresh dish presented to him at the Grand Duke's banquet,

and how displeased the barbarous Muscovites were at his show of spirit and conscious superiority. He even allows himself a little joke in discovering in the loaf of bread the Grand Duke handed to him 'an emblem of the hard yoke and perpetual servitude of those who eat it', since it was shaped like a horse's collar.

The Continent had other writers on Muscovy beside Herberstein, the Italian Paulus Jovius, for instance, but for the Tudor English it was their own men who discovered for them that strange, half-barbarous country.

Hakluyt introduces them. When he was in Paris, as chaplain to our ambassador there, he was outraged to hear that 'in voyaging, exploration and adventure' his countrymen were despised for their 'sluggish security'. To refute this he collected, with tremendous industry, *The Principal Navigations, Voiages and Discoveries of the English Nation, by sea or overland, to the most remote and distant quarters of the earth, at any time within the compass of these 1,500 years*, a work he published in 1589.

He wants, he says, to preserve certain English exploits from 'the greedy and devouring jaws of oblivion'. True, the Portuguese had found a new way to India, the Spaniards had discovered lands westward of the Pillars of Hercules, but their way was never barred by ice, mist and darkness. Our sailors

'exposed themselves unto the rigour of the stern and uncouth Northern seas, made trial of the swelling waves and boisterous winds, which there commonly do surge and blow, sailed by the ragged and perilous coast of Norway, the unhaunted [i.e. unfrequented] shores of Finmark, the dreadful and misty North Cape.'

Hakluyt cites a letter to Henry VIII from Robert Thorne, a London merchant living in Seville. Thorne was envious of the achievements of the Spaniards and Portuguese; the English compared to them, seemed to be 'without activity or courage'. There was a route to the fabulous East still undiscovered, a way 'shorter to us than to Spain or Portugal', namely by the north-east. By this passage 'ships may have the clearness of the day without any darkness of the night', and from thence proceed to Cathay and all the Indies. Thorne was not the only one to believe in this north-east passage. Among others there were the mathematician and astrologer, John Dee and, most important of all, the veteran explorer, Sebastian Cabot, governor of the Company of Merchant Adventurers. He knew the 'perils and travails' of the expedition from his own experience. He had searched for a passage to Cathay, not by the north-east but by the north-west and, instead of the magical Cathay, had discovered only the barren Newfoundland.

It was on Cabot's advice that, in 1553, in the seventh year 'of our most dread sovereign lord Edward VI . . . certain grave citizens of London, men of great wisdom and careful for the good of their country', raised between them (each giving £25) the sum of £6,000, and fitted three ships for the exploration of the north-east passage 'for the discovery of Cathay and divers other regions'. The three ships were the *Bona Esperanza* of 120 tons, the *Edward Bonaventure* of 140 tons and the *Confidenza*. Sir Hugh Willoughby, 'a most valiant gentleman and well-born' was appointed captain of the *Bona Esperanza* and admiral of the little fleet, 'both by reason of his goodly personage (for he was of a tall stature) as also for his singular skill in the services of war' (he had fought under Henry VIII against the Scots). Richard Chancellor was appointed captain of the *Bonaventure*.[1]

The moment when Chancellor accidentally 'discovered' Muscovy was singularly auspicious for both countries. England was badly in need of new markets. Ivan the Terrible, surrounded by enemies both at home and abroad, was desperately anxious for new friends and allies—and also to import instruments of war. The Tudor adventurers did not know this, and the joy with which they were at first welcomed and the honours and favours heaped on them may have caused them some mild surprise, but they took them in their matter-of-fact way—and as the rightful due of their great nation and their great sovereigns—and were not deterred from writing critically of what they saw. It is time, now, for them to tell their own stories.

[1] Hakluyt gives us the tale of Chancellor's adventures partly in his own words but mostly in those of Clement Adams, Chancellor's friend. Adams was a learned man, who had studied at King's College, Cambridge, and then became tutor to the king's henchmen in Greenwich. Chancellor recounted his adventures to him. Adams wrote them in elegant Latin, afterwards translated. The two accounts corroborate each other, but as Adams tells us more about Chancellor than modesty allowed him to tell of himself, in the following account Adams' words are generally preferred.

RICHARD CHANCELLOR

*Discovered Russia 1553. Second journey to Russia 1555.
Drowned 1556*

THE English merchants, who at such pains and expense
had equipped the three ships for their journey to Cathay,
were anxious to have the best men available in charge of the
expedition. Hugh Willoughby was well known and had excellent
credentials. It was Master Henry Sidney (the father of Sir Philip)
'a noble gentleman, much beloved of Edward VI' who recommended the merchants to employ Chancellor.[1] Addressing the
merchants with great eloquence, Sidney said that the nobility wished
to help them in their serious enterprise, which he hoped would
prove profitable to the nation and that he could not 'profit and
stead' them in this worthy action better than by recommending to
them Chancellor whose wit had been maintained and nourished
in his own house. As he said:

'I do now part with Chancellor, not because I make little reckoning
of the man, or that his maintenance is burdenous and chargeable
unto me, but that the authority and estimation which he deserveth
may be given him. You know the man by report, I by experience;
you by words, I by deeds; you by speech and company, but I by
the daily trial of his life have a full and perfect knowledge of him.
And you are also to remember into how many perils for your
sakes and his country's love he is now to run. We commit a little
money to the chance and hazard of fortune: he commits his life to the
raging sea and the uncertainties of many dangers. We shall here live
and rest at home quietly with our friends and acquaintance: but he,
in the meantime, labouring to keep the ignorant and unruly mariners
in good order and obedience, with how many cares shall he trouble
and vex himself? We shall keep our own coasts and country: he shall
seek strange and unknown kingdoms. He shall commit his safety to

---

[1] Hakluyt is mistaken. It was Sir William Sidney, Henry's father, who
recommended Chancellor.

barbarous and cruel people, and shall hazard his life amongst the monstrous and terrible beasts of the sea. . . . If it fall so happily out that he return again, it is your part and duty also, liberally to reward him.'

After this speech the merchants began 'secretly to rejoice with themselves and to conceive a special hope that [Chancellor's] virtues already appearing and shining to the world would grow to the advancement of the kingdom'.

Cabot had drawn up instructions for the mariners under thirty-three headings. The first items dealt with discipline, but it is notable that the captain was told that he must consult with the pilot, masters and mates, although in the last resort all must obey him. The sick must be properly looked after and if any man die his widow should have his effects. Log-books must be strictly kept up, the names of the people of every island discovered be duly entered, with what commodities they had and what they wanted in exchange. They must 'be used with gentleness and courtesy, not provoked by any disdain, laughing or contempt'. Note must be taken if they appear to be scratching the sand for gold or metal. There was to be no missionary spirit in the adventurers: they were not to disclose to any nation the state of our religion, but pass it over in silence and be tolerant of other peoples' laws and rites. But on board ship, true religion was to be observed with morning and evening prayers; the Bible read Christianly to God's honour; blaspheming and ungodly talk be punished as well as dicing, cards and other devilish games. When possible, natives should be allured on board and plied with drink so that they should reveal the secrets of their land. Finally they must remember that sailors above all other creatures are nearest to God and daily remember the great importance of their voyage and that the honour and glory of the noble realm of England depend on it.

On May 20th the three ships were towed down to Greenwich by rowers dressed in sky blue. The mariners had bid farewell to their wives, their children and kinsfolk and some to friends dearer than kinsfolk. The court was at Greenwich (though not, alas, the good King Edward, who was sick and soon to die) and here they were given a tremendous reception, the courtiers running out and the common people standing very thick upon the shore. The ships shot their guns and the mariners shouted so that the sky rang again with the noise. At Harwich they paid their last adieu to their native country and, not knowing if they would ever see it again, many could not refrain from tears. Chancellor (who was a widower) was especially troubled, both because he left behind two little sons who might become orphans and because part of his victuals were putrefied and the hogsheads leaking but, though 'tormented with a multiplicity of sorrows and cares', he sailed up the coast of Norway.

Sebastian Cabot had adjured the mariners to keep within sight of each other but unfortunately 'because of the violence of the wind and thickness of mists' this was impossible. The ships were separated off the Lofoten Islands. Sir Hugh Willoughby's ship made better sail and was soon lost to view. Chancellor never saw the *Bona Esperanza* or the *Confidenza* again, and continually worried about their masters and crews. He wrote:

> 'If the rage and fury of the sea have devoured these good men, or if as yet they live and wander up and down in strange countries, I must needs say they were men worthy of better fortune, and if they be living, let us wish them safety and a good return; but if the cruelty of death has taken hold of them, God send them a Christian grave and sepulchre.'

A year later Chancellor learned that neither of his prayers were answered: Hugh Willoughby and his men were granted neither safe return nor Christian burial, for they had no chaplain with them. They perished of cold in an inlet off the Murman Coast, where Willoughby had decided to winter. Some Lapland fishermen found the ships, their holds still full of the woollen goods intended for sale in China (these by the Tsar's order were brought to Colmagro) and, in the cabin of the *Esperanza*, Sir Hugh's log-book and last will and testament. In this Sir Hugh explained how the 'very evil weather with frost, snow and hail' decided him to await the spring before sailing further and how he had sent men in all directions to find natives, without results.[1]

---

[2] The most imaginative account of what happened to the two ships and their crews is in a letter from Michiel, the Venetian ambassador in England, to the doge and senate in Venice. The ships, he writes, were found 'with the men on board all frozen . . . some of them seated in the act of writing, pen still in hand, and the paper before them; others at table, platter in hand and spoon in mouth; others opening a locker, and others in various postures, like statues, as if they had been adjusted and placed in those attitudes. They say that some dogs on board displayed the same phenomena. They found the effects and merchandise all intact in the hands of the natives and brought them back hither with the vessels.' (Calendar of State Papers, Venetian, 1555–56, p. 240.)

Chancellor, left alone in those unknown waters, 'became very pensive, heavy and sorrowful', but his men, though troubled because of their doubtful course, agreed with him that they must continue

> 'to make proof and trial of all adventures. Which constancy of mind in all the company did exceedingly increase their Captain's carefulness for he, being swallowed up with like good-will and love towards them, feared lest through any error of his the safety of the company might be endangered.'

Chancellor sailed on

> 'and sailed so far, that he came at last to the place where he found no night at all, but a continual light and brightness of the sun shining clearly upon the huge and mighty sea.'

Helped by this perpetual light, he sailed into 'a great bay' (the White Sea) where he found some fishermen, who were so terrified by the 'strange greatness of his ship' that they fell before him, offering to kiss his feet. Chancellor, 'according to his great and singular courtesy', raised them up, comforting them by signs and gestures. His gentleness was well rewarded. The governor of the place came on board and the common people brought victuals and were eager to trade, but did not dare without permission of their tsar.

The settlement Chancellor had found was Colmagro at the mouth of the River Dwina. (This was later replaced in importance by nearby Archangel.) Its governor told them that the country where they had accidentally landed was called Muscovy or Russia and that it was ruled over 'far and wide' by their King Ivan Vassilievitch, whom we know as Ivan the Terrible. Messengers were sent to him and, after exasperating delays, Chancellor (who had already started on his journey) received an invitation to come to the court in Moscow and an order that post-horses should be provided for him at the Tsar's expense. This overland route was for Chancellor and his men the 'strangest and most troublesome' part of their journey. They were used to venturing on uncharted seas in cockle-shells of 140 tons, but not to travelling over the tundra, the marshes, through the dark forests of northern Russia, and then over everlasting snow and ice—driven moreover in unfamiliar sledges by barbarians in sheep-skins whose language they did not understand, to a completely unknown destination. Chancellor never troubled to describe this journey in detail. All he said of it was that it was very long and most troublesome and the cold extreme and horrible. One good experience he had: the peasants when they heard of the Tsar's commands fought with each other for the honour of supplying post-horses; and so, 'after much ado, they come to Moscow, the chief city of the kingdom and the seat of the king'.

Chancellor started his report by attempting to describe the geography of Russia, 'a very large and spacious country, every way bounded with divers nations'. He was rightly impressed by its special glory, its very many and great rivers of which the Volga, falling by divers passages into the Caspian Sea, was the most famous. Moscow was bigger than London but very rude and without order, although the nine churches in the Kremlin 'were not altogether unhandsome'. These were used by certain religious men, over whom there was a patriarch. 'As for the king's palace it is not of the neatest but much surpassed by the beauty and elegance of the houses of the kings of England.' But when, after twelve days, Chancellor and his men were summoned to the Court, they were dazzled by its splendour. A hundred courtiers were dressed all in gold, down to the ankles. As for the Tsar, they wondered at his majesty. He was not only dressed in gold, he had a gold crown on his head and held a sceptre in his hand, garnished with precious stones. Chancellor, though he might well have 'been dashed out of countenance by so much splendour was nothing dismayed!' He saluted after the manner of England and gave the Tsar King Edward's letter. In this, Edward reminded whatever potentates might read it that

'every man desireth to join friendship with other, to love and be loved and also to give and receive mutual benefits; that our fathers have ever gently and lovingly entreated such as of friendly mind came to them, especially merchants who, wandering about the world search both the land and sea to carry such good and profitable things as are found in their countries to remote regions and kingdoms and to bring from the same such things as they find commodious for their own countries; that the God of Heaven and earth had provided that not all things should be found in one region, to the end that one should have need of another.'

When the Tsar had read this, he invited the newcomers to supper. The banquet was as grand as everything else, the table spread with vessels and goblets of gold. The Tsar, after crossing himself, gave each one of the courtiers bread, calling him by his name and title. (That he should remember these, Chancellor thought miraculous.) Then roasted swan was distributed and other dishes, and mead which they had to drain to the last drop.

The outcome of Chancellor's mission was highly satisfactory. The Tsar, Ivan Vassilievitch, gave Chancellor a most friendly letter to take back to his sovereign. In this, after first calling upon the mighty power of God, the incomprehensible Holy Trinity and rightful Christian belief and giving his own titles, not only as great lord of Russia, but of more than twenty cities and places in it (the repetition that had so bored Herberstein) he related how he had welcomed Chancellor into his country and would give permission to all merchants sent by our rulers to trade freely, without let or impediment, throughout his whole dominions and to come and go at their pleasure. The letter was written in the Muscovite tongue, with letters like the Greek, but it was accompanied by a translation into Dutch. Chancellor took this letter back with him in 1554 and handed it to Philip and Mary, who then declared themselves officially the discoverers of Russia and granted a charter to the Merchants of Russia or the Muscovy Company, as it became known in London. The opening up of trade between the two countries had come at an opportune time for them both. As Clement Adams points out, England in the 1550s was finding it difficult to export her textiles and desperately needed new markets. Ivan IV needed military supplies to help him in his war with the Tartars and could not get them from his Western neighbours, who were jealous of his victories, but this, of course, Adams did not know.

Before Chancellor returned to London with his important documents he learned as much as he could about the country which he had so unexpectedly discovered. The first thing that he described was the Tsar's army.

'He never goes to the field himself with under two hundred thousand men, yet does he never take to his wars either husbandman or merchant. All his men are horsemen, all archers. Their armour is a coat of mail with a skull on their heads. Some of their coats are covered with velvet or cloth of gold: their desire is to be sumptuous in the field. Partly I have seen it or else I would scarcely have believed it.... They are a kind of people most sparing in diet and most patient in extremity of cold, above all others. For when the ground is covered with snow and is grown terrible and hard with the frost, this Russ hangs up his mantle or soldier's coat against that part whence the wind and snow drives and so, making a little fire, lies down with his back towards the weather; his drink is cold water from the river, mingled with oatmeal, and this is all his good cheer, and he thinketh himself well and daintily fed therewith; the hard ground is his feather bed and some block or stone his pillow; and as for his horse, he is, as it were, a chamberfellow with his master, faring both alike.[3] How justly may this barbarous and rude Russ condemn the daintiness and niceness of our Captains who, living in a soil and air much more temperate, yet commonly use furred boots and cloaks? . . . As often as they are to skirmish with the enemy they go forth without any order at all, but lying for the most part in ambush do suddenly set upon their enemy.'

No soldiers, except foreign mercenaries, receive any wages but some are rewarded for especial valour in the field, with some farm or estate which, however, reverts to the Tsar if there is no male issue. Daughters receive nothing.

Chancellor was awed and at the same time shocked by the great power of the Tsar. If a man, because 'he was stricken in age or maimed', could do no service to him, he would take away his possessions

'and he may not once repine thereat and cannot say as we the common people of England say, if we have anything: that it is God's and our own. . . . Oh! that our sturdy rebels were had in the like subjection to know their duty towards their princes.'

As for the administration of the law, it was commendable that the Tsar heard the important cases himself, but he is 'wonderfully abused by his magistrates', commendable too that no lawyers plead in court, but every man pleads his own cause. Still, from the account of the beatings a man receives until he has confessed his guilt, and the fate of the debtor, who becomes a slave to his creditor, life in Muscovy does not appear rosy. In fact 'the poor are innumerable and live most miserably'. Chancellor heard a Russian say

'that it was a great deal merrier living in prison than forth, but for the great beating. For they have meat and drink without any labour and get the charity of well disposed people: but being at liberty they get nothing.'

[3] This hardiness of the Russian soldier is perennial and helps to explain why the most efficient army in the world did not conquer him in World War II.

In fact many sold themselves to gentlemen or merchants so that they have meat, drink and clothes. In one point only was Russia in advance of England: no one was hanged for his first offence but only for the third.

Chancellor has much to say about religion in Russia, for which he has great contempt, seeing in it 'such excess of superstition, as the like hath not been heard of'. He notes that they follow the law of the Greeks, that services are in their own language, that their priests know neither Latin, Greek nor Hebrew, that though they read passages from the Old and New Testaments every day 'they have such tricks in their reading that no man can understand them'. There are no pews: 'When the priest is at service they gaggle and duck like so many geese.' He sees idolatry in the honour paid to the ikons (though they reject 'graven images'), and notes that it is the ikon that is first saluted when a man comes into his neighbour's house. He is shocked that they don't know the Ten Commandments, holding that they were abolished by the death and blood of Christ. Few of them know the creed, holding that such holy things should not be communicated to the common people. Priests must be married, but if their wives die they must become monks and embrace chastity. Monasteries are rich, possessing a third part of the Muscovy empire. Monks are allowed no meat during fasts, only the herbs and cucumbers which they grow themselves. There are four fasts in the year, enjoined on all believers. Of this the severest is in Lent. Every Wednesday and Friday are also days when they may only eat salt fish and herbs.

The most ridiculous custom is that, when a man dies, the priest will put into the fingers of his corpse a certificate to assure St Peter that he died in the true faith and should be placed higher than Christians of the Latin church.[4]

Chancellor did not neglect his chief task. Russia could offer us

[4] Chancellor, seeing nothing in Russian religion except superstition and idolatry, gloriously certain of the superiority of his own Protestant church, set the pattern to many generations of observers. Until the twentieth century it was rare indeed for foreigners to see any virtue in the Russian Orthodox Church. Few, if any, noted that in the ceremonies of Holy Week the common people were participating in the passion of their God, living it day by day in fasting and tears until the supreme moment of joy and release, when the priest at Easter midnight, told his sorrowing congregation that Christ had risen, had risen indeed, that all now was light, joy and forgiveness, for did not each one of them on that day forgive those that had sinned against them and feel themselves bound together in love and unity? This *sobornost* (sense of unity) was at length seen to be the supreme gift of the Russian Church.

tallow, flax, hemp, wax, honey and hides. In the north they had great store of oil which they got from seals and of furs, as sable, fox, beaver, mink and ermine, and salt from sea-water. As for English wares, our woollen goods were most in demand. He described some of the towns. Novgorod, after Moscow, was the chief city of Russia. The Flemings had established a house of merchandise here, but had lost their privileges, because of their 'ill-dealing'. The Tsar did not listen to their warnings that the English were pirates but rather believed King Edward's letter. Yaroslavl, 200 miles from Moscow, was an important centre for corn, which it sent to Moscow. ('Sometimes in a forenoon a man shall see seven or eight hundred sledges, going and coming, laden with corn and salt fish', for people came from a thousand miles away to buy and sell in the Moscow market.) Vologda was another important centre; in fact this was a better market for our merchants than Moscow, because all other towns traded with it and it was cheaper by half than Moscow.

In 1555 the Muscovy merchants in London equipped the *Edward Bonaventure* for its second expedition to Russia, appointing Richard Chancellor again as grand pilot. This time they printed orders under twenty-three headings to Chancellor and the two agents who accompanied him. The most interesting of these was the admonition not only to these three but

'to the pilots, masters, merchants, clerks, boatswains, stewards, skafemasters and all other officers and ministers of the present voyage to study the instructions and acquire a perfect knowledge of the people of Russia, so that they should know the laws and customs, manners and behaviours of the people of the countries where they shall traffic, not only of the nobility, lawyers, merchants and mariners but of the common people'.

(Tudor merchants were more acutely aware than those of our day of what a study of their customers' needs and idiosyncracies could do to help their export drive.) They had not given up their longing for Cathay and begged their envoys to discover 'by conferring with well-travelled persons' if it were possible to pass from Russia by sea or land to that desired country.

Killingworth, one of the agents, reported ('in a rude letter, for lack of time') that they had been received with cheerful words by the Tsar's secretary and given a house in Moscow, where every two days they were sent eight hens, some honey and mead. On the ninth day they were invited by the Tsar to a banquet. They handed him a letter from their new sovereign Mary Tudor, whom the Tsar called his cousin. Although busy preparing for new wars, the Tsar gave them a letter to the English merchants in which he listed all the privileges he was granting them for trade in Russia. In a splendidly magniloquent preamble, he pointed out that men need amity as much as they need air and fire, in fact cannot live in quietness without it, and that this amity is increased if men traffic with one another, that merchandise furnishes men with what they need in *nourriture*, clothing, trimming and the satisfying of their delights so that they become as men living in a golden world. He not only gave the Muscovy Company the right to buy and sell all over his realm but promised that the Englishmen they sent should be within the jurisdiction of their own factor and that they should not be liable to arrest or imprisonment for debt if their factors would go surety for them. If they were robbed, the Tsar would do all he could to get reparation for them, if slain (which God forbid) the evildoers would be sought out and punished. Altogether a most satisfactory letter. Moreover Ivan Vassilievitch, by the grace of God, Emperor of Russia, Great Duke of Novgorod, promised these things not only for himself but also for his heirs, giving 'his imperial and lordly word instead of an oath'. What could be more reassuring?

In 1556 Ivan IV made a momentous decision: he would send an ambassador to the English court. Hakluyt gives the man's name as Osip Napea[5]. To Chancellor was entrusted the delicate and dangerous task of conveying this important personage and several of his suite from St Nicholas on the White Sea to England, in his cockle-shell of a ship, the *Edward Bonaventure*. She was laden with valuable merchandise; wax, train oil, furs, felts, yarn and such like, as well as sables and other costly furs and a large, fair, white falcon, for use in the hunt of wild swans and cranes, gifts which the Tsar was sending to his 'cousin' Mary Tudor.

They set sail in July. On November 10th, the *Edward Bonaventure* was driven by storms on to the rocks of the Scottish shores in a bay near Pitsligo, where she broke in pieces. The ship's boat was lowered; Chancellor used 'all carefulness for the safety of the body of the ambassador and his train' but the boat was 'by rigorous waves of the sea in the dark night overwhelmed'. By God's preservation and special favour the noble ambassador and a few

[5] He was Osip Grigorevich Nepea of Vologda. The Tsar had just given him the purely honorific title of Governor of Vologda.

others got to shore. Chancellor, with many of his mariners and seven Russians, was drowned.

It is John Innocent, secretary to the Tsar's ambassador, who gives us this brief account of the fate of the *Edward Bonaventure*, her Captain Richard Chancellor and many of her crew. John Innocent wastes no words on the loss; Hakluyt includes no comment on it. It was a ruthless age, used to danger, daring and sudden death. We who read of Chancellor in the twentieth century may feel a pang at his loss, for, of all the sixteenth-century travellers to Russia, it is he whom we know best. Henry (or William) Sidney has told us of his wit and shining qualities and of how ill he could spare him from his household, Clement Adams has stressed the heaviness of his grief at the loss of Willoughby, his continual carefulness for the welfare of his men, and his gentleness and courtesy to the natives when, in the Arctic regions of Russia, they fell at his feet in terror and he raised them up, reassuring them with kindly gestures. It is true that there is, to us, something all too arrogant in the way Chancellor describes the manners and customs of the barbarous Russians whom he has discovered. But we must remember that he had the immense pride in being English of the Tudor gentleman; when he saw nobles trembling in the presence of those of higher estate, even great princes falling to the ground before their Tsar, he was conscious of the greater dignity of our manners. Like the other adventurers of the period he was a pious man; he was convinced of the superiority of the reformed faith, so recently acquired, and of its greater purity. When he pours scorn on the superstitions of the Russians, who 'gabble and duck like so many geese' in their churches, it is because religion is not a matter of indifference to him. Moreover, matter of fact and critical as Chancellor was in his descriptions of natives and customs so alien to him, he had a moment of vision and wrote these strangely prophetic words of the Russian people:

> 'If they knew their strength, no man were able to make match with them, nor they that dwell near them should have any rest of them. But I think it is not God's will; for I may compare them to a young horse that knoweth not his strength, whom a little child ruleth and guideth with a bridle, for all his great strength, for if he did know it neither child nor man could rule him.'

We are not told how London received the news that the gallant Chancellor, the 'discoverer of Muscovy', had perished on the

B

Scottish shore. No doubt the loss was forgotten by the sensation-loving populace in the excitement of seeing their first live Russians riding through their streets in one of the most gorgeous processions the capital had ever witnessed. It was headed by the Lord Mayor and Aldermen in scarlet and a great number of merchants. Osip Napea looked grand too, for outside London, he had been given velvets and silks for a riding garment. He was travel-stained from his long, hazardous journey, not only by sea but through the muddy tracks of Scotland and England. It was difficult to move for the vast crowds 'plentifully running on all sides'. Later Napea was presented at Court and graciously received by Philip, who was on one of his rare visits to England, as well as by Mary. He was feasted and cosseted, taken to a fox hunt, shown the sights of London, the Tower and the Investiture of the Order of the Garter in Westminster Abbey, but he remained suspicious and disgruntled.

'He is not as reasonable as we at first hoped,' the Muscovy Merchants complained to their agents. 'He thinks that every man will beguile him. As the Russians do not always speak truth themselves, they think that other people are like them'. The fact was that Osip could not get over the loss of the *Edward Bonaventure's* valuable cargo, which he rightly suspected had been rifled and hidden away by the rude and ravenous Scots people. The Queen sent commissioners to Pitsligo; they, with stern threats, ordered the Scots to give up their plunder but nothing was recovered except some small parcels of wax. Unlike most Russians, who throw away possessions as gaily as they acquire them, Osip kept harping on the loss. Everyone was thankful to see him and his Russian suite safely embarked at Gravesend on board the *Primrose*, in charge of the well-travelled Antony Jenkinson, Gentleman.

ANTONY JENKINSON

First journey to Russia 1557; second journey 1562;
third journey 1566; last journey as ambassador 1571

ANTONY JENKINSON was chosen to be captain of the
Primrose (to which the precious Osip Napea was entrusted
for safe conduct back to his own country) because he was
a seasoned traveller, merchant and seaman. The Company also
appointed him agent for three years. The list he gives us of his
journeys includes Spain, Portugal, Greece, Turkey, Asia Minor,
Syria and most of North Africa. In 1546, as a young man, he had
been sent into the Levant as training for a mercantile career.
In 1553 he was at Aleppo and wrote an account of the entry into
that city of Solyman the Great, whose permission he received
to trade in Turkish ports, free of customs' duties. He was always
eager to explore new countries and carried with him dispatches
from Queen Mary to Ivan IV, requesting the Tsar to help him on
his way to Persia and even to Cathay. Sumptuous presents were
sent to the Tsar, mainly of velvet and satin but also a lion and
lioness, and Osip Napea was also given a number of valuables, for
which one hopes he was grateful.

Three other ships sailed with the *Primrose*. The Muscovy
Merchants gave instructions to the masters and mariners of the
fleet similar to those given before, except that there was an added
urgency in their admonition to keep within sight of each other;
in dark or misty weather they should make a great noise with trum-
pets, drum, horn and gun. They sent an important letter to their
agents in Russia giving a list of the cargoes in the four ships:
mainly cloth (kersies and cotton) but also nine barrels of pewter.
The most useful merchandise to be obtained in Russia, they said,
was still wax, tallow, flax and train oil (from seals). As for hemp, it
was best to make ropes of it in Russia. Of furs they desired no
great plenty because they were dead wares; sables and rich furs

were not 'every man's money' though they could do well with
mink. Search must be made for herbs and earth that made good
dyes such as Turks and Tartars use. They were sending a young
man with knowledge of wood to get samples of yew, near the
Pechora River, and coopers to make casks, also ten young appren-
tices to be trained either to keep accounts or to buy and sell and
'some to be sent abroad to the notable cities of the country for
understanding and knowledge'. They wanted samples of steel
and copper from Tartary. They affirmed that they had been given
by Philip and Mary the monopoly of trade with Russia.

In his first letter Jenkinson related how, on May 12, 1557,
he embarked at Gravesend, and arrived safely in the bay of St
Nicholas on July 13th. The Russian ambassador and his company,
he tells us with obvious relief, 'with great joy got to shore'.
They were welcomed home with splendid presents, 'not only
rye bread and pancakes but also swans, geese and ducks and all
manner of victuals both fish and flesh, in the best manner that the
rude people could devise'.

Jenkinson himself went on to Colmagro, a hundred versts
away, and sailed in a small boat up the swift River Dwina (noticing
that the natives made 'tar' from the trees which grew by its sides)
until he came to Vologda, a great city where the houses were all
built of firwood, as also the churches, two for every parish—one
for summer, the other to be heated in winter. All the way, he never
entered into a house but lodged in the wilderness by the river's
side. 'And he that would travel that way must carry with him a
hatchet, a tinder box and a kettle to make fire and seethe him meat,
when he hath it, for there is small succour in these parts.' On
December 1st, he left Vologda in a sledge, as the manner is in
winter, with post horses. He changed fourteen times before Moscow.

On Christmas Day the Tsar invited him to a banquet at his
palace in the Kremlin. Six hundred were present, heathen as
well as Christians. Two places from the Tsar sat a boy of twelve,
the heir to the emperor of Kazan whose country Ivan had conquered eight years earlier. In another hall were feasting 2,000
Tartars who had recently surrendered to the Tsar. It was all
immensely grand and festive. The Tsar kept handing Jenkinson
dishes of meat and goblets of wine and mead. Every time the Tsar
drank or tasted a dish of meat, he crossed himself and all the company stood up. (Where Herberstein had been irritated, Jenkinson
only marvelled.)

1 Antony Jenkinson's Muscovy, 1562.

On Twelfth Night, Jenkinson witnessed the gorgeous ceremony
of the blessing of the waters. First came the long procession from
the church with lighted tapers, followed by men carrying the cross
and ikons of Our Lady and St Nicholas; then a hundred priests
and the Metropolitan himself. Last of all came the Tsar with a
crown on his head and all his nobles richly apparelled with gold,
jewels and furs. This immense crowd gathered bareheaded,
in spite of the fearful cold, round a hole that had already been
hacked out of the thick ice on the river. The priests sang, the
Metropolitan blessed the water, then cast it on the Tsar, his son
and his nobles.

> 'That done, the people with great thronging filled pots of the water
> to carry home and divers children were thrown in, and sick people,
> and plucked out quickly again and divers Tartars christened. All
> which the Emperor beheld. Also there were brought the Emperor's
> best horses to drink the hallowed water.'

Jenkinson was surprised by the prestige of the Metropolitan
and greatly impressed by the authority of the Tsar ('No prince
in Christendom is more feared of his own nor yet better beloved').
He did not admire the Russians in general.

> 'They are great talkers and liars, flatterers and dissemblers. The
> women be very obedient to their husbands and go not often abroad.
> I heard of men and women that drank away their children and all
> their goods at the Emperor's taverns.'

He noted, as innumerable visitors hereafter were to note, that
in Russia it was accounted no shame to be drunk.
There follows a long account, given by one of Jenkinson's
companions, of religion in Russia. This is, on the whole, objective,
without the contempt shown by Chancellor and later foreign
visitors. On Palm Sunday there is a very solemn procession, the
Tsar leading the horse on which the Metropolitan sits, young men
spreading garments in front of it. For, after Our Lady and St
Nicholas, the Metropolitan is next to God and of higher dignity
than the Tsar himself. In matters of religion he gives sentence as
himself lists, 'whether it be to whip, hang or burn'. There are a
great many rich monasteries. 'They keep great hsopitality and re-
lieve much poor people day by day.' At Easter, after the fasting
and mourning of Holy week, they have the resurrection

> 'whereof they rejoice. For when two friends meet during the Easter
> holy days, the one of them says, the Lord of Christ is risen, the other

answers, it is so of a truth and then they kiss and exchange their eggs, both men and women continuing in kissing four days together.'

At christenings the godfathers and mothers all spit to exorcize the devil. The godfather hangs a cross round the baby's neck. This he wears all his life 'else he is no Christian'.

The thing that rouses real indignation in honest English breasts is the way marriage is solemnized. This is in most points abominable. First the man sends the woman a small box in which there is a whip, needles, cotton, scissors, etc., and perhaps some raisins or figs, 'giving her to understand that if she offend she must be beaten with a whip; by the needles, etc., that she must apply herself diligently to sew; by the fruits, that if she do well, no good thing shall be withdrawn from her.' When the marriage day is appointed, the bride makes a great show of resistance, shutting herself up, sobbing and weeping, until she is dragged to the church by two women. The marriage ceremony is much as ours. Afterwards there is drinking, singing and dancing that lasts for three days. However poor they are the bridegroom is called a duke, the bride a duchess.

'One common rule is amongst them, if the woman be not beaten with the whip once a week she will not be good, and the women say if their husbands did not beat them they would not love them.'

When a man or woman dies, they stretch him out and put a new pair of shoes on his feet because he has a great journey to go, then they wind him in a sheet as we do and put a testimony in his right hand which the priest gives him to testify to St Nicholas that he dies a Christian man or woman. Their friends follow the corpse, always laid in an open wooden coffin, to the church carrying wax candles, weeping and howling. When a man is hanged he is given no testimony; 'how they are received into heaven, it is a wonder, without their passport.'

'There are a great number of poor people among them which die daily for lack of sustenance, which is a pitiful case to behold. . . . A great many are forced in the winter to dry straw and stamp it to make bread thereof. In the summer they make good shift with grass, herbs and roots; barks of trees are good meat with them at all times. There is no people in the world, as I suppose, that live so miserably and the most part of them that have sufficient for themselves are so unmerciful that they care not how many they see die of famine in the streets.'

They believe that in a country full of diseases the best thing is to go to their hot baths twice a week and sweat the evil out.

In 1558, Antony Jenkinson got permission from the Tsar to explore the Volga, down to Astrakhan on the Caspian Sea, which he had recently conquered. From him we get the first English account of the Tartars. Unlike Captain John Perry and many Englishmen after him, he does not admire them but considers them a wicked people. He is shocked that they have no towns or houses but move from place to place with their wives, children and cattle. (They say to their children who do not want to move, 'Will you smell your own dung, like the Russians?') They eat no bread, which they say is made from the top of a weed and makes the Christians weak, but only meat, especially horse. For drink they have blood from their horses and fermented mare's milk. They delight in no art or science except wars. When Jenkinson came to Astrakhan he found it a desert, for famine and pestilence had followed the long wars and 100,000 had died. The surviving Tartars were so miserable they might easily have been converted to the Christian faith 'if the Russians themselves had been good Christians, but how should they show compassion to other nations when they are not merciful unto their own?' Jenkinson could have bought many goodly Tartar children for the price of a loaf of bread but he 'had more need of victuals than of any such merchandise'.

Jenkinson crossed the Caspian Sea, penetrating to Bactria and Bokhara, where we cannot follow him except to note that even in these countries, outside his jurisdiction, the Tsar's fame was such that his letters saved Jenkinson on many occasions from being killed or made a slave. He could not get to Persia because it was too unsettled, but he did some trade with the Tartars and rescued six Tartar ambassadors and twenty-five Russians from the prospect of slavery to the king of Samar. On his return to Moscow he kissed the Tsar's hand, gave him the men he had salvaged, a white cow's [yak's] tail from Cathay (which he hadn't reached) and a Tartary drum. Having got the Tsar's leave to depart he arrived safely at Colmagro in May 1560, and from thence sailed to England.

Jenkinson's second journey to Russia, in 1561, is of little interest for the purpose of this enquiry as he was only crossing to Persia and his account tells mainly of his experiences there. His third journey, started in 1566, was of great importance because he gained great privileges from the Tsar for English merchants. Calling upon God, the only strengthener of all things and the helper of all Christian believers, the Tsar promised his 'sister' Queen Elizabeth to grant certain valuable privileges to the Muscovy Company. Not only did he permit them to buy and sell in all part of his kingdom without paying any custom duties, but he gave them complete monopoly of trade in Russia. If any other merchants, out of what countries soever they might be, came in with their ships or waggons, their goods would be confiscated. Moreover the Company was permitted to buy houses in Vologda and Colmagro or whatever other places they liked and set up trading centres there. Jenkinson was triumphant. The Company had obtained all that their hearts desired. Moreover, the Tsar again sent an embassy to London. They presented Elizabeth with some fine sables and other rich furs, which in our climate, her courtiers felt, 'were wholesome, delicate, grave and comely, more dignified and comforting to age than the new silks, shags and rags' on which latterly we had been wasting our money.

Unfortunately the new friendship did not fulfil its promise. The first coolness came in 1567. Ivan, feeling menaced by enemies at home and abroad asked Elizabeth both for asylum in England, if he were forced to flee, and for alliance with him in his wars. Elizabeth readily promised him asylum (he would do the same by her, he said, if she needed it—she thanked him but said she did not) but she had no wish to get involved in his quarrels with his neighbours. Ivan was furious. He threatened the Muscovy Company to open trade with English merchants who did not belong to them. Elizabeth immediately sent another embassy, headed by Thomas Randolph but, though he succeeded in getting all the Company's privileges confirmed, the truce was only temporary. Ivan was still hoping for an alliance. In 1570 he wrote an angry letter to the Queen:

> 'We thought that you lord it over your domain and rule by yourself . . . but now we see that there are men who do rule beside you, and not men but trading boors, who do not think of the profit of our safety, honour and lands but seek their own merchant profit. And you remain in your maidenly estate like a common maid.'

It was to soothe the angry Tsar and patch up trade relation again that Jenkinson was sent on his fourth and last journey to Russia in 1571—this time as ambassador.

As soon as he arrived in Russia, he sent his interpreter to Moscow to tell the Tsar of his arrival. In the meantime the English agents gave him most alarming reports; they had heard it said that if ever Jenkinson came back to Russia he would lose his head. For a moment Jenkinson hesitated, wondering if he had better not return home again, but he was a brave man. Sure of his innocence, he was determined to face it out, to seek an interview with the Tsar, to hear of what he was accused and have a chance to justify himself.

For six painful months Jenkinson waited in Colmagro, with no bodyguard, no lodging appointed for him and no victuals supplied, 'according to the fashion for ambassadors, which argued his [the Tsar's] grievous displeasure towards our nation'. For four months he had no news of what had happened to his interpreter. Later he discovered that, because the whole country was 'sore visited by the hand of God with the plague', no one was allowed to travel and his interpreter, after he had gone half way, had been held in quarantine. Jenkinson sent another messenger, with a guide, by an unknown way through the wilderness, although he knew that it was strictly forbidden to travel by indirect ways. The two men were caught by a watchman who might lawfully have burned them, with their horses, but was persuaded (presumably by bribes) not to do so.

At last, on January 28, 1572, the plague having abated, a message came from the Tsar that Ambassador Jenkinson should be given post-horses and await his pleasure in Pereslav. Here he remained under house arrest for seven weeks, not allowed to see anyone, not even his own people. At last, on March 23rd, he was summoned to the court. The Tsar received him graciously, allowing him to kiss his hand. He then dismissed his courtiers all except his chief secretary and one other and told Jenkinson to come near him with his interpreter. He then, in somewhat obscure language, explained the reason for his displeasure. In 1567 he had sent Jenkinson back with a secret message to Elizabeth and had expected he would return with a favourable answer. Instead, the Queen had sent Randolph, 'but all his talk with us was about merchants' affairs and nothing touching ours'. (The secret message, as explained above, was the request for an alliance and, if necessary, asylum.)

Jenkinson replied that he had given the secret message to the Queen and that she had sent an answer back with Randolph. He could not come himself because he had been sent on another mission. He reminded the Tsar that the merchants of the Company had now been trafficking in his dominions for nineteen years and had always been ready to serve him. It was grievous that His Majesty had withdrawn all privileges from the Company's merchants (he asked that these should be restored) and that he had allowed, to trade on their own in his kingdom, rebellious agents who had given England a bad name. They were traitors who should be handed over to Jenkinson to take back home. The Tsar said he could not read the Queen's letters yet nor give an answer, because it was the week before Easter which must be spent in fasting and prayer. He then dismissed Jenkinson to his lodging but sent him a dinner 'ready dressed with great store of drinks of divers sorts'.

Jenkinson received a reply from the Tsar only six weeks after he had presented him with a detailed list, in writing, of complaints. These were mainly that English merchants could not recover their debts, not even from the imperial treasury, and were not allowed to pass down the Volga to Astrakhan and over the Caspian Sea to fetch their fellow traders out of Persia with their goods, and that English artificers had been kept in Russia against their will.

The Tsar replied most reasonably, promising to redress nearly all of the grievances. One thing he refused and that was to compensate the English for what they had lost in a Moscow fire, 'for that it was God's doing' and not his. Jenkinson left his interpreter behind to collect the debts and receive the letters of privilege. The Tsar sent him a gentleman 'charged to conduct him and provide boats, men, post horses and victuals all the way to the seaside, an enormous distance for such a provision'. At Colmagro he waited for a month. The Tsar had promised to send back for punishment the agent who had traded on his own and sown dissension, but he never turned up. On July 23rd, Jenkinson sailed for home. He wrote;

> 'And thus, being weary and growing old, I am content to take my rest in mine own house, chiefly comforting myself, in that my service hath been honourably accepted and rewarded of Her Majesty and the rest by whom I have been employed.'

That Jenkinson felt old and weary after his last exhausting experience in Russia, where his very life was in danger (as it had been many times on his travels), is scarcely surprising, although he was destined to live another forty years. (In 1572, when he retired from his travels, he was probably still under fifty.) One hopes that he enjoyed taking his rest in his own house. He had, in 1568 married Judith Mersh, a relative of Sir Thomas Gresham, by whom he had five daughters and a son, all of whom married.

Jenkinson was the first of our merchant seamen to cross the dangerous and unknown Caspian Sea and penetrate into central Asia, even to the legendary Bokhara, which in the nineteenth century was to become part of the Russian Empire. He was an acute and accurate observer and added considerably to geographical knowledge. England had already had, from Chancellor, a picture of manners and customs in Muscovy but he added many significant details. He wrote of his experiences in such a matter of fact style, avoiding all grandiloquence and exaggeration, that one is apt to forget how extraordinary they were, and what courage and tenacity were needed to face them.

His country made some acknowledgement of the debt they owed him. In 1568 Jenkinson received a grant of arms. The preamble described him as 'one who for the service of his prince, weal of his country and for knowledge sake, hath not feared to adventure his life and to wear his body with long and painful travel into divers and sundry countries'.

STEPHEN BURROUGH

*First journey with Chancellor, 1553; second journey
towards the Ob, 1556; third journey 1557*

STEPHEN BURROUGH'S title to fame is that he was the
first of our merchant seamen to discover Novaya Zemlya
and to make contact with the Samoyeds. He had been master
of Chancellor's ship on the first voyage and was now sent by the
merchants to explore further into the North-East Passage and at
least penetrate as far as the River Ob. The English of that time
believed that Cathay, or China, was a little to the east and south
of this river, and the merchants passionately wished to reach it and
to exploit its fabled riches. The discovery of Russia had been
incidental, a deviation which must not distract from the original
grand scheme.

Although, as we shall see, Burrough did not get as far as the
Ob, and indeed only crossed a quarter of the vast distance
between Norway and the Bering Straits, no other explorers after
him got much farther east until the nineteenth century.

Burrough wrote a factual and lively account of his experiences.
In April 1556 he sailed down the Thames on the pinnace
Searchthrift. The good old gentleman, Master Cabot, came aboard
the ship at Gravesend, giving the mariners right liberal rewards
and a feast for Burrough at 'The Christopher', after which he
danced amongst the rest of the young and lusty company. 'Which
being ended, he and his friends departed most gently, commend-
ing us to the governance of Almighty God.'

Almighty God did indeed help Burrough in many ways and
fashions, especially by sending him Gabriel, a friendly Russian
mariner bound for Pechora to fish for salmon. He guided Burrough,
pointing out the shoals, and lent him two anchors, for his own were
too big. A nasty fellow called Keril quarrelled with Gabriel and
complained to Burrough that one of the anchors was his. When

Burrough threatened to report him he kow-towed, telling him that he was the son of a gentleman whereas Gabriel was only a priest's son, so that he, Keril, could 'do him more pleasure'. This did not go down well with Burrough, who considered Keril vainglorious. He gave Gabriel two small ivory combs and a steel mirror, but to Keril only a dish of figs. In July, off the mouth of the Pechora, they met their first iceberg, 'a fearful sight to see', and 'a whale' which would have upset the pinnace if the sailors had not scared it away with loud shouts. They discovered the island of Novaya Zemlya, and on the mainland met their first Samoyeds. The Russians told them that this name meant that they eat each other and they warned Burrough against them. On shore he found a heap of hideous Samoyed idols, with stones covered with blood in front of them. The people went about in carriages drawn by reindeer, they were dressed in reindeer skins, had no houses, no corn or bread. They appear to have been gentle enough, bringing the newcomers wild geese and white bear-skins, but Burrough thought of them with horror. (Captain John Perry, in the eighteenth century, found them gentle indeed and their religion sensible, for they worshipped the sun. He thought their reputation as cannibals exaggerated.) On the way back, harried by storms and ice, Burrough made Colmagro, where he wintered, giving up further exploration.

Richard Johnson, who sailed with Burrough on the *Searchthrift*, wrote an even more terrifying account of the Samoyeds, whose devilish rites he witnessed. He saw their priest stab himself with a sword after singing as 'we use here in England to hallow, whoop or shout at hounds'. He fell down as dead when his god spoke to him, yet none could tell Johnson what the god had said. In Novaya Zemlya itself they saw no people, only white foxes and white bears.

Burrough was forced to winter at Colmagro. 'Without the great help of God, who never faileth them at need that put their sure trust in Him', his bark would 'never have been able to brook such monstrous and terrible seas'. Moreover, there was a great and terrible abundance of ice, and in late August 'the nights waxed dark and the winter began to draw on'. He hoped to be able, the next summer, 'to proceed further in the intended discovery of the Ob'. In this he was not successful.

Burrough's abortive voyage had an interesting sequel. His factual account of his discoveries was not forgotten by the

Muscovy Company. In 1580 they fitted out another expedition. One ship was under the command of Arthur Pett, a second under Charles Jackman. This time the merchants were so sure that the ships would get through to Cathay that they sent with the sailors a letter from Elizabeth, in Latin, to the Mighty Prince and Emperor of Cathay. They were advised to find some small island which they could plant and fortify and where they could keep their stores, 'from whence we might feed those heathen nations with our commodities without cloying them or venturing our whole mass in the bowels of their country'. When they got to Cathay they should get maps of the country and books about the language, to see if it was true that they had printing before it was devised in Europe. They might even be able 'to sail over to Japan Island, where you shall find Christian men, Jesuits of many countries of Christendom and perhaps some Englishmen'. In the Arctic circle they were sure to find a good market for warm woollens and might in return get masts, pitch, tar and hemp for the Navy. They might even settle some Englishmen there, 'the offals of our people', as the Portuguese had done in Brazil. From Cathay they must bring back with them, besides the maps and books, 'seeds of all strange herbs and flowers which will delight the fancy of many for their strangeness, coming from so far off'.

Particularly curious is the list of the samples of goods which they were to take with them to dazzle the Chinese. This is very long but, besides every kind of woven and knitted goods, one may note girdles, gloves and shoes of leather, great and fair mirrors for women, glasses of English making, spectacles, ivory combs, needles and buttons, pewter goods, knives of good edge, gold and silver coins. They must also take the sweetest perfumes, 'marmelade' and dried fruits, apple John, sack and vials of good sweet waters with which they might besprinkle guests when they came aboard their ships. Most important was a map of England and a large map of London 'to make show of your city, with the river drawn full of ships' and a herbal 'which may much delight the Great Khan'.

Needless to say the Great Khan never saw the herbal, nor were Chinese guests besprinkled from the vials of good sweet waters or dazzled by seeing the number of ships on the map of the Thames. The boats had to turn back even before they got to the Ob. Golden Cathay was as far off as ever.

JEROME HORSEY

Several journeys to Russia from 1572 to 1591

OF all Tudor visitors to Russia, Horsey was the one who knew her best. The Muscovy Company sent him there as one of their agents in 1572, and there he spent the best part of eighteen years. Although, in the end, he had a very bad reputation both with the Russians and the Company and was accused of fraudulent dealings, he managed to survive and even to retain the favour of Queen Elizabeth.

Though an unscrupulous knave, Horsey is worth quoting because he tells us things that no other Tudor visitor relates. He is the first, for instance, to comment on the beauty and richness of the Russian language, which he spoke fluently. He said it was 'the most elegant and copious in the world'. When Horsey gave Elizabeth a letter from the Tsar, she was fascinated by the script which, she said, 'had some affinity with the Greek. I could quickly learn it.' She prayed Essex who was standing by her, to learn 'the famousest and most copious language in the world'. Essex pretended to be delighted by the idea and said that he would, when he had more time to spare.

Horsey's longest and most revealing account he called *A Relation or Memorial* and dedicated to Sir Francis Walsingham and to other loving friends who desired some account of his travels. It contained many things that the Company would not have liked to have had broadcast to the public; it might have closed the doors of Russia to them. With the caution of a wise editor, Hakluyt published extracts only from the duller of Horsey's writings. (Most of the *Relation* was published by Purchas in 1626.)

Horsey writes in horrifying detail of the hideous cruelties and orgies of Ivan the Terrible. In the end he sums him up as 'a right Scythian, full of ready wisdom, cruel, bloody, merciless'. At the same time he puts some of the blame for his actions on his

subjects whom he castigates as 'wicked and vile'. 'If the old
Emperor had not held so hard a hand and severe a government
over them, he could never have lived so long.' (Our other
merchants and emissaries had usually written with politic
enthusiasm of Ivan IV, even kissed his bloody hand with deference
although, shrewd men that they were, their eyes were probably not
blinded by his gracious reception of them.)

It is from Horsey's *Relation* that we learn how seriously Ivan
took Elizabeth's promised asylum in England, for 'he lived in
great danger and fear of treasons and being done away with'.
He had many large barges built in Vologda ready to carry treasure
down the Dwina and be conveyed, with himself, on to English boats
for the escape to London. We learn, too, that Ivan consulted an
English magician[1]

> 'to know his likelihood of success if he should be a suitor for the hand
> of the Queen. And though he was much disheartened, not only that he
> had two wives living and that many kings and great princes had been
> suitors to Her Majesty and could not prevail, yet he magnified himself
> his person, his wisdom, greatness and riches above all other princes
> and said he would have a try and presently put his last wife into a
> nunnery.'

We have an account of the Tsar's wooing, in 1582, through
Pisemski his ambassador, of the Lady Mary Hastings, the Queen's
relative. Elizabeth tried to put the ambassador off by telling him
that the lady was pockmarked. Eventually she arranged an
interview in York House garden. The ambassador, whom Horsey
describes as a 'noble, grave, wise and trusty gentleman', fell
prostrate at her feet,

> 'rose, ran back from her, his face still toward her; she and the rest
> admiring [astonished] at his manner. Said, by an interpreter, it did

[1] We are indebted to the researches of J. Hamel, the learned Russian, for
information about this English magician, Dr Bomelius. He quotes the letter
which Bomelius wrote from the Queen's Bench Prison to Sir William Cecil,
begging him to set him free, so that he could accept an invitation to go to
Russia, which had been transmitted to him by the ambassador in London.
This was accordingly done and Bomelius lived for a time 'in favour and pomp'
in Muscovy, for he gained great power over the superstitious Tsar. He caused
him to commit 'many rash acts', persuaded him, also, that Elizabeth was
younger than had been reported and was willing to marry him. In the end,
accused of plotting against the Tsar with the Poles, he was tortured and 'roasted
to death' as Horsey reports. His widow was eventually allowed to return to
England. (See J. Hamel, *England & Russia*, 1st edition, 1854; new impression,
1968, Frank Cass.)

suffice him to behold the angel he hoped should be his master's spouse; commended her angelical countenance, state and admirable beauty. She afterwards was called by her familiar friends in court the Empress of Muscovy.'

(Lady Mary Hastings, although at first pleased, was later frightened by hearing of the ferocious character of her suitor and persuaded Elizabeth to save her from the proposed honour.)

Horsey tells us of the terror of the dying Tsar. He was immensely superstitious. He sent for sixty witches from northern Russia (Shakespeare's *Lapland witches*) 'where there was great sorte of them', to make divinations as to his fate.

Horsey was proud of the influence he had had over the terrible Tsar. He had found some scores of poor Scots soldiers and three Englishmen living in a most miserable manner, piteous to behold. They had been fighting for Sweden against Russia and had been made prisoners. Horsey told Ivan that they belonged 'to a venturous and warlike people, ready to serve any Christian prince for maintenance and pay'. The Tsar took them into his army and sent them against his mortal enemies, the Crim Tartars, who, armed only with bows and arrows, cried out, 'Away with these new devils that come with their thundering puffs';'whereat the Emperor made good sport'.

Ivan entrusted Horsey with a very dangerous mission. He desperately needed gunpowder, saltpetre, lead and brimstone, and wanted Elizabeth to supply him. The quickest way to get his petition through was by the land route through the Baltic states and Poland, all enemy countries. Horsey knew Polish and Dutch as well as Russian. The Tsar had the letters to Elizabeth concealed in the false side of a wooden brandy bottle, worth threepence, to be hung under a horse's mane. Horsey was twice arrested as a spy for Muscovy, but managed to persuade his captors that he was fleeing from that country. At Danzig and Königsberg he was received with honour, because he had ransomed several of their merchants out of captivity. When he came to his journey's end and opened the brandy bottle, he took out and sweetened the Tsar's letter and directions as well as he could 'but yet the Queen smelt the savour of the aqua vitae when I delivered them to Her Majesty'. The mission was successful. In 1581 Horsey was back in Russia, with munitions of war to the value of £9,000. He sailed in the company of thirteen ships, delivered the goods and received prompt payment for his masters.

Horsey was now in high favour with Elizabeth who, in 1584, sent him as envoy to the new Tsar, Feodor Ivanovitch, the weakling son of Ivan IV who had just died. Horsey gives an elaborate account of Feodor's coronation (published by Hakluyt).

Horsey, to begin with, was in high favour at court. He was especially indulged by the 'noble prince' Boris Goudunov, who 'always affected him with special liking'. Boris, the brother-in-law of the half-witted Feodor, was all-powerful, so his patronage was important. Horsey gives, as a proof of this, his triumph over a Dutch merchant who, as a subject of the king of Spain, said that he should be presented to the Tsar before an Englishman. Horsey retorted that 'he would have his legs cut off by the knees, before he would yield to such indignity to his sovereign, the Queen's Majesty of England'. Boris Goudunov got the message and Horsey was 'first in order (as good reason) admitted and presented to the Tsar', who accepted 'with good liking' the gifts sent him by his sister Queen Elizabeth. In return, the same day the Tsar sent Horsey seventy dishes of sundry kinds of meats, with three carts laden with all sorts of drinks very bountifully'. More important, the Tsar renewed the privileges granted by his father to the Muscovy Company.

Horsey tells us that no man seemed fitter than himself to take this 'message of amity' back to England. Throughout his journey to Archangel he and his servants were treated with the greatest honour. They were 'sumptuously feasted in every town' which they passed and, when they arrived at the coast, they found that provisions for their voyage included a whole menagerie of live animals and birds. Besides 16 live oxen and 70 sheep, 3 young bears and a wild boar, there were geese, hawks, cranes, and swans— and, of course, rich presents of furs and gold cloth for Her Majesty.

Elizabeth was so delighted by Horsey's success that she sent him back to Moscow in 1586, again as her ambassador. Unfortunately for Horsey, as well as making powerful friends, he had also made powerful enemies, amongst them the Chancellor. Several highly placed Russians were, like the Chancellor, restive at the English merchant's arrogant demands for a monopoly of the Muscovite trade for members of their Company, to the exclusion, not only of Dutchmen and all foreigners, but also of other Englishmen. Elizabeth was horrified to receive angry letters not only about the bad behaviour of her merchants in Russia but about the 'lewd practices' of Horsey, who was enriching himself by private trade and, worse still, was said to be have treacherous dealings with the Poles[2]. It was all very sad. Horsey had, this time, brought especially pleasing presents from England, not only lions, bulls and dogs but organs and virginals—musical instruments which delighted the Tsarina, who had never seen nor heard the like before. 'Thousands of people resorted and stayed about the palace to hear the same.' Elizabeth, although protesting her confidence in her 'well-beloved servant Jerome Horsey', was obliged to dismiss him from his post and send the man who, of all her ambassadors to Russia was the most highly qualified by his learning and experience, Giles Fletcher.

But we have not yet done with Horsey. Although he had now no official position, he lingered on in Russia, which was providing him with such pleasing opportunities of enriching himself. He was fortunate enough in 1589 to get back to England alive under the aegis of Fletcher, although many Russians were thirsting for his blood. Mysteriously enough, he was back again in Muscovy the same year and lingered on long enough to give us a dramatic account of how he heard of the death of Demetrius (Dimitri), youngest son of Ivan the Terrible, who, as he was heir to the throne, stood in the way of the ambitious Boris Goudunov.

'One night, I commended my soul to God above other, thinking verily the time of my end was come. One rapped at my gate at midnight. I was well furnished with pistols and weapons, I and my servants, some fifteen went with these weapons to the gate. "O my good friend Jerome, ennobled, let me speak with you." I saw by moonshine the Empress's [dowager's] brother. . . . "The Tsarevitch Demetrius is dead; his throat was cut about the sixth hour by the *diaks*; some one of his pages confessed upon the rack by Boris's setting on; and the Empress poisoned and on the point of death, her hair and nails and skin fall off; help and give some good thing for the passion of Christ his sake." . . . I ran up, fetched a little bottle of pure salad oil (that little vial of balsam, which the Queen gave me) and a box of Venice treacle, "Here is what I have, I pray God it may do her good." Gave it over the wall; who hied him post away.'

Soon after this happened (in May 1591) Horsey also 'hied him post away'. He never ventured back to the country where, he

[2] The Muscovy Company took notice of Russian complaints against her agents. Hamel quotes a letter to them from their employers accusing them of unseemly behaviour—amongst other things of coursing, bull and bear baiting, and going about in silks and satins.

tells us, people had been hired to poison him. (Possibly he did not think the salad oil he had so generously given the Empress a sufficient antidote.) In England he flourished like the green bay tree, serving for thirty years in Parliament. 'No kingdom of the world', he wrote, 'was comparable for happiness to this thrice blessed nation, the angelical Kingdom of Canaan, our England.' When near his end, he could not resist a pious flourish: 'The experience of this wicked world,' he wrote, 'both at home and abroad, makes me now the more willing to live in a better.'

GILES FLETCHER

Ambassador to Russia 1588–89

GILES FLETCHER, the son of a clergyman, was educated at Eton and at King's College, Cambridge, where he remained for twenty years, lecturing in Greek. He then turned to law in which he gained a doctorate. He served in Parliament and on embassies both in Scotland and Hamburg. His qualifications for the difficult mission in which Elizabeth sent him to Russia could not have been higher, yet no ambassador was as scurvily treated as was Fletcher on his entrance to that country. It took him two months to travel from the Dwina estuary to Moscow. There was no welcome for him here; he was given quarters he describes as 'very unhandsome and unwholesome.' He had to cool his heels for three weeks before he was granted an audience at the Kremlin. It was December of 1588, yet news was so slow and unreliable in those days that Russians believed a rumour that we had been defeated by the Spanish Armada, although our 'glorious victory' had occurred in June.

The audience at the Kremlin got off to a bad start because Fletcher haughtily refused to recite all the titles of the Tsar. (These included about twenty unpronounceable cities.) It was impossible for a foreigner to remember them all, he said. The real reason was because his own sovereign was content with a short title. In the end he gave in, but the next day the presents he had brought the Tsar were unceremoniously dumped back in his quarters. The interview had not lightened the atmosphere.

For months Fletcher was kept hanging about. He was no tidle. He studied the country, talked with all and sundry and made notes for the book he published on his return to England, *Of the Russ Commonwealth*, the most penetrating account of Russia made by any foreign visitor in the sixteenth century and at the same time the most hostile. It was so black that the Muscovy Company petitioned Lord Burleigh to suppress several passages, not because they were untrue but because they feared that if the Russians got hold of the whole book they would refuse to trade with us. This was accordingly done and the complete book, with all its exposures, was not printed until 1643.

Fletcher abhorred tyranny and was well aware of the bloody deeds of the late Tsar Ivan the Terrible, although, oddly enough, he did not present as an atrocity his killing of his son. 'That he meant him no such mortal harm when he gave him the blow may appear by his mourning and passion after his son's death, which never left him till it brought him to the grave.' He hints that now another son, Demetrius, was in danger. Russia he says, was in such a desperate state, 'under such oppression and slavery' that the people longed for foreign invasion. (In later centuries Napoleon and Hitler believed the same.)

Fletcher dedicated his book to the Queen, telling her that in it she would see the 'true and strange face of a *Tyrannical State* (most unlike to your own) without true knowledge of God, without written law, without common justice'. Her Majesty (unlike the Tsar, he implied) was 'a Prince of subjects, not of slaves, that are kept within duty by love, not by fear'. This splendid pronouncement of Fletcher's belief that England was a free country, its liberties safeguarded (presumably) by the working together of sovereign, lords and commons, Hakluyt did not dare to include in his extracts because of its fierce indictment of Russia.

The opening five chapters on Russian history and geography are nowadays of little interest. It is what Fletcher learned from his own observation that is of value. There are sometimes flashes of poetry in his descriptions as when, after giving sombre details of the effect of the winter frost—if you hold a metal in your hand your fingers will freeze to it and 'you may see many travellers brought into town sitting dead in their sledges'—he suddenly breaks out:

'Yet in the summertime you shall see such a new hue and face of a country, the woods (for the most part of fir and birch) so fresh and so sweet, the pastures and meadows so green and well grown (and that upon a sudden), such variety of flowers, such noise of birds (especially of nightingales) that a man shall not lightly travel in a more pleasant country. The speedy growth of the spring seems to proceed from the benefit of the snow.'

When Fletcher writes about the Tartars and their zeal in slave-making, he is not, like other foreigners, struck only by their cruelty but also by their more estimable characteristics.

'Although the Tartars have no written law they hold by the traditions common to all their horde. They must obey their Emperor when he demands their service but, apart from that, every man is free. He owns no private land, the whole country is held in common. He must despise daintiness and wear coarse clothes, the more patched the better. . . . They must be true in word and deed to their own horde and nation. . . . They are said to be true and just in their dealings; and for that cause they hate the Russ people, whom they account to be double and false in all their dealings. Of money they have no use at all and therefore prefer brass and steel before other metals (for their weapons). As for gold and silver they neglect it of very purpose (as they do all tillage of their ground) to be more free for their wandering kind of life and to keep their country less subject to invasions.'

(We are reminded of More's Utopians, whose only use for such things was as toys for their children and as chamber pots.) About the Tartar's devotion to his friend, Fletcher notes that when his friend dies he kills his best horse and takes its skin to the place of burial. The Russians think that this is so that the friend may have a good horse to carry him to heaven; Fletcher thinks that it is a sign of his love for his dead friend that he gives the best thing he had to die with him.

The most original part of Fletcher's book is not in the picturesque details he gives about manners and customs, but in his analysis of how the government worked. He attempted to find out how the Tsar retained his power. All other travellers had noted that the Tsar was a tyrant who could dispose of the lives and property of his subjects as he wished; Fletcher was the first to enquire how he managed to do it.

Fletcher stressed that the Tsar took into his own hands every function of the state. He made the laws, appointed and dismissed all officials and judges. He kept the nobles in a state little better than slavery. Many he forced to leave their estates and go to distant provinces

'where they might have neither favour, nor authority, not being native nor well known there. Some are sent into Siberia, Kazan or Astrakhan under pretence of service, and there either made away with or else fast clapped up. Some are put into abbeys and forced to take vows because of some pretended crime.'

Fletcher mentions by name several princes known to him who were banished in this way. The Tsar prefers to them the poor sons of the gentry who, as they have no land, are dependent on his favour and will therefore he more likely to serve him loyally in war and peace. No office is hereditary. Officials are changed at the year's end. 'They are men of no credit nor favour with the people where they govern, being neither born nor brought up among them, nor yet having inheritance of their own there or elsewhere'. Noble girls also were forced into convents so that their stock might die out. (Both titles and property could descend through the female line in Russia.)

As the nobles hold all at the Tsar's pleasure—land, office, life itself—there is no chance of their challenging his authority. Neither is it likely that the Church would stand up to him as he appoints all the bishops, choosing them out of the monasteries, which Fletcher considered hotbeds of corruption and ignorance. They were extremely rich both through the management of their huge estates and through trade; they were the greatest merchants in the land; in fact the Company had more dealings with the monasteries than with anyone except the Tsar. Fletcher shared the scorn of his Protestant countrymen for religion as practised in Russia, seeing in it only superstition and deploring the ignorance of the clergy.

As for the common people, they had no incentive to perfect themselves in their skills or to follow their trades with diligence

'for that the more they have, the more danger they are in, not only of their goods but of their lives also. And if they have anything, they conceal it all they can, sometimes conveying it into monasteries, sometimes hiding it under the ground and in woods, as men are wont to do where they are in fear of foreign invasion. . . . This maketh the people (though otherwise hardened to bear any toil) to give themselves much to idleness and drinking.'

Fletcher did not despise the common people; on the contrary he stressed their 'natural wit'. 'They are of reasonable capacities if they had those means that some other nations have to train up their wits.' It is a matter of policy to keep them ignorant. If they were better educated they could not bear the cruelty of their

magistrates and superiors. 'They are kept from travelling, that
they may learn nothing, nor see the fashions of other countries
abroad.' Moreover, it is almost impossible for them to change
their social status. Every man has to 'keep to the rank wherein his
forefathers lived' as this is easier to keep him 'in servile subjection'. For 'a man of spirit and understanding, helped by
learning and liberal education, can hardly endure a tyrannical
government'.

The army is completely subservient to the Tsar and alienated
from the common people, who they are encouraged to 'wrong and
spoil, to make them have a liking of the present state'. For this
reason there is no hope of their making common cause with the
people and overturning the régime. 'It would be a hard matter to
alter the state of the Russ government as it now stands.'

The Tsar has a huge income, not only from the rents and dues
of the vast Crown lands and from customs' duties, but from the
frequent confiscation of property he makes from those who 'are
in his displeasure'. Ivan IV was reputed to have said that 'the
people were like sheep that must needs be shorn once a year at
least, to keep them from being overladen with their wool'. The
officials are encouraged to rob the people and then arrested and
forced to give up their ill-gotten gains.

The result of this lawless, cruel and oppressive régime is an
utterly depraved people, overflowing with sin. 'And no marvel as
having no law to restrain whoredoms, adulteries and like
uncleanness of life[1].' Moreover a Russian cannot be trusted.

---

[1] George Turberville, in the three chatty letters he wrote in verse to friends in
England, gave as acid an account as Fletcher of the barbarism and vice of the
Russians.
   'Perhaps the muzhik hath a gay and gallant wife
   To serve his beastly lust, yet he will lead a bugger's life.
   The monster more desires a boy within his bed
   Than any wench, such filthy sin ensues a drunken head.'
As for his wife, he gives her 'harlot dyes' for her face but
   'he mews her to be sure she lie by no man's side.'
Finally Turberville damns the whole Russian race by comparing them with
England's most hated and despised neighbours
   'Wild Irish are as civil as the Russies in their kind;
   Hard choice which is the best of both, each bloody, rude and blind'.
Turberville was Secretary in Randolph's Embassy in Moscow (1568–69).
His poems were first published in *Tragical Tales* (London, 1587) and reprinted
by Hakluyt in his *Principal Navigations* (London, 1589). They have been
reprinted in *Rude and Barbarous Kingdom*, ed. Berry and Crummey (University
of Wisconsin Press, 1968).

'It may be said truly (as they know best that have traded most with them) that from the great to the small (except some few that will scarcely be found) the Russ neither believeth any thing that another man speaketh, nor speaketh anything himself worthy to be believed.'

It is small wonder that the Muscovy Company requested Burleigh to suppress such passages. But the value and originality of the book is great. No such exposure of the workings of what we now call a totalitarian régime, of its effects upon the people it governs and the difficulty of overthrowing or changing it, had ever been made.

The shabby treatment meted out to Fletcher on his entry to Russia may have jaundiced his view and prevented him from seeing the great qualities of its suffering people: their native generosity and quick sympathies, their capacity, when called upon, for heroic deeds and unbelievable endurance, their unusual intensity of feeling. Like so many other foreign visitors he could not see below the surface—but what he did see, he saw vividly and analysed brilliantly.

Fletcher's mission, begun so badly, had an unexpectedly auspicious conclusion. By January 1589 the news of the English victory over the great Armada had been confirmed and relations improved. He was granted another audience at the Kremlin and, in April, a third and final one. This time he was given a new charter of privileges for the Company. This was on the whole satisfactory, although it did not renew their monopoly of trade with Russia by the northern route. Still more important for Fletcher, he was allowed to depart and also to take Jerome Horsey with him. Horsey was by now as odious to the Russians he had defrauded as he was to the Company. The Russians considered him worthy of death but allowed Fletcher to have him, forbidding him re-entry to their country. (Horsey, we have seen, was a wily knave and managed to get back to Russia in 1591.)

Fletcher, on his return to England, is reported by Thomas Fuller to have expressed his thankfulness to God for his safe return from so great a danger; for 'the poets cannot fancy Ulysses more glad to be come out of the den of Polyphemus, than he was to be rid of the power of so barbarous a prince'.

What impression did the newly discovered Muscovites make on the English at home, with their traditional contempt of foreigners? We catch a glimpse of it in the plays which they flocked to see. When Shakespeare, in *Love's Labour's Lost*, made the King of Navarre and his courtiers disguise themselves as 'frozen Muscovites' he knew that he could raise a loud laugh from his audience, as he does to this day, by what Rosaline called their 'ridiculous rough carriage' and 'shapeless gear'. Since the reign of Philip and Mary, Londoners 'had run plentifully on all sides' to see them riding through their streets and looking, in spite of their ambassadorial pomp, shapeless and ridiculous. No ambassadors had ever been received more magnificently, but none had seemed so exotic in dress and manners.

The manner in which the Muscovite ambassador Pisemski had wooed for his master, Ivan the Terrible, the hand of the Lady Mary Hastings, the Queen's relative, in the garden of York House, was fresh in the memory of Elizabethan courtiers when they saw the play. Pisemski had prostrated himself at her feet, then run backwards facing her and, in fulsome language, praised 'her angelical countenance, state and admirable beauty'. Because of the account published by Hakluyt of the impressions of the 'discoverers of Muscovy', Elizabethans believed that the Russians were all slaves and that they gloried in their slavery, that, as a sign of this, the peasants beat their heads against the pavement in front of their lords and the pictures of their saints, and the lords in front of their Tsar. Jenkinson had told them that their foreheads had lumps the size of eggs because of these prostrations.

The strange Russian language fascinated them too. Elizabeth, as we have seen, had called it 'the famousest and most copious language in the world' but to ordinary men it seemed merely comic and they liked to hear it in garbled form, as Shakespeare put it in the mouths of soldiers pretending they were Muscovites in

All's Well that Ends Well. Nash, the satirist, in his *Have with you to Saffron Walden* had even made a pun of it on his name, threatening those who might curse and rail upon him with being compelled to fall down and worship him 'crying upon their knees *pomuloi nashe,* which is, in the Russian tongue, "Have mercy upon us" '.

At the end of the century London welcomed a real monster of an ambassador, Grigori Ivanovitch Mikulin. He was attended by his colleague Ivan, and sixteen other monsters. The alderman and Muscovy Company merchants had accompanied them from the City to Richmond, where they were received by Elizabeth in her palace. At Richmond, Mikulin alighted from his coach.

> 'His company, being some sixteen, went before him two and two together, being very great, fat men, especially he himself, a man of tall stature, very fat, with a great face and a black beard cut round; of a swarthy colour his face and his gait very majestical.'

A still greater honour awaited Mikulin and Ivan, his colleague. Elizabeth summoned them to dine with her in Whitehall on Twelfth Night, the evening of the first performance of Master Shakespeare's new play. Elizabeth sent to fetch them a man as tall and magnificent as they were, though not so fat, Sir Jerome Bowes, estimated to stand 'three storeys high'. Bowes had been well known in Russia (when he had been ambassador there) for his haughty airs, his courage and his insistence on his high dignity as the Queen's representative. When Ivan the Terrible had told Bowes 'with a stern and angry countenance' that he did not reckon the Queen of England to be his fellow, for there are [some] that are her betters', Bowes had replied that the Queen, his mistress, was as great a prince as any in Christendom. When the Tsar had retorted that were he not ambassador he would throw him out of doors, Bowes had told him to do his will, his Mistress would avenge him. The Tsar had roared at him to get out, but later, when he had recovered from his rage, he told his courtiers that he wished he himself had such a servant, 'for he would not endure one ill word to be spoken against his mistress'. (Stories of Bowes' defiance of the Tsar persisted into the next century. Eighty years later, Pepys told how Bowes had refused to go upstairs so see the Tsar unless two noblemen who had dared to go in front of him were pulled down, knocking their heads on every stair. When the Tsar, to show Bowes his power, told a courtier to jump out of the

window and break his neck, Bowes, unimpressed, remarked that
his Queen had better uses for the necks of her subjects On
another occasion he threw down his gauntlet, challenging the nobles
in the name of his Queen to fight for their Tsar.)

The 'great fat man' was not invited to see *Twelfth Night* but
he had achieved his ambition—he had eaten bread and salt with
Her Majesty. The banquet was almost as magnificent as the one
that Ivan IV had given to Chancellor. The chamber was hung with
gold tapestries and there was a plentiful display of gold and silver
vessels. The distinguished Italian guest, Don Virginio Orsino,
who, to his chagrin, was not banqueting in the royal presence but
in a neighbouring room, explained in a letter to his wife, that 'if
he [the Muscovite] had not been seen eating in the Queen's
presence, the Great Duke would have had him beheaded'. He
promised, maliciously, to describe later the Muscovite's 'ridiculous
manners' (*costumi ridicolosi*).

Mikulin was in London when Essex rushed into the streets to
start his rebellion. Used to such dangers at home, he gallantly
offered to fight for Her Majesty, 'the Tsar's beloved sister'.
Elizabeth, in a letter to Boris Goudonov full of praise for his
ambassador, wrote that although his help was not necessary—
all trouble was over in twelve hours—she took it in very kind and
thankful part. Mikulin gave a glowing account of his reception in
England and took back with him assurances of the renewal of the
old friendship between Russia and England. He and the other fat
men in his train had given us a new symbol of their country, the
rugged Russian bear which Macbeth would rather have met than
Banquo's ghost.

PART II
1600–1698

SEVENTEENTH-CENTURY
EXPLORERS OF MUSCOVY

Above: 'No art or science except wars.' (p. 40). Tartars exercising.

Below: The wife of the deceased is obliged to howl most pitifully.' (p. 80). A Russian funeral.

II

Above left: Early visitors were fascinated by the Samoyeds (p. 83).

Above right: 'The poor princess deserved a better fate' (p. 88).

Below right: Another band of Tartars, crueller than the first' (p. 91).

INTRODUCTION

In the first years of the seventeenth century, not many Westerners braved the dangers of travel in Muscovy. This was the Time of Troubles, following on the death of Boris Goudunov in 1605. Boris had been a strong ruler, but the belief that he had gained the throne through ordering the murder of the rightful heir to it, the Tsarevitch Dimitri, haunted his subjects (to whom, because of his title, he was sacred) and made them only too willing to believe that the conspiracy had miscarried and that Dimitri had turned up in Poland. When he entered Moscow at the head of an army of Poles, he was welcomed with wild enthusiasm but later suffered from his sponsors. The Poles were Catholics and the perennial enemies of the Orthodox Russians. They outraged the Muscovites. Because of them the hapless Dimitri, an engaging figure, was murdered. For years Russia was in chaos. In 1613 the pious Muscovites, who believed so profoundly in the divine right of emperors, had at last an accredited tsar. The boyars elected to the throne a lad of sixteen, Michael, the first of the Romanovs. This did not end the confusion. There was a second False Dimitri. The Poles fought on. The peasants and peaceable citizens were a prey to marauders.

It is a relief to know that, by 1618, enough law and order had been restored for James I to send an embassy to his 'brother', the new Romanov tsar. This embassy is chiefly notable for the ambassador's chaplain, Richard James, and his companion Tradescant. James, a Fellow of Corpus Christi College, Oxford, compiled a Russian–English vocabulary and transcribed specimens of Russian oral literature. (This early Cecil Sharp made his collection of songs a hundred years before the Russians did.) As for Tradescant, founder of the first Natural History Museum and the first Botanical Garden in England, he brought back with him Arctic berries and plants, a new kind of helebore, a purple geranium and several rose bushes (all single) whose scent was 'marvellous sweet'. One became known as the wild briar of Muscovy. It is encouraging and rather touching to think of these two mild, scholarly Englishmen collecting songs and plants in barbarous Muscovy, so soon after the tribulations of the Time of Trouble.[1]

[1] See J. Hamel, *England and Russia*, trans. J. S. Leigh (London, 1854); S. Konovalov, *Oxford and Russia*, an Inaugural Lecture (Oxford, 1947).

C

In 1636 the Duke of Holstein sent an embassy to Moscow. This enterprising duke hoped to steal a march on the rest of Western Europe and secure special trading privileges for his little country. In this he failed, but his embassy is important because with it went the learned young German Olearius, charged with the duty of gathering information about the peoples, manners and customs of Muscovy. Olearius is the first of the seventeenth-century Westerners worth considering at some length.

The Tsar Michael is a shadowy figure; not so his son Alexis, who succeeded to the throne on the death of his father in 1645. He earned the gratitude of the Royalists in this country by sending money to the exiled Charles II and asking in tender terms after 'the disconsolate widow of that glorious Martyr, King Charles the First'. When Charles II was safely on the throne, Alexis sent an embassy to congratulate him and (in 1662) London enjoyed the sight of the Tsar's three envoys driving in great pomp through their streets, their attendants with hawks on their wrists, 'in their habits and fox caps very handsome', according to Pepys, 'but Lord! to see the absurd nature of Englishmen, that cannot forbear laughing and jeering at everything that looks strange'. Charles, 'mindful of the Tsar's brotherly kindness to him in the time of his affliction', gave the Russians a reception unmatched in splendour (as the French ambassador noted rather ruefully) and received with pleasure gifts of gold cloth, furs, hawks, and horses. In 1664 he sent a return embassy to Moscow under the Earl of Carlisle, in the hopes of renewing the friendship broken in the time of Cromwell and regaining the lost trade privileges. Unfortunately, the Earl of Carlisle was a stupid, arrogant fellow who knew nothing of diplomacy but had accepted the post in the hopes of some good hunting in a wild country. He behaved so insolently that the Tsar was stung into throwing back the King of England's gifts, although he must have especially regretted the watches and pistols. Even Andrew Marvell's beautifully composed Latin epistles—the poet was in the earl's train—did nothing to smooth over the rift. The embassy served only to embitter Anglo-Russian relations. Its only good result was a lively account of Muscovy given by its secretary Guy Miège, a Swiss who had lived long in England. The Tsar's court was almost grander than in the days of Ivan the Terrible. The Tsar was like a sparkling sun, his throne silver-gilt, his crown and sceptre covered with precious stones; the four lords standing beside him were clothed in white ermine and had great chains of gold; 200 boyars were clothed with vests of gold, silver or velvet set with jewels.[2]

But Alexis was less celebrated, in Russia, for his grandeur than for his extreme piety and his insistence on the rigorous keeping of fasts and attendance at divine service. Poor Macarius, Patriarch of Antioch and his son Paul of Aleppo experienced this in their bones and flesh. They had come to Holy Muscovy to beg for alms and they did not enjoy its holiness. Macarius and his suite nearly died of starvation during the frequent fasts of the Church, when a little pulse, or a dried herring, was put before them; they nearly dropped dead when forced to stand upright, for four hours in a cold dark church, listening to endless intoning. For them, used to the more relaxed, more festive holiness of their Syrian dioceses, Muscovite holiness seemed overdone. It is something of a shock to find the Russian Orthodox Church criticized, not by Protestant or Roman Catholic bigots but by those of its own hierarchy.

Alexis was extremely pious yet, by a well-meaning effort to purge the mistakes which, through ignorant copyists, had crept into the Bible and the Church ritual, he caused the first great schism of the Russian Church. The Patriarch Nikon, by making these corrections, alarmed the conservatives.

The result was that the Razkolniks, or Old Believers, formed their own church and, in spite of bitter persecution, became the first and largest group of Russian non-conformists.

Perhaps Alexis' great gift to his country was the encouragement he gave to foreigners. In this respect he was the precursor of his more famous son Peter. Not only did a number of Scotsmen fight in his wars (the most famous of them was General Patrick Gordon) but his own personal doctor was the Englishman, Samuel Collins. For us this is gain: Collins was uninhibited in his comments on life in Muscovy.

Uninhibited too, was the Dutch sailor Jan Struys, but more exciting as his adventures led him farther afield. From Struys we have a first-hand account of the Cossack brigand, Stenka Razin, folk-hero of Russian song and legend, forerunner of Mazeppa and Pugachev. Startled, we glimpse another Muscovy, wild, passionate, full of colour, as improbable as the most fantastic work of art; but now we are in Russia and this is real life.

[2] G. Miège, *A Relation of Three Embassies . . . in 1663–1664* (London, 1669).

ADAM OLEARIUS

*Voyages and Travels of the Ambassadors from the
Duke of Holstein to the Great Duke of Muscovy
and the King of Persia*

Translated by John Davies

London 1662

ADAM OLEARIUS' account of his travels as member of the
Duke of Holstein's embassy to Muscovy and Persia was
first published in Schleswig in 1647. It had a wide success.
By the end of the seventeenth century it had gone through
several German editions and had been translated into French,
English, Dutch and Italian. Olearius' book influenced European
opinion on Russia in the seventeenth century, as much as
Herberstein's had in the sixteenth century.

Olearius, the son of a tailor, had studied at Leipzig, where he
was awarded the degree of Master of Philosophy and had then
become an assistant in the university's Faculty of Philosophy. The
Thirty Years War forced him to leave Saxony for Holstein, where
he entered the service of its enlightened Duke Frederick, who
appointed him secretary, later counsellor, to the embassies he
sent to Moscow in 1634, 1636 and 1639. He made his last trip
to Moscow in 1643, carrying a special message from the Duke of
Holstein to the Tsar Michael Feodorovitch.

Olearius' duty was to gather information about the peoples,
manners and customs of Muscovy. The report he produced shows
his eager curiosity and a scholarly attempt to verify his observation.
At the same time a learned man, a German and a Protestant, he
was so profoundly convinced of the superiority of his countrymen
and their culture, that he regarded everything Russian from his own
high platform and his account streses their abject slavery, super-

stition, gross habits—in short, their pitiable barbarism. Our own Tudor merchants and travellers had noted these things in the sixteenth century but had been more aware of positive qualities. They had, for instance, written with genuine admiration of the hardihood and self-sacrifice of the soldiers. With poetic and prophetic vision Chancellor had seen Russia as 'a young horse that knoweth not his strength'. Olearius had no such insight.

Olearius quotes Herberstein very often. He also knew the Italians Possevinus, Paulus Jovius and Guagninus but, except for Clement Adams, who wrote in Latin, he knew nothing of the English narratives published by Hakluyt. This is not surprising as until the end of the seventeenth century the leaders of European culture, notably the French, considered English a barbaric language not worth the learning. It makes more impressive the similarity of German and English accounts of the manners and customs of the Russians. One cannot doubt the prevalence of terror, slavery, superstition and drunkenness, when all travellers say the same thing. Olearius is not simply repeating his forerunners; he saw things with his own eyes. He was a student of science, especially of astronomy and mathematics. There is no reason to doubt the devotion to truth which he claims in his preface. It was not his fault that this devotion did not enable him to see below the surface.

It would be idle to cite the accounts Olearius gives of the Tsar's traditional reception of ambassadors, of the ceremonies and ritual of the Orthodox church, baptism, marriage and funerals, of the fierce winter, the burning summer, the wolves, wild beasts, small swift horses and daring *izvoztchiks* (coachmen)—all these things we have heard already. But although Olearius noted the same 'barbarities' as our Tudor travellers, he sometimes gives a new and rather amusing slant on them and is worth quoting.

To begin with, it is instructive to compare the rules of conduct given by Duke Frederick to his ambassadorial suite with those given by Sebastian Cabot to Richard Chancellor's mariners. Apart from injunctions of implicit obedience to the Marshal who acted for the ambassador, the suite was ordered to attend divine worship regularly, to pray to all-powerful God for the success of their important enterprise, to eschew swearing and coarse vices, such as gluttony, drunkenness and other excesses, quarrels, fights—and duels. They must not insult or ridicule foreigners but rather treat them with courtesy and friendliness. Unfortunately, Olearius notes, not all observed these rules. Godlessness, insolence and licentiousness crept in. He does not particularize, but evidently Germans were not entirely free from the vices and failings he criticizes so ruthlessly in the Russians.

On their first journey from Narva to Moscow it was summer, and the ambassador and his suite went mainly on horseback, sending their baggage in fifty waggons. The villages they passed which had recently suffered from disbanded mercenaries, many of them English and Scotch, were often extremely hostile.[1] In one,

'the horses began to wince, stand upon their hinder feet and beat the ground as if they had been bewitched, whereof we could not imagine what should be the cause till that, having alighted, we found them covered all over with bees, which were beginning to fall upon us and prosecuted their animosity so far as to force us to keep them off with our cloaks and to go and take up our quarters in the fields. We understood since that it was a strategem of the inhabitants, who had incensed the bees purposely to prevent our lodging in the village.'

[1] Many foot-loose Scotsmen fought in Russia in the seventeenth and early eighteenth centuries and not just as common soldiers. Patrick Gordon, outstanding as he was, is in some ways typical. He tells us in his diary that he decided to go to a foreign country, partly to be free from his loving parents but mainly because his patrimony was small, as he was 'the younger son of a younger brother of a younger house'. Moreover, although he had had an excellent schooling he was, as a Catholic, excluded from study at a university. He took ship from Aberdeen to Danzig in 1651. After several misadventures he decided to return home but fell in with a cornet and quartermaster of the Swedish army who told him that riches and honour lay at a soldier's feet and that of all soldiers Scotsmen were the best. He enlisted in the Swedish cavalry and, in the true spirit of a soldier of fortune, fought alternately with the Swedes against the Poles and with the Poles against the Swedes, learning, in the process, both skill in the art of war and in the art of loot. (Loot furnished him not only with horses and armour but with a valuable extension to his library, for he was a learned man.) In 1661 he fell in with some Russians who induced him to take service with their Tsar. In Muscovy he was often in despair with a country where the people were 'morose and niggard, yet overweening and valuing themselves above all other nations', where, besides, strangers were not, as in the rest of the Continent, open 'to all honour, military and civil', but looked on as hirelings. Warned by friends that petition to leave would mean Siberia or worse, he took command of a regiment and, in the end, served the Romanovs for nearly forty years, gaining victories for them over Tartars, Turks and rebellious Cossacks. He helped the young Peter the Great to suppress two Muscovite insurrections, and when he died in 1699 it was Peter who stood weeping by his bedside and who later headed the most magnificent funeral procession ever granted to a foreigner. Patrick Gordon was only one of the many brilliant Scotsmen—Bruce, Hamilton, Ogilvy, Leslie and Drummond— who helped to modernize the Russian armed forces and gain them victories over their enemies, whether Swedes, Poles, Tartars or Turks, and incidentally vastly extend their empire. See *Diary of General Patrick Gordon* (Aberdeen, 1859).

In Moscow, Olearius was present on the occasion of the festival celebrating Christ's entry into Jerusalem on Palm Sunday. The procession moved from the Kremlin to the Jerusalem Church, the Tsar leading the Patriarch's horse, which was adorned with long ears to make it resemble an ass. On the night before Easter, the Tsar went into prisons and gave each prisoner an egg and a sheepskin coat saying, 'Let them be happy. For Christ, who died for their sins, has indeed risen.' Then he ordered that the prison gates should be shut again and went off to church.

About Moscow, Olearius says that there were more than 2,000 churches, monasteries and private chapels in it. Every fifth house was a chapel, as every magnate 'builds a private chapel and maintains a priest at his own expense'.

He was impressed by the variety of fruit and vegetables found in the Moscow market: apples, pears, cherries, plums, red currants, asparagus as thick as a thumb, cucumbers, onion and garlic—but the Russians had never planted lettuce or other salad and even laughed at the Germans who did, saying that they eat grass. Now some were beginning to try it. They grew melons in enormous quantities, most sweet and delicious. The seeds they planted in horse manure and straw after softening them in milk or rain water. At night they covered the mounds with mica, against the frost. Formerly Moscow had had few herbs and flowers but the last Grand Prince had had a fine garden planted with them, even with double Provence roses (before that, they had only wild roses).

Birds were so plentiful that the Russians did not value them. The peasants got little for grouse, wild ducks and geese. Cranes, swans and small birds like thrushes and larks were not considered worth hunting and eating. As there was ample pasture, there were many horned cattle and sheep which were sold for very little. Among minerals, mica was the most important, used all over Russia for windows. Recently, Germans had started iron-mining in Tula.

Olearius has a long section on the Russian people, their looks and dress, manners and customs. The men

'are for the most part corpulent, fat and strong and of the same colour as other Europeans. They much esteem great beards when the moustaches hide the mouth, as also great bellies. . . . The great lords shave their heads [but] those that are out of favour at court let their hair grow and hang negligently about their heads, thereby showing their affliction. The women are well proportioned, having passable good faces, but they paint so palpable that if they had a handful of meal cast in their faces, they could not disfigure themselves as much as the paint does. . . . Married women put up their hair within their caps, but the maids let theirs hang down their backs in two tresses and tie it at the ends with a piece of crimson silk. Children under ten years of age as well girls as boys have their hair cut, so that there being no difference in their habits, their sex is only discovered by the brass or silver rings which the girls wear in their ears.

'The Muscovites never change their fashion, nor can I remember more than one lord, who took a fancy to the French mode. . . . If a man consider their nature and manner of life, he will be forced to avow there cannot be anything more barbarous than that people. Their boast is that they are descended from the ancient Greeks, but there is no more comparison between the brutality of these barbarians and the civility of the Greeks than there is between night and day. They never learn any art or science, on the contrary they are so ignorant as to think a man cannot make an almanack unless he be a sorcerer, nor foretell the revolutions of the moon and eclipses unless he have some communication with the devil.'

(For this reason Olearius refused the Tsar's invitation to become his astronomer. He heard it rumoured that the Tsar was going to bring a magician into his court, who had correspondence with the devil [himself], and he feared for his life.)

Although the Muscovites admired physicians, they would not allow the dissection of corpses nor the study of skeletons. A Dutch barber narrowly escaped lynching because the skeleton he had hanging on his wall danced when he played the lute.[2]

Olearius recognized that Russians were clever and shrewd, but said that they used their intelligence for their own advantage and profit. False witness was so prevalent among them that strangers were in danger from it, as well as their own relatives and neighbours Recently a law had been passed that people bringing accusations must be willing to maintain them under torture. When Olearius was in Moscow a spiteful wife accused her husband, a cavalry-man, of plotting to poison the Tsar's horses and stuck to the charge

[2] Not till 1697 did a Russian take a medical degree and this was in Padua. In the sixteenth century there were English physicians in Russia and, in the seventeenth, Germans as well as Scots and English. When, on one occasion, a German physician asked leave of the Tsar to return to his country to take his doctor's degree, the Tsar replied: 'I know your skill and will give you a certificate larger than you would receive abroad.'

even when tortured. The husband was exiled to Siberia, no further proof being required.

'The Russians are in general a very quarrelsome people who assail each other like dogs, with fierce, harsh words. . . . When their indignation flares and they use swearwords, they do not resort to imprecations involving the sacraments, as unfortunately is often the case with us. Instead they use many vile and loathsome words. They have nothing on their tongue more often than "son of a whore", "son of a bitch", "cur", "I fuck your mother" to which they add "into the grave". Little children who do not know the name of God have on their lips "fuck you", and say it as well to their parents as their parents to them. Recently this foul and shameful swearing was strictly forbidden upon pain of knouting. Certain secretly appointed people were sent to mix with the crowd and with the help of *streltsi* [the Tsar's bodyguard] and executioners were to seize swearers and punish them on the spot by beating but they soon gave it up as a bad job.

'One should not seek great courtesy and good manners among the Russians. After a meal, they do not refrain, in the hearing of all, from releasing what nature produces, fore and aft. Since they eat a great deal of garlic and onion it is rather trying to be in their company. Perhaps against their will these good people fart and belch noisily.

'Just as they are ignorant of the praiseworthy sciences, they are little interested in memorable events or the history of their fathers and they care little to find out the qualities of foreign peoples. . . . They tell all sorts of shameless fables, and he who can relate the coarsest obscenities and indecencies, accompanied by the most wanton mimicries is accounted the best companion. . . . So given are they to the lusts of the flesh that some are addicted to the vile depravity of sodomy not only with boys but also with men and horses. People caught in such obscene acts are not severely punished. Tavern musicians often sing of such loathsome things, while some show them to young people in puppet shows.'[3]

As in the more civilized West, smoking had, in seventeenth century Russia, become a menace.

'The Russians greatly love tobacco and formerly everyone carried some with him. However it was remarked that people got no good of it. Slaves lost much time in their work, many houses went up in smoke because of carelessness with the flame and sparks and, before the ikons, worshippers emitted an evil odour. Therefore, in 1634, at the suggestion of the Patriarch, the Grand Prince banned the sale

[3] Translated by H. S. Baron, Stanford University Press, 1967.

and use of tobacco, along with sale by private taverns of vodka and beer. Offenders were severely punished by slitting of the nostrils and the knout. We saw marks of such punishment on both men and women!

(Peter the Great repealed the ban when he sold the monopoly of the tobacco trade with Russia to an Englishman.)

Olearius notes as others had done the pitiable life of women secluded in their chambers after marriage, submitting to frequent beatings (yet not taking these, as Herberstein asserted, as signs of intense love) liable to be shut up in a convent if childless or 'found guilty of something dishonourable', but it was its utter futility that really shocked him.

> 'Since the daughters of the magnates and merchants receive little or no training in housekeeping, when they are married they merely sit and sew beautiful handkerchiefs of white satin and pure linen, embroidering them with gold and silver, and make little purses for money and the like. [They] ride in the summer in closed carriages lined with red satin, with which they also decorate their sleighs in winter. They sit pompously in their sleighs, as if they were goddesses, with a slave girl at their feet. Occasionally they arrange recreations with their maids, for example riding on swings.'

Moreover women were considered more unclean than men. Even after wedlock, sexual intercourse was considered sinful and defiling; ikons were covered, the little crosses, received at baptism, removed from the neck, during coitus.

Olearius thought the people lazy.

> 'Russians of high and low estate are in the habit of sleeping after the noon meal. The Russians determined that False Dimitri was not the Grand Duke's son, nor even a Russian by birth, because he did not take an afternoon nap. Nor did he often go to the bath, as the Russians do.'

Olearius notes one or two more pleasing things.

> 'During the great fast, when the time of confession approaches, some of them purchase birds which they then set free again. They suppose that on that account God will liberate them from their sins.'

He also notes that the Orthodox had some hope for the sinful after death. Though they do not believe in purgatory,

> 'they do believe in two special places that souls reach as soon as they are loosed, where they await the Last Judgment and the resurrection

of their bodies. The pious reach a cheerful and charming place, the godless a gloomy, frightful valley but a soul on its way to the latter place may be brought into the true path by the zealous prayers of his former confessor, priest, monk or anyone else. To this end they also give alms.'

Like Giles Fletcher, Olearius saw that Russians were not allowed to travel abroad, 'so that they might stay tranquil in slavery and not see the free institutions that exist in foreign lands'.

All the same, things were not as bad as under the former tyrants.

'The present Grand Prince [the Tsar Michael] is a very pious ruler who, like his father, does not want a single one of the peasants to be impoverished. If one of them is stricken by misfortune, the court to whose jurisdiction he is subject gives him assistance. And if someone is sent in disgrace to Siberia, even this disfavour is mitigated by providing the exile with a tolerable livelihood. Magnates are given money, scribes positions in the chancelleries of Siberian cities soldiers given places as soldiers. The most oppressive aspect for most of them is that they are banished from His Majesty's countenance and deprived of the right to see his bright eyes. Moreover there have been instances when such disgrace worked a great advantage, namely when the exiles' professions or trades were more fruitfully pursued than in Moscow.'

Olearius gives a detailed account of his embassy's journey to Persia. They sailed down the Volga and at last neared Astrakhan. He writes:

'On September 13th, while we were, after morning prayers, reading chapters out of the Bible and among others Numbers XIII where Moses speaks of the fertility of the land of Canaan and the excellency of its fruits especially of its grapes, brought thence by the spies, there came two boats from Astrakhan, which brought us some fruits to sell. . . . I am in doubt whether that of the Holy Land could be better; so delicious were the melons and peaches and the kernels of the grapes were as big as nuts.'

Grapes were something new in Russia. They had been recently introduced by Persians, and Olearius met an Austrian-born monk, aged 105, who had laid out vineyards which now produced wine. He had when a boy been captured by Turks and sold into Muscovy, where he had changed his religion and become a monk.

'He was a very goodnatured man . . . but as soon as he had taken two or three dishes of aquavitae, he was subject to the ordinary weaknesses of those of his age, threw away his staff and fell dancing, though not with overmuch confidence.'

The Holstein embassy ended in failure. Duke Frederick had wanted to gain the right to transport Persian silks and other wares through Russia and, although the Tsar had been willing to grant him this right in return for a large sum of money, the Shah refused to co-operate. Moreover, the Holstein ambassador had behaved so badly that on his return to his country he was tried and executed. But Olearius had fulfilled his duties beyond all expectation and his book was for decades the standard work on Russia, not just for little Holstein, but for all Europe. Not until Peter the Great, more than half a century later, had opened his Window on the West, did Europeans have another picture of the mysterious Muscovy, and even then it was in many aspects much the same picture.

DR SAMUEL COLLINS

*The Present State of Russia in a letter to a friend
at London*

London 1671

SAMUEL COLLINS, the son of the vicar of Braintree, studied in Cambridge and took his medical degrees in Padua and Oxford. While travelling in Holland in 1660, he met a commissar of the Russian Court, who was looking for talented foreigners to serve the Tsar, Alexis Mihailovitch. Collins was persuaded to go to Moscow where his qualities were soon noticed. He was appointed physician to the Tsar, an office he kept, with many honours and rewards, for nine years. He died in Paris a year after he left Russia, and his book was published in London in 1671, and eight years later was translated into French.

The publisher, in his preface to the book, wrote that Dr Collins was

'a gentleman of large parts. . . . His genius led him to be curious and inquisitive mostly of those things that were difficult to be attained to. . . . He had the happiness to be a favourite of the great Tsar and his Patriarch (things not usually compatible) and, it may be, has made a further discovery of Russ affairs than any stranger has been capacitated to do, before or since. He projected a life of Ivan Vassilievitch, but an acute unkind disease put a period to that and his life.'

Curious and inquisitive Collins certainly was. He gives minute details of the daily life of the Tsar. He notes that Alexis was so anxious that justice should be done that he had at his palace a special box in which petitions could be placed and 'in the night season' he visited 'his Chancellor's desk, to see what decrees were passed and what petitions unanswered'.

'He is a goodly person, about six foot high, well set, inclined to fat . . . of a stern countenance, severe in his chastisements, but very careful of his subjects' love. Being urged by a stranger to make it death for any man to desert his colours, he answered, "It was a hard case to do that, for God has not given courage to all men alike." . . . His sentinels and guards, placed round about his court, stand like silent and immovable statues. No noise is heard in his palace, no more than if uninhabited. . . . He never misses divine service. If he be well, he goes to it; if sick, it comes to him in his chamber. On fast days he frequents midnight prayers, standing four, five or six hours together, prostrating himself to the ground, sometimes a thousand times, and on great festivals fifteen hundred. In the great fast he eats but three meals a week; for the rest he eats a piece of brown bread and salt, a pickled mushroom or cucumber, and drinks a cup of small beer. He eats fish but twice in the great Lent and observes it seven weeks together. . . . In fine, no monk is more observant of canonical hours, than he is of fasts. We may reckon he fasts almost eight months in twelve.'[1]

[1] Macarius, Patriarch of Antioch, found the piety of the Muscovites excessive. In 1654 he came to Holy Russia with his son Paul, Archdeacon of Aleppo, to beg for money for his poor diocese from the wealthy Russian Church. 'Now', Paul complains in his diary, 'we were entered on our travail and labour! For all their churches are void of seats. There is not one even for the Bishop; you see the people all through the service standing like rocks, motionless or incessantly bending with their devotions (God help us for the length of their prayers and chants and masses, for we suffered great pain, so that our very souls were tortured with fatigue and anguish).' Paul found the abstemiousness of the Holy Muscovites also excessive. 'For every person in this land of Muscovy confines himself to only one meal a day.' 'We had indeed been forewarned by our friends and we kept up appearances before them in spite of our inward rage and suffering. For we had been told that anyone wishing to shorten his life by five or ten years should go into Muscovy and walk there as a religious man, making a show of perpetual abstinence and fasting, continual reading and prayer and rising at midnight for devotions. He must also banish all mirth and laughter and jokes and renounce the eating of opium for they set guards over the bishops and archimandrites, observing whether they practise devotional humility, fasting and prayer, or whether they get drunk and amuse themselves. Whenever they perceive any person guilty of great or small offence, they send him away forthwith, with troops of other prisoners, to the land of darkness, whence there is no escape, to Siberia; there to be employed in collecting furs. It is a journey of three and a half years to the shores of the frozen ocean.' The Patriarch and his son were especially alarmed on hearing that people were put to death for using tobacco. They managed to survive the worst plague Muscovy had ever known, by being confined to their room for five months (without the comfort of a drop of wine). After five years, their painful pilgrimage ended and they were restored to the jollity and laxity of their Syrian home and to Turkish overlords, who were so much more indulgent to them than Holy Moscow.

Collins tells us, in his matter-of-fact way, information about the Tsarina's origins that make her sound like a character from a fairy tale.

'Ilya, the present Emperor's father-in-law, was of so mean account that within this twenty year he drew wine to some Englishmen and his daughter gathered mushrooms and sold them in the market.'

'The Imperial Palace is built of stone and brick, except some lodgings wherein His Majesty sleeps and eats all the winter. For they esteem wooden rooms far wholesomer than stone. They have some reason to think so, because their stone rooms being arched brick, reverberate a dampness when the stove is hot [i.e. there is condensation]. The Emperor lodges three storeys high. His drink is *brague* [beer] made of oats. His bread is made of rye, which the Russians esteem stronger nourishment than wheat. The Tsar lies in no sheets, but in his shirt and drawers, under a rich sable coverlet and one sheet under him.'

'Whensoever he goes forth, the east gate of the inner wall [i.e. the Kremlin wall] of the city is shut till he return. He seldom visits any subject, yet the last year he did, but went not in the common way, for the side of a wall was pulled down.'

'The scents of musk and ambergris are not much esteemed, but rose water is much used at court. . . . Cinnamon here (you must know) is the *aroma imperiale.*'

Collins' admiration for the Tsar seems to have survived intact nine years of intimacy as his private physician. He even writes tolerantly of his excessive piety, although he had no respect for the Orthodox priests (or popes). 'That priest is counted the best fellow that can mumble most in a breath.'

'The pope's priesthood is wrapped up in his wife's smock; for when she dies he must officiate no longer, which makes them indulge their wives more than ordinary, for their office sake.'

Collins describes marriage and funeral ceremonies in detail. He notices that when the bride comes out of the church, the clerk showers her with hops, 'wishing her children as thick as hops', another, in a sheepskin coat,

'prays she may have as many children as there are hairs on his coat. . . . They sit at table with bread and salt before them, but eat nothing; in the meantime a choir of boys and girls standing aloft sing *epithalamiums* or nuptial songs, so bedaubed with scum of bawdry and obscenity that it would make Aretine's ears glow to hear them.'

'Their burials are strange. As soon as the breath is out of the body, they carry the corpse into the church, where it abides not long before it is buried in the church yard. The wife of the deceased is obliged to howl most pitifully and hire others to do the like, but little reason have they to do it, considering their severe usage. . . . The Russians count that the greatest funeral where are most women mourners. These, therefore, in a doleful tone cry out (as the wild Irish do *ohone*) "*Timminy Dushenka*, Alas, my dear, why hast thou left me, was I not obedient to thee in all things? Was I not careful of thy house? Did I not bring thee fine children? Hadst thou not all things in abundance, a fair wife, pretty children, much goods, good clothes and brandy wine enough?" As soon as anyone is dead, they open the windows and set a basin of holy water for the soul to bathe in, and a bowl of wheat at the head of the corpse, that he may eat, having a long journey to go. After this they put on his feet a pair of black shoes and some kopecks or pieces of money in his mouth, with a certificate in his hand (from the Metropolitan of the place) to St Nicholas, of his life and conversation.

'Thirty days after burial, they read the psalter over daily upon the grave, having a little booth made of mats to shelter from the weather, but what their meaning is in this I cannot understand.'

England was notorious for drunkenness; Russia, says Collins, is her equal.

'In the carnival before *Quadragesima* or Lent, they give themselves over to all manner of debauchery and luxury, and in the last week they drink as if they were never to drink more. . . . Some of these going home drunk, if not attended with a sober companion, fall asleep upon the snow (a sad cold bed) and there they are frozen to death. If any of their acquaintance chance to pass by, though they see them like to perish, yet will they not assist them, to avoid the trouble of examination if they should die in their hands.'[2]

To Collins, Russian singing was unbearably harsh.

'All the beggars here beg singing as well prisoners as cripples, and a strenuous voice loseth nothing by its harsh notes. For the Russians love nothing smooth but their womens' fat sides. . . . You must know they have music schools where children are brought up with great

[2] Henry Morley, travelling in Russia in the 1860s, saw people standing round a wounded man but not daring to help him. According to Russian law, a dead body or person in danger of life must not be touched or helped, except by the police. 'If anyone interferes and the man dies, he may pay for it with Siberia or, if he is rich, with an enormous fine. . . . The Russian law is terribly foolish and inhuman on this point,' Morley comments. See Henry Morley, *Sketches of Russian Life* (London, 1866).

diligence and much severity. . . . Finally when they have brought up these children to a perfection, what with basses, tenors, counter-tenors and trebles, you shall hear as good a concert as ever was sung at a cats' vespers! . . . It has been thought state policy to forbid all music or jollity among the commons to prevent effeminacy.'

Like other Englishmen, Collins is shocked by the 'severe usage' of women. 'If a man thinks his wife barren, he will persuade her to turn nun, that he may try another; if she refuses, he will cudgel her into a monastery'. If the Empress had not brought a second tsarevitch or prince [Peter the Great] born June 2, 1661, after four girls together, 'tis thought she would have been sent to her devotions'.

'If a man kill his slave, or his wife, in correcting them, there is no law against them.' On the other hand, 'A woman that kills her husband is buried alive, put into the ground up to her neck and there suffered to die, which is soon done in winter'.

He has a chapter on crime and punishment.

'Their judiciary proceedings are very confused. The accused cannot be condemned although a thousand witnesses come in against him, except he confesses the fact; and to this end they want not torments to extort confessions.'

Collins gives horrible details of these, for example: 'The punishment of coiners is to melt some of the coin and pour it down their throat'.

'If there be secret conspiracy contrived, and disclosed in the acting, the traitors are severely tormented and afterwards sent towards Siberia, and in the way, a hundred or two hundred versts off, softly put under the ice.'

'Hanging has not been in use (until lately) . . . for the dull Russ thought if the malefactor were strangled his soul was forced to sally forth at the postern gate, which made it *pogano*, viz. defiled. The hangman's place is hereditary and he teaches his children to strike upon a leathern bag.'

He obviously does not find Russian women physically attractive.

'The beauty of their women they place in their fatness: God make me fat and I'll make myself beautiful. A lean woman they count unwholesome, therefore they who are inclined to leanness give themselves over to all manner of epicurism, on purpose to fatten themselves. and lie abed all day long drinking Russian brandy (which will fatten extremely), then they sleep and afterwards drink again, like swine designed to make bacon.'

Collins' book is sprinkled with things which, as his publisher said, were 'difficult to be attained to' but which he found out in the course of his practice. 'The ecclesiastical law commands their abstinence from venery three days a week, viz. Monday, Wednesday, and Friday. After coition, they must bath before they enter a church.'

> 'It is a grand sin with them to omit *lotionem post mictum* [washing after urinating]. As we use paper in our cacking-office to clear accounts, so *Juan de Rusco* [Russian Ivan] uses a little spade made of fir, thin-shaven, like the ivory spatula which merchants and scriveners use to fold up letters and smoothe them.'

Collins observes the remarkable homogeneity of the Great Russians. 'The mode [i.e. clothing] of men and women, rich and poor, is all one, all over the Empire, from the highest to the lowest, and their language one, yea and religion too, which certainly must hugely tend to their peace and preservation'.

As Collins was anxious to write a history of Ivan the Terrible he picked up anecdotes about him.

> 'This Ivan Vassilievitch nailed a French ambassador's hat to his head. Sir Jerome Bowes, a while after, came as ambassador and put on his hat and cocked it before him, at which he [the Tsar] sternly demanded how he durst do so, having heard how he chastised the French ambassador. Sir Jerome answered, he represented a cowardly King of France, "But I am the ambassador of the invincible Queen of England, who does not vail her bonnet nor bare her head to any Prince living, and if any of her ministers shall receive affront abroad, she is able to revenge her own quarrel." "Look you there!" quoth Ivan Vassilievitch to his boyars. "There is a brave fellow indeed, that dares do and say thus much for his mistress; which whoreson of you all dare do so much for me, your Master?" This made them envy Sir Jerome, and persuade the Emperor to give him a wild horse to tame; which he did, managing him with such vigour that the horse grew so tired and tamed that he fell down dead under him. This being done, he asked his Majesty if he had any more wild horses to tame. The Emperor afterwards much honoured him, for he loved such a daring fellow as he was, and a mad blade to boot.'

Like so many early visitors to Muscovy, Collins was fascinated by the Samoyeds and believed the legend that they were called man-eaters.

'for they eat those whom they conquer in battle. Their food is most fish, their riches deer, of which they have great herds, and so tame that at whistle they will appear at hand and suffer themselves to be harnessed and put to the sledges by pairs, which they will draw as swiftly as wind, eighty miles a day. When they hunt for new deer, they consult the priest who, after many ceremonies and conjurations, tells them to what quarter they must go, and most commonly they find his predictions true.

'There is no distinction in the clothes of male and female, but both are made of deerskins, with the hair side outward, which, by experience, they find the warmest. You can hardly distinguish the men and women by their visage, neither wear beards and both have faces like baboons.

'One being asked if he thought not an Englishwoman (then present, young and handsome) as pretty and fair as his lady ugly, answered, "No, surely, thy wife's complexion is pale like the belly of a fish; our women's colours are natural and genuine".'

Collins did not forget Cathay, the fabulous country which still haunted the dreams of English explorers.

'Siberia is a vast unknown province, reaching to the walls of Cathay. I have spoken with one that was there who traded with the Chineses, and another also, who said he saw a sea beyond Siberia, wherein were ships and men in strange habits, like the Chineses, by their description, rich in cloth of gold and jewels, no beards but on their upper lips. From hence the latter brought *tchai* and *Bom Diam*. The *tchai* is that which we call *teah* or *tey* and *Bom Diam* is *Anisum Indicum Stellatum* [aniseed]. It is brought over in papers about one pound weight, written on with Chinese characters.'

It is a misfortune that Collins died of 'an acute and unkind disease' before he had had time to write the history of Ivan the Terrible. For the courtiers of Charles II, it would have been the best horror story in their repertoire; for us who have supped too full of horrors to want any more it would assuredly have added many of those intimate and picturesque details, which Collins had such a knack of picking up, and which kept alive the legend of the Monstrous Tsar nearly a century after his death. But, thanks to his publisher, we have what is more important: a first-hand account of Muscovy in the reign of the Tsar Alexis.

JEAN STRUYS

Travels in Muscovy[1]

French Edition, Amsterdam 1718

GLANIUS published the French edition of this book in 1718, because—he writes in his introduction—although the author Jean Struys was distinguished neither by birth nor education, he was a 'natural genius', who had succeeded in all he had undertaken and had written of his experiences in an easy style that would please those who look for what is 'solid and authentic' in what they read. The descriptions of the places he visited are so exact and detailed that they would be useful to the reader while his adventures would amuse them.

Struys started on his travels in December 1647, but did not arrive in Muscovy until October 1668.

Struys tells us in his introduction that from his earliest years he was obsessed with the desire to travel, but that his father insisted on his learning an honest trade and would not hear of his going to sea. He bore this until he was seventeen. Then, finding his father inflexible, he ran away from home and, at Amsterdam, as a common sailor, boarded a ship bound for Genoa. For ten years he travelled far and wide, to Sierra Leone, Madagascar, Siam, Japan and Turkey. In Troy he was seized by the Turks and for six weeks was in the galleys.

It was here that Struys met his first Russian, an old man who had been a galley slave for twenty-four years and had lost his ears and nose as a punishment for trying to escape. With the help of a file which Struys had managed to conceal, they both got rid of their chains and shortly before dawn, 'slipped softly into the sea'. The Turkish sentinels shot their arrows after them, one of which

[1] *Voyage en Muscovie*. The extracts are translated by the Editor.

pierced the thigh of the old Russian, 'to the bone'. In spite of this he swam with his comrade for two hours, till they reached the Venetian ship, the *Sacrifice of Abraham*, which received them kindly. Here, by the goodness of Heaven, the Russian was soon healed of his dangerous wound, and both men took part in the ensuing battle with the Turks in which the Venetians won a glorious victory. From this experience Struys learned, among other things, the phenomenal physical strength, power of endurance, courage and trustworthiness of the Russian peasant, and one hopes that he remembered his old comrade later when he was in his most critical mood in barbaric Muscovy.

The battle against the Turks was fought in June 1656. The next year Struys returned to Holland, intending to stay there for a few days but, as he put it, 'fate decided' that he should marry and that for more than ten years he could not leave his family. After this, nothing could hold him and he left in another *Sacrifice of Abraham* en route for Muscovy and Persia. At Riga their ship was unloaded and its cargo put on thirty carts to be taken overland to the Caspian Sea, where they hoped to obtain silk from Persia. (Struys does not tell us what wares were on the carts to be given in exchange, only that they were grossly overloaded.) He was horrified by the extreme poverty and nakedness of the peasants round Riga, treated, he says, by their lords worse than the Turks treated their slaves. He was glad to get to Pitsiora, his first Russian village, where the inhabitants were well fed and had a flourishing market. At Pletscow, the next town they arrived at, they sent back their Riga carts, as they had received the Tsar's order that horses and waggons or sleighs should be provided for them for the rest of their journey to the Caspian. It was already the end of October. On November 12th the snow was so deep that they had to proceed in sleighs. Struys recounts many details of his journey to Moscow: the terrors of the forest where he met a bear, packs of wolves and bands of robbers; the miserable wooden huts the peasants lived in. He was not much impressed by Novgorod, in spite of its former glories and the Monastery of St Anthony. Here was preserved the millstone on which the saint had sailed from the Tiber, through the Baltic and down the Volga. This attracted thousands of worshippers, but not Struys although, as a Catholic, he should have believed in saints and their miracles.

Struys had a guide who spoke German; he himself began to learn Russian of which he says he soon knew as much as was suitable for a foreigner. He found his journey through gloomy forests and wretched villages extremely melancholy. The *izbas* (cottages) where they sometimes stopped had neither food for them nor beds, so that they spent the night smoking their pipes. They were glad when at last they got to Moscow. Struys gives a careful description of this city, noting the horrors of its winter, in which many people are frozen to death or, unless they rub themselves with snow, lose their ears or noses through frost-bite. The summer, he hears, is about as bad because of its extreme heat and the unwholesome bogs surrounding the city, which were a breeding place of fevers.

He writes a chapter or two on the manners and customs of the Muscovites for whom he conceived a great contempt, finding them ignorant, brutal and vicious. Since 1634, tobacco had been forbidden them because, through smoking, many families had been ruined and many houses burnt down. Struys was scandalized by their arranged marriages and maintained that they were often unhappy and led to divorce. If a woman was sterile or had only daughters, she could be forced by her husband to enter a convent and he was free to remarry after six weeks. If one of the partners was accused of adultery, he or she could be forced by a judge to become monk or nun. The Russians are lascivous but so superstitious that when they take a woman they remove the cross that, since their christening, has hung round their neck and hang a veil over the ikon. He notes that if a man takes a foreigner, it is a great sin, but not so bad in a woman, since if she has a child she will undoubtedly bring him up in the Orthodox faith. Struys even finds it superstitious in Russians that they wash before going to church, as though water would take away their sins. At the baths men and women mix without scruple 'as naked as one's hand'.

Struys left Moscow in May (He arrived in Astrakhan in September). He met the officers and crew of his ship in a boat on the River Oka, and it was by boat that most of the journey was made. He was impressed by the great apparent fertility of the land beside the Volga (which he said was like the Nile). 'Yet it is a desert, having never been inhabited since the army of Tamerlane put it to fire and sword to punish the insolence of the Muscovites who had plundered and burnt one of his frontier cities.'

Astrakhan, Struys writes, is for its size and beauty, one of the most famous towns in Muscovy. Ivan the Terrible had conquered it after he had taken Kazan, and since then it had grown enormously and brought great revenues to the Tsar in customs' duties.

Not only Kalmucks and Tartars, but Armenians, Persians and even Indians trade here with the Russians. There was fruit of all sorts and since the Persians had given vines to a German monk, grapes and wine.

Struys considers the Tartars, whom he found in the winter camp around Astrakhan, less hideous than the Kalmucks, their sworn enemies, but apart from that, has little good to say of them. In return for a promise to fight for the Tsar, they pay him no tribute. This suits them. War gives them the chance to loot.

In Astrakhan, Struys was received by Stenka Razin. The captain of his ship, hearing of his fame, decided to visit him and asked Struys to go with him. Struys tells the hero's story as he learnt it from the Muscovites. Stenka Razin was a Don Cossack, a proud race who fought for the Tsar on condition that they kept their freedom to rule themselves. No slave who fled to them could be recaptured. In this way they had attracted to their ranks many brave and desperate people. Stenka Razin had revolted against the Tsar to avenge his brother, who had been hanged by the Russian General Dolgoruki for withdrawing his regiment, against orders, after a successful campaign against the Poles. Stenka could make himself feared. He could also make himself loved. He gathered hordes of willing followers, seized ships laden with merchandise on the Volga, sacked towns and monasteries on its shores and terrorized the whole country-side. When the governor of Astrakhan sent a fleet against him, Stenka, although he had only twenty-two boats to the governor's thirty-six, had the best of it, and Tsar Alexis offered to forgive him the past if he would return to his service. Stenka, who was at the end of his resources, accepted with joy and camped near Astrakhan. From time to time his troops marched into the town all superbly dressed, wearing crowns covered with pearls and precious stones. Stenka was recognized by the respect shown him; people approaching him on their knees, calling him *Batushka* or father. He was tall, his carriage noble, his looks proud, his only flaw that his face was slightly pockmarked. At first the people of Astrakhan were delighted with the newcomers, as they sold at ridiculously low prices the things which, during four years, they had stolen from Persians, Russians and Tartars. Struys himself bought from them a massive gold chain for forty roubles and silk for a song.

Stenka received Struys and his captain kindly, and was delighted with a gift of two bottles of brandy, since his had run out. He

found by enquiry that they were Dutch sailors and merchants,
under the protection of the Tsar. This was all right at the moment
but later when Stenka, tired of inactivity, retired from Astrakhan
and again turned rebel, it proved disastrous. Before that happened they visited him in his ship on the Volga where he was drinking and making merry with his officers.

'Near him was a Persian princess whom he had seized with her
brother on one of his last raids. He made a present of the young man
to the governor of Astrakhan but kept the princess, whom he loved.
. . . At the end of the day, he became very drunk and leaning over the
ship's side and looking with a dreamy air at the water of the Volga,
he cried after a moment's silence, "No river can be compared with thee.
What do I not owe thee who have given me so many triumphs and
such treasures? I owe thee all that I possess and all that I am. Thou
hast made my fortune and crowned me with benefits but I have
shown ingratitude. . . . I seem to hear thy reproaches, that I have never
given thee anything. Pardon me kind river; I confess that I have
offended and if this confession is not enough to appease thy just anger,
I offer thee with all my heart what is dearest to me in the world."
At which he ran to the princess and threw her into the river, all dressed
as she was in gold cloth and adorned with pearls and precious stones.
The poor princess deserved a better fate and there was no one who
did not pity her in his heart. And, although she was of such a high
rank, and suffered at finding herself in the power of a cruel and brutal
man, yet she had felt an infinite indulgence for him and had never
shown resentment at her captivity. However brutal Razin was, one
must believe that if drink had not maddened him he would not have
done this cruel deed, for until then he had seemed rather just than
inhuman.'

Struys, whose great merit as a travel writer was his inexhaustible
curiosity, tells us that he sought out Razin's followers and got
them to tell him how they had gained such power. It was from
them presumably that he had heard the story of the Persian princess, or did he insert it later on when it had become the famous
Russian folk-tale and song? Certainly it embellishes his memoirs.
When Stenka withdrew from Astrakhan to raise revolt again
among his people, he took with him a large number of officers
and men, whom he had won over to his side. The governor sent
an emissary to him demanding their return. He replied that they
would soon be returning—in a different manner. 'Tell your governor', he said, 'that I am a prince, born free and independent, and
that perhaps his power is not so great as mine.' Soon the people

of Astrakhan were horrified to see a fleet of eighty sail, each boat armed and filled with soldiers 'all eager for loot' and, although the Tsar sent a larger fleet against the rebels, it did him no good, for the Muscovites who had joined Stenka penetrated his ships, inducing the sailors to mutiny and throw their officers into the river. Others penetrated the army; the common soldiers cut the throats of their officers and joined Stenka, who made them an impassioned speech:

'At last, my friends you are free; what you have just done liberates you from the yoke of your tyrants. This yoke is so heavy and cruel that it is amazing that you have borne it so long. Heaven, touched by your tears, has sent you a liberator who, after freeing you from the oppression under which you have been groaning, will love you as his own children and will have for you the heart of a father. In gratitude for this, he asks only sincere affection, inviolable fidelity and a steadfastness proof against the wiles of your enemies. It is to destroy them that Heaven has put you under my protection. Help me and we will finish what we have begun.'

After this speech, the Muscovites whom his gifts had already suborned, swore that they were ready to follow Stenka wherever he might lead, that their zeal was unquenchable, that he would soon see the sort of people he had won to his side. These words were followed by the applause of the whole army and a general cry of 'Long live the prince. Long live the father of his soldiers and may Heaven destroy all tyrants.'

Struys continues:

'Whilst Stenka was triumphing, there was sorrow in Astrakhan where the governor, surprised at the treachery of his fleet, thought vainly of winning it back. To crown his anger he discovered that the people despised him; they had praise only for Stenka; the soldiers said out loud that they were going to quit the service, that they did not receive their pay because it was put to other uses, that it was not fair that they should risk the lives of which so little care was taken.'

Stenka Razin's success alarmed our Dutch sailors exceedingly. It was clear that Astrakhan would soon fall into his hands and that they, being under the Tsar's protection, would all be massacred. They noted that the governor had so little confidence in his own people that he promoted the foreigners—Germans, Dutch, and an English captain, Robert Heut (sic). He put Germans in charge of the city's artillery. The captain of Struys' ship confided in him his plan to cross the Caspian Sea, stealing away secretly in the dead of night. He was a harsh man and forbade him to warn the two sailors, Cornelius Brak and Jacop Trappen, because they had their wives and children with them, and they might be an encumbrance. 'However I thought that this command was contrary to Christian charity and that it was cruel to abandon our compatriots to the rage of a people who would give them no quarter, so I warned them and saw to it that Brak came on board with his wife and child.' Trappen, who hadn't enough money for the journey, was forced to stay. 'We recommended him to divine Providence.'

They set off through the arms of the Volga and, although in their small sloop they were in great danger from storms as well as of losing their way, Struys noted everything that they passed and was especially interested in how the fishermen at the mouth of the Volga, caught sturgeon. They planted stakes in triangles to trap the fish. They killed them with javelins and made caviar from their roe,

'which is the only part which they value; as to the fish, they care little for it and salt only some of it, as the lower orders in Moscow buy it. The sale of caviar here is as great as the sale of butter in Holland. The Muscovites do not eat butter during their fasts, using caviar instead for all their sauces, so that they consume vast quantities of it.'

They sailed into the Caspian Sea, whose water, Struys noted, was sweet and excellent to drink. They landed for a while at Terki, which had been well fortified by a Dutch engineer in 1636 and was now being strengthened by an English colonel.

They next landed in Circassia, where Struys was dazzled by the beauty of the women and their lack of false shame. The breasts which the lower orders expose are

'two globes, well placed, well shaped and of an incredible firmness, and I can say without exaggeration that nothing is so white or so clean. Their eyes are large, sweet and full of fire, their nose well-shaped, their lips vermilion, the mouth small and smiling; . . . their hair of the most beautiful black, sometimes floating and sometimes tied up, and frames their faces most agreeably. They have lovely figures, tall and easy and their whole being seems free and relaxed. In spite of these exquisite gifts they are not really cruel and are not afraid of the approach of men, no matter from what country.'

Their husbands are good-natured and not jealous but it is hard to understand how such beautiful women can love men so ugly. Although they are easy-going, one must not go too far with them. Struys has seen some of his comrades, taken in at first, lose all confidence by their rebuffs. These people appeared to be Mohammedans, but had neither mosques nor mullahs. He saw them celebrate the feast of Elijah.

When Struys and his companions were near Derbent, they decided to abandon their sloop and go on to Persia by land. At first they walked through the bush by night, eating only dry bread without water, but on the fourth day it was decided, against the advice of Struys, to travel by day. Here again the poor Brak with his wife and child would have been abandoned, being asleep when the decision was taken. Struys told his comrades that they were worse than Tartars and woke up the little family. Soon they were all seized by Tartars and taken to their Sultan, Osmin, who after stripping them of most of their belongings (leaving Struys, however, his gold chain and bag of money) let them go on their way. They had not gone far when they fell into the hands of another band of Tartars, crueller than the first lot. One after the other they raped Brak's wife and stripped the party naked, except that they left Struys two pairs of drawers, which he wore one over the other. One pair he gave Brak's wife to help to hide her nakedness. (Later on Brak was sold as a slave and his wife taken into a prince's harem.)

A little farther on Struys and two of his companions were captured by another band, who believed that they were some of Stenka Razin's men, whom they detested. They were tortured and put into chains and eventually brought before Sultan Mahomet, the son of Osmin, who kept them as his slaves.

Once Struys is out of Muscovy his story can be briefly told. By this time we are accustomed to find him always behaving in an exemplary manner; not only is he charitable, willing to disobey orders when these are unkind, but we also notice that when his advice is not taken the consequences are always disastrous. While he was a slave to Osmin's son, he was even more heroic—remaining not only faithful to the wife he had not seen for years but also to his Christian faith. Osmin's son told him that if he would embrace the true faith and become a Mohommedan, he would not only free him but also give him two beautiful wives and make him head of his army. The two women, who were not bad looking, came twice to try to seduce him. He politely declined their kind offers, pointing out that his faith, which he refused to abjure, allowed him only one wife and she awaited him in Holland. This they thought exaggerated and indeed ridiculous. Struys was finally sold in Derbent to a Persian, Hadji Biram. He was in luck, for Persians were kinder to their slaves than Turks. Moreover he was lucky enough to save his master from drowning in the sea. After this his master treated him very humanely and promised to take him to Isfahan, where he would find his fellow countrymen. In the meanwhile he had caught the eye of Aline, the principal wife of his master, a Dutch captain's daughter who had been abducted at the age of twelve. She had plenty of money and told Struys that they could escape and together make the journey to Holland where, if his wife happened to be dead, she would marry him. The plan tempted him extremely. Not only was Aline charming and a Christian, she had also a vast quantity of jewels and bags full of money which she showed him. He knew of a boat they could take and he knew the Caspian Sea. But he was not a Dutchman for nothing. He did not dare to go to Astrakhan as long as Stenka Razin was ruling it. His adventures continued as various as ever and, as always, he noted the manners and customs of the people with whom, though a slave, he came into contact. The religion of an Indian tribe struck him as most extraordinary. On one of their fêtes they went to a river, throwing into it rice and beans for the fishes and then did the same for the insects

'of whom they took a singular care. For they would rather die than kill a single animal. They stir up the water to save the fishes from the nets and cry with all their might to make the birds fly away. And this great pity they have not only for beasts, but also for their own kind, whom they refuse to fight. They will not even light candles, for fear that flies will get burned in them.

(If anything makes one believe in Struys' experiences and the accounts of the people he met, it is this description of a religion which, of all others must at the time have seemed the most incredible to the Western mind.)[2]

Struys, for his sins left his kind master for the Polish ambassador, who nearly starved him to death. In October 1673 he borrowed

---

[2] Today we are used to these beliefs though we are sometimes brought up against them in a way that touches us. When the Tibetan children came to England they were acutely distressed by our brutal ways with flies and would respectfully follow round the swatters, picking up their victims and trying to bring them back to life.

money, bought his master a horse and was liberated. Hadji Biram, remembering how he had saved his life, gave him presents and so did his sad wife Aline, lamenting as she handed him a well-filled purse that she was destined to spend the rest of her life among infidels. Although Struys had by this time heard that Stenka Razin had been captured and taken prisoner to Moscow, and that Astrakhan was liberated, he was no longer tempted by Aline's plot. As a free man he could return home in a less adventurous and dangerous manner and in the meantime could visit Isfahan. And it is here that we take our leave of Struys, still enquiring, still wondering, still trusting to a kind Providence which did, indeed, bring him back safely to his home in Holland.

POSTSCRIPT TO J. STRUYS' *Travels in Muscovy*

Volume III of J. Struys' *Voyage en Muscovie* takes us away from Russia. It starts with a description of Isfahan, tells us how Struys took ship and came to Batavia; how, at last, longing for his home, he embarks for Holland, is taken prisoner by the cruel English in St Helena and is eventually put ashore by them in Ireland. This, compared to Muscovy and Batavia, is next door to home. Struys, only interested in his picaresque adventures in all quarters of the world, wastes no time in describing his reunion with his wife and children, nor on what it felt like to settle down to a respectable, quiet life in one of those neat, bright, houses with their polished tile floors and the sun coming through the windows which we know so well from Vermeer's pictures. The wholesome loaves and cheeses depicted by Pieter Hooch and Ter Borch must have been especially acceptable to Struys whose most sensational chapter in this third volume describes his shipwreck on the Indian coast and the torments of hunger which he suffered there with his comrades. He spares us nothing; not even the digging up and devouring of corpses. Accustomed as we are to find Struys always siding with virtue and reinforcing it with reason, it is no surprise to find him dissuading a comrade from cannibalism, first on the grounds that God had given formal instruction against killing, secondly that the proposed victim, a woman, was only a skeleton covered with skin and would not make a juicy morsel and thirdly that, once human flesh was tasted, the appetite for it increased and none of the ship-wrecked party would feel safe. When the temptation came again to the famished men, it was scotched by the reasonable suggestion that they should draw lots amongst themselves for their victim. No one felt willing to let Providence decide his fate in this haphazard manner. After innumerable adventures, including fighting for the Great Mogul, building ships for him and sailing down the Ganges, Struys managed to get out of India; he neglects to tell us how. It does not much matter. We know that he always escapes from his tight corners. What we should have liked to hear is what he does when he is at home and no longer in one. About this he is silent.

PART III
1698–1801

THE WINDOW INTO EUROPE

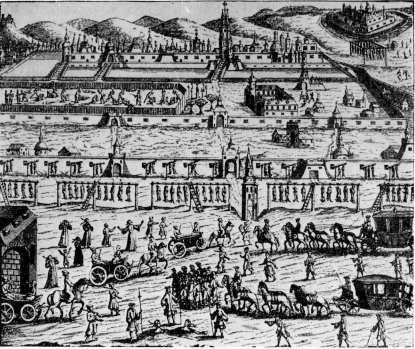

I

Above: Fire, the scourge of town and village (p. 110).

Middle: The 'purge' of the *Streltsi* (p. 107).

Below: Voronezh at the beginning of the eighteenth century (p. 101).

IV

Ice slides (p. 115).

INTRODUCTION

In the eighteenth century, after Peter the Great's opening of his 'window', Western visitors to Russia increased enormously. They were very articulate and many of their memoirs, letters and books have come down to us. We are faced by the difficulty of choice. The secret dispatches of ambassadors are a valuable source of information for students of international relations and court intrigues. Often they seem no more than the gossip columns of history. These are discarded as in the main, irrelevant to the object of this book which, as pointed out in the Preface, is to show how the Russian people lived and how they faced the problems set them by their inexorable climate, the geography of their vast country and the arbitrary rule of their masters.

Many eighteenth-century ambassadors throw incidental light on these subjects. Sir George Macartney is an instance. He was a pleasure-loving, witty, handsome young man, who (if Casanova is to be believed[1]) was recalled by our Foreign Office at the request of Catherine the Great, because he had had the impertinence to fall in love with one of her maids of honour. Macartney has apt things to say, not only about the courtiers with whom he mixed but about the common people, whom he described as extremely docile when properly handled and as 'having a greater share of honesty than we have any right to expect'. He is said to have been £6,000 in debt when he left Russia.

Sir James Harris, ambassador at the difficult and humiliating time when we were losing our American colonies (1778–83) is mostly concerned with diplomatic relations, the rise and fall of court favourites, and whom (and how much) to bribe. In a letter to a friend he summarizes the miseries of an ambassador to Catherine II.

> Now for a word on this country; you know its extent, its high reputation—nothing but great deeds are done in it. The monarch is an arrant wonan—a vain spoilt woman. . . . the men in high life, monkeys grafted on bears . . . Religion, virtue and morality nowhere to be found; honour cannot be expressed in this language. There is no reward for good actions, no punishment for any crimes. The face

[1] Casanova was leading his adventures in St Petersburg while Macartney was English ambassador there (1765): *Mémoires de Casanova*, VII.

D

of the country in this neighbourhood is a desert, the climate never to be lived in. . . . You will naturally suppose living here not very comfortable.'

We can put aside the ambassadors to make room for people less exalted. Most interesting of these are Captain John Perry, the hydraulic engineer employed by Peter the Great to build a canal and scrape his warships, and John Cook, a Scottish doctor who came to Russia, he tells us, for a change of air. Both these men stayed for fourteen years and wrote graphic accounts of their experiences and the people they worked with.

Dr John Bell is another Scottish physician who worked for several years in Russia, accompanying Peter the Great's embassies to Peking, Persia and Istanbul. He wrote good descriptions of the regions through which he passed. But, with apologies to Dr Johnson who warmly recommended his *Travels* to Boswell, we have preferred Dr John Cook's experiences to Dr Bell's, as more personal, fuller of incident and odd characters.

Jonas Hanway is another visitor whose travels through Russia are omitted. Hanway is an endearing figure, best known as the inventor of the umbrella and for his courage in carrying it through hooting crowds in London (less remembered for his efforts to reclaim fallen women and improve the condition of chimney sweeps and foundlings). From this generous, eccentric Englishman one might expect a picturesque book on Russia, but the book we have is disappointing. He was sent, in 1743, by the Russia Company, to improve our trade relations with that country and with Persia. He was a good choice from their point of view, for he had an almost religious feeling about the value of commerce, and the supremacy of England as a mercantile nation as well as in all other ways. He travelled, he writes, 'about four thousand miles, through a variety of adventures and accidents', and the journal which he wrote should have been a thrilling story. But he wrote it to convince the public of the all-importance of Anglo-Russian trade relations, to remind English merchants of the happy employment they were in, for 'few callings are so free and independent', and to remind them, too, that the Almighty had chosen their island not only to be the granary of Europe and America but also 'to befriend mankind in clothing them in every quarter of the globe'.

Mrs Vigor's letters to a friend are included because they are entertaining and shrewd. Like her admired Lady Mary Wortley

Montagu, she lost none of her advantages as an intimate of court circles.

The distinguished astronomer and scientist, the abbé Chappe d'Auteroche, urging his *izvoztchiks* across muddy steppes, along frozen rivers and through gloomy forests in carriages and sledges that were always breaking down, takes us with him all the way. We share his panic lest he miss his rendezvous with Venus, on June 6, 1761, in Tobolsk. He carries the culture and gallantry of eighteenth-century France into the wilds of Muscovy and through him we see many Russian things with new eyes.

Another Frenchman, Masson—who with his brother served Catherine the Great in her armies for ten years, only to be expelled by her son the Tsar Paul—wrote amusing secret memoirs on his experiences and observations, but his portraits of Catherine's favourites and his court gossip are more relevant to historians than to the purpose of this book.

We end with the scholar, William Richardson, who spent four years in St Petersburg as tutor to the sons of Lord Cathcart, the English ambassador. He wrote a shocking account of the slavery of the serfs as well as some entertaining anecdotes. This yields better extracts than the weighty book of William Coxe, another tutor, accompanying his pupils on the grand tour. This was famous in its day and necessary reading for ambassadors and other visitors to Russia. But it is a pedestrian work and we leave it respectfully behind.

CAPTAIN JOHN PERRY

The State of Russia under the Present Tsar

London 1716

WHEN Peter the Great came to London in 1698 to study shipbuilding, John Perry was recommended to him as a 'person capable of serving him in his new designs of establishing a fleet, making his rivers navigable . . . particularly the making of a communication between the River Volga and the Don'.

Perry was pleased at this opportunity of exercising his skill in a far-away, foreign country under an enterprising, unconventional young ruler. This was not merely because he was a spirited, adventurous fellow but also because he was under a cloud in his own country. He had entered the English Navy at an early age and advanced so rapidly that when only twenty-three, he was put in sole command of a ship. Unfortunately he fell foul of the captain of a larger vessel, was court-martialled, fined £1,000 and sentenced to ten years imprisonment in the Marshalsea. His release after five years coincided with Peter the Great's arrival at Deptford and his request for an experienced naval engineer. Perry was promised a salary of £300, over and above a subsistence allowance, and a promise of further liberal rewards if he should give good service.

Perry's account of Russia is the most vivid, detailed and factual after those of the Tudor adventurers recorded by Hakluyt or the even more widely famous book of Olearius. It is indeed more valuable than these because, for fourteen years, Perry was working with the commoners of Russia on practical jobs. He would have stayed on in Russia indefinitely, his design being, he tells us, to marry a woman of that country 'for whom he had long had a great esteem', but he could never get the money he had been promised, and was continually hampered in his work by reactionary boyars who hated the Tsar's innovations. In the end, he made so many enemies among the great lords of the land that, in fear of his life, he fled the country (in 1712) under the protection of the British ambassador, Mr Whitworth.

Perry's book, although a record of personal frustration and failure, was in itself a great triumph. It was widely read, and influenced both English and French opinion about Russia throughout the century. It can still be read with enjoyment, as a story of adventure as well as for its first-hand account of a great period of Russian history.

Perry's first assignment was the making of a canal between the Volga and the Don. This would have enabled ships to sail from the Caspian to the Black Sea. The canal was to run between the Camishinka (Kamyshin), a tributary of the Volga, and the Lavla, a tributary of the Don, a distance of three miles. It had been begun by a German engineer who had fled the country soon after starting it. Perry worked on it for three summers but only received half of the 30,000 men promised him, and neither the necessary artificers nor materials. Moreover, he made an enemy of Prince Galitzin, the governor of the district, who declared it 'as his opinion, that God had made the rivers to go one way, and it was presumption in man to think to turn them to another'. Most of the old boyars, Perry adds, 'had a dislike to all new undertakings which the Tsar by the advice of strangers engaged in'.

After three years, with 'several sluices near finished and the canal half dug', Perry was ordered to leave the work and come to the Voronezh, a tributary of the Don, to rescue His Majesty's ships which, being built of green timber, were decayed and like to sink in the river. Here he embarked on what turned out to be his most successful task in Russia. He built sluices and locks and in sixteen months he placed fifteen ships (some of them with fifty guns) on dry land to be refitted, stripped down and repaired. He also made the Voronezh navigable to a farther distance.

With the works of the good Captain John Perry (whether projected, left half done or achieved), with his enemies, the unfulfilled promises, the unpaid arrears, we are not concerned. Those who in our days have worked in 'developing countries' will not find his frustrations and disappointments hard to believe. What is new and remarkable in his book is the way he describes the people he worked with, and the things he saw with his own eyes. He had the same curiosity and unsophisticated pleasure in seeing new things as the Tudor sailors but, belonging to the age of Locke and Newton and the Royal Society, he was less naïve than they had been and brought the tales he heard to the test of reason.

He travelled widely, and his first account is of the Samoyeds of Novaya Zemlya. He is full of respect for these hardy people who have adapted themselves so well to the Arctic regions where they were born that they refuse to live anywhere else. Perry gives a detailed description of the houses they make in the snow and the ovens they heat them with, regretting that Captain Willoughby and his crew had not left the ship where they froze to death and, instead, taken shelter in them or built themselves the like. (Although this had taken place 150 years earlier, it was not forgotten.) The Samoyeds are not cannibals as their name implies but a friendly, neighbourly people. They can neither plough, nor sow, nor breed cattle, but live principally on deer and bears, on the fowls of the air and dried fish, with turnips for their bread. They acknowledge the Tsar but refuse the Christian faith, 'taking their rules of life from such of their elders who have lived justly'. Perry was duly impressed by the reindeer 'which God and Nature seem to have designed on purpose for this frozen country . . . they have flat hoofs which spread so much that they run over the top of the frozen snow without sinking into it', whereas Russian horses sink if they go off the beaten track. Moreover, the natives tie thick boards to their feet and run over the snow without sinking into it. These reindeer, which feed on the mosses that grow on trees, serve the natives not only for transport and food but also for raiment and their boots. The bears and wolves are not as dangerous as people imagine, as they do not attack unless threatened.

It was during the three summers when Perry was working at Camishinka that he observed the manners and customs of the Asiatic tribes living on the east of the Volga. Of the Kalmucks he writes that they own protection from the Tsar and

> live in good amity with the Russians and come every year on the east side of Volga and trade with the Tsar's people. . . . They live in tents and move northward and southward according to the season of the year with their flocks and herds and their wives and families. . . . Their way of life is like that which Moses relates in the first ages of the world; they neither plough nor sow but move from place to place for fresh pasture and take the fruits of the earth as they find them. They keep time with the fowls of the air and move back southward

in the winter to the borders of the Caspian Sea. As soon as the snow melts away and the spring appears in its verdure they move on, sometimes to the latitude of 2 or 3 and 50 degrees North, and some sooner and some later spread the country in parties, sometimes 20,000 of them in a body and pitch their tents in streets and lanes in the same regular manner as in a town or village and every one knows their due place and order, so that I have seen the cows stop at their own tents, when they drive them home to milk them. As they go backward and forward they usually come on the east side of the Volga and stay 2 or 3 weeks or more and barter their sheep, horses and cattle with the Russians for corn and meal, for copper and iron, kettles, knives scissors, etc., and take also some cloth and linen from the Russians.

In a footnote Perry records that their sheep make very good mutton, that they have a flap of hard fat instead of tails and that the skin of the black lamb is sold for two or three times the price of the lamb itself, having a strong, smooth curl with a beautiful gloss.

The wives and children, Perry tells us, are transported in covered waggons drawn by

'dromedaries, which is a large beast, bigger than a camel, with two humps on the back which serve as a saddle for men to ride on; they have a pace easy and smooth and these creatures carry the tents and baggage and are taught to kneel down and receive their burden, though they do it usually with a grumbling sort of noise.

With their hair, cloth is woven, and the Russians make hats of this material.

Perry describes their tents made without poles, covered with a stuff like felt, with a hole at the top to let out smoke, as warm as a stove when the door is shut.

He makes little distinction between these Kalmucks and the Tartars. He does not realize that the Kalmucks are Buddhists. He thinks that, like the Tartars, they are Muslims. He writes:

'When I was employed in making the communication at Camishinka, above half the labourers that were sent to dig the canal there were of these Tartars, and most of the horse that were sent to cover the workmen were of the gentry or better sort of the same people. I have often taken occasion to ask them about their religion and they say that the Russians using of images is too great a terror to them to think of embracing their religion, for that there is but one God and that He cannot be pictured or described by men: they are afraid to do evil or change their religion for fear that He will not afterwards bless them . . . . As to these Tartars, I must do them the justice that as often as I had occasion to trust or make use of them, both I and all my assistants have observed that we have found them sincere and honest in their lives and ingenuous in their conversation, above what we have observed in the Russian nation.'

Perry, firm Protestant that he was, says that he had often told these men that 'were the Christian religion to be laid down to them in that purity as it was delivered by our Saviour and his Apostles and as it is taught by the doctrine of the Church of England . . . they would very readily and gladly, long ere this, have embraced the Christian religion.'

Perry takes this occasion for one of his customary diatribes against what he considers the superstitious and corrupt nature of the Russian Church. He inveighs against the drunkenness both of priests and people on all Church festivals. He notes, as most foreigner travellers do, that it is not considered a scandal to be drunk, that a man lying in the gutter will say, 'What will you, Father, it is a holiday and I am drunk.' Unlike many foreigners who found tipsy Russians good-natured, happy and non-violent, Perry says that they (for want of being better taught by the priests) commit all sorts of wickedness, not only robbery and murder but 'even the horrible sin of sodomy, being scarce looked on as a crime in this country'.

The sceptical Perry had already seen the millstone on which St Antony had sailed in four days from the Tiber, through the Ocean and Baltic Sea. This was kept in the monastery dedicated to him, near Novgorod. Perry saw it and remarked, 'I believe no cork will swim like it.' But the monks would not show him the uncorrupted body of the saint—a miracle, it was said, accorded to many men of saintly life in Russia. St Antony's feat was outdone, he felt, by the Mother of God who 'had come through the air from Constantinople in 24 hours' and swept a monastery from one side of the River Tiffin to the other, where it would be more convenient for worshippers—both miracles equally possible, the Russians said, to the omnipotent power of God, 'and it is as much as a man's life is worth to dispute the validity of these things with them'.

Perry had little respect for the 'popes' or priests, who 'never preach to the people, for it is a thing they have no skill in'. He had known men bred to the handicraft trades to be admitted to the priests' office, their main qualification being that they had a good clear voice 'and can say over *"Gospodi Pomilui"* twelve or fifteen times in the same breath'. Only in Kiev, 700 miles from Moscow, was there a school for priests. He notes the custom that

> 'when any person comes into a room to pay a visit, the first thing they do as soon as they get their feet within the door is to cross themselves, saying *'Gospodi Pomilui';* at the same time with great reverence bowing to he pictures and then to turn to make their compliments to the master of the house and so round to the rest of the company. . . . For it is a thing very reasonable that you should first make your compliment to God.'

It happens that Russians going into a very poor house blackened by smoke and with no candle burning under the ikon, for this can only be afforded on holidays, 'cannot see the picture and presently enquire *'Gdye Bog?'* (Where is God?) and then pay their devotions, sometimes knocking their heads on the floor, which is often done also to great men'.

Perry looking down from his superior Protestant heights on what seemed to him mere ridiculous superstition naturally felt great sympathy with the Tsar in his attempts to check religious

2   Revering the ikons.

extravagances and to drag his people out of the medieval quagmire in which they had sunk, and to bring them into line with Western civilization. Scattered throughout his book are accounts of how the Tsar did this. He never blames the Tsar for all the obstructions his work encountered, the failure to pay his arrears and so on, but always the boyars and administrators whom the Tsar, busy with his wars first against the Swedes and then the Turks, could not control.

'The occasion of his [Peter's] first falling upon the thoughts of shipping and of his travelling to inspect the improvements of other countries was owing chiefly to his early genius and curiosity to enquire into the reasons and causes of things; which method in his common conversation he still uses with indefatigable application in minutest things.'

Perry had seen the Tsar, dressed like a workman, in the shipyards of Deptford and Amsterdam.

'His humour did not lead him to the courts of princes but he employed his time conversing with common artificers, that were masters of such arts as were wanting in his country. . . . He wrought one part of the day with the carpenter's broad axe among the Dutchmen and for the better disguise wore the same sort of habit as they did.'

Sometimes he went to

'private entertainments where he would be very free and merry with a few persons, which to this day is his way and is most agreeable to him. . . . And I have often heard him say when he has been a little merry that he thinks it a much happier life to be an Admiral in England than Tsar in Russia.'

Peter admired the beauty and proportion of English ships and vowed he would only have English-built ships made in his country and therefore took back with him several builders and artificers.

'He would sometimes be at the smiths and sometimes at the gunfounders and there was scarce any art or mechanic trade whatsoever from the watch-maker to the coffin-maker but he inspected it. He even visited our churches and had the curiosity to see our Quakers.'

The practical Perry was delighted with the Tsar's innovations: that the boyars had to send their sons abroad to be educated; that he took away many young monks for his armies and for building St Petersburg; that no man should beome a monk till he was fifty; that monasteries being useless he took away some of their lands; that he cut short the long coats that the nobles wore; that he ordered that women should be entertained in the same room as the man; and even that beards should be shaven off or a fine paid, for wearing one.[1] When the Tsar came to Voronezh there was a great slaughter of beards.

'One of the first that I met with just coming from the hands of the barber was an old Russian carpenter, that had been with me at Camishinka, who was a very good workman with his hatchet, and whom I always had a friendship for. I jested with him a little on this occasion, telling him that he was become a young man and asked him what he had done with his beard? Upon which he put his hand upon his bosom and pulled it out, telling me that when he came home he would lay it up to have it put in his coffin and buried along with him, that he might be able to give an account of it to St Nicholas, when he came to the other world and that all his fellow workmen had taken the same care.'

Although these changes were considered a sin in the Tsar and a breach of their religion, more particularly as being brought in by strangers, the women liked their husbands and sweethearts better. They were also pleased because the Tsar forbade forced marriages 'and made an order that no young couple should be married together without their own free liking and consent'.

---

[1] J. G. Korb, secretary to the imperial envoy, describes Peter the Great's return to Moscow after his visits to Holland and England. Vast crowds of boyars flocked to pay him court and show their loyalty by casting themselves on the ground to worship him. Barbers were present to shave off beards. 'Nor was there anybody left to laugh at the rest. They were all born to the same fate. Nothing but superstitious awe for his office exempted the Patriarch. . . . The General-in-Chief of the Tsar's troops was the first who submitted the encumbrance of his long beard to the razor.' Korb goes on to describe how this same general so excited the Tsar's anger that, at a banquet at which he and other distinguished foreigners were present, Peter drew his sword and would have killed him had not General Lefort, 'catching the Tsar in his arms, drawn back his hand from the stroke'. Lefort, a foreigner, Swiss in origin, was the only one who could have done this for he was more beloved by Peter than any Muscovite. 'Merriment followed this dire tempest.' Korb's account of the manners and customs of the Muscovites in this early period of Peter the Great's reign is invaluable. It was published in Vienna in 1700, but because of its bloodcurdling account of the execution of the *Streltsi* (illustrated with realistic engravings) it was suppressed by order of the imperial court, at the request of the Russian government. (The *Streltsi* were old Muscovite soldiers who had risen against the 'foreign' Tsar and his 'Germans', as all strangers like Lefort and Gordon were called.)

See *Diary of J. G. Korb, an Austrian Secretary of Legation to the Court of Tsar Peter the Great,* translated from the Latin by Count MacDonnell (London, 1863).

3   A great slaughter of beards.

Before this they had not been allowed to see each other till the day before the wedding.

His greatest admiration for the Tsar was for the way he created his navy out of nothing and reformed his army from top to bottom, learning everything himself the hard way.

'He is from the drummer to the general a complete soldier; besides his being engineer, cannoneer, fire-workers, ship-builder, turner, boatswain, gun-founder, blacksmith, etc. All which he frequently works at with his own hands and will himself see that everything is performed to his own mind, as well as in these minutest things as in the greater disposition of affairs.'

For once he has a good word to say for the Russians; 'As to the common foot soldiers, there are some very remarkable things which render them as fit for service as any in the world.' When they travel on the steppes they make a fire 'and sleep in the time of severest frosts and do not catch cold'. He attributes this to their habit of taking a weekly sweating bath and then coming out naked to jump in the river. 'With rye bread and water they will march fourteen days together. Moreover they do not seem to value or be discouraged by death.' The sixteenth-century sailors had noted the same hardiness, as indeed did our allies and their German enemies in the Second World War.

Perry had an eye for the beauty of the country, even of the steppes, which so many travellers found monotonous and dreary.

'The country all the way from Camishinka to Terki [the Crimea], as it is in the best climate of the world, so it is for the most part extremely fertile and pleasant to inhabit. In the spring of the year as soon as ever the snow is off the ground, which usually does not lie above two or three months in these parts, the warm weather immediately afterwards takes place; and the tulips, roses, lilies of the valley, pinks, sweetwilliams and several other flowers and herbs, spring up like a garden, in very great variety. Asparagus, the best I ever eat, grows so thick that you may in some places mow it down and the common grass in the meadow is up to the horse's belly. Liquorice, almonds and cherries the fields are covered with, but the trees are low and the fruits small. And also in autumn appear ripe several sorts of grain and fruits of the earth which by cultivation might be much improved. There is great variety of birds and wild-fowl in abundance of all sorts both of land and water; and also small fallow deer, reindeer, elks, wild boar, wild-horses, wild sheep of which I once eat part of one, that being chased by a wolf was taken by a fisherman in his boat on the River Volga; it eat tenderer and was much preferable to common mutton.'

After this, Perry describes the terrible steppe fires which he has often seen, 'the flames reflected on the clouds in a dark night and in a cloud of smoke by day', the fires running on sometimes for 20

or 40 miles until they come to a river. The grass neither mowed
nor eaten by cattle for want of inhabitants grows dry and is lit
by the fires which Russians or Tartars make, when they stop to
bait their horses and rest and prepare their victuals.

'It is a thousand times to be lamented that so rich and noble a
country, situated on the side of the great River Volga, which is
perhaps the best stored with fish of any river in the whole world . . .
should now lie in a manner waste without inhabitants, while the
Samoyeds pass their days in misery, and even many of the Northern
Russians I have seen, for want of sun enough to ripen their harvest,
mingle roots of grass and straw with their corn to make bread.'

As the Tsar has 'fallen on thoughts of improving sailing vessels
for the use of the Caspian sea' he will be able to trade not only with
Persians and Armenians but also with Great Tartary, and 'English merchants whom I have talked with in Moscow believe it
might be a means to vend considerable quantities of English cloth'.
Describing the fruits on the Caspian Sea (apricots, peaches,
grapes, etc.), Perry is eloquent about the two sorts of melon,
especially the water melon, 'of a beautiful rose colour, full of juice
with an exquisite taste which quenches thirst and never surfeits'.
About fires, the great scourge, because of their frequency, of
Russian towns and villages, Perry has much to say. In Moscow

'I have seen it in less than half a day's time burn above a Russian
mile in length and destroy many thousand houses before it has been
quenched and often without giving the inhabitants opportunity to
carry off the tenth part of their goods. This has often brought many
people to the last degree of poverty,'[1]

He blames the habit of paving the streets with wood, also the
lords, counsellors and their creatures for putting a tax on bricks,
'whereby many men who would willingly build their houses with
bricks to preserve themselves from ruin by fire are unable to do it'.
Life in Russia is not all hardship and melancholy.

'There are two remarkable times of the year when the Russians
express their joy: the one is when the snow first falls on the ground
and the winter is so strongly set in, that the rivers are so frozen up,

[1] 'Hardly any great festival of the year passes without being followed by a
conflagration. Some of the Germans who had run to put out the last fire' by
which six hundred houses were devoured, being falsely accused of theft, were
cast into the flames and immolated to the fury of the people.' J. G. Korb.

that they can pass with their horses and sledges upon the ice. Then they have an opportunity of land-carriage by sledge, which is certainly the most commodious and swiftest travelling in the world either for passengers or goods. The whole winter through there come several thousand sledges every day laden into Moscow, usually but with one horse, the cost of land carriage not above a fourth or fifth so much as it is in summer on wheels.

'The other time of their rejoicing is in the spring of the year: after the ice has been some days rotten and dangerous and then breaks away, the river becomes open and free for the boats to pass. On these two occasions the Russians hold a kind of festival and are merry with their neighbours.'

Perry was a kind man as well as a shrewd and practical one. He grieved at

'the many and sinister ways the governors and men in power contrive some pretended fault to be charged upon a man and examine him with threats of the knout or battocks; let justice be as it will, every man according to his substance must either suffer stripes or buy off his punishment with money. . . . The common boors and peasants who have been sent upon the works under my command have complained to me, with tears, of wrongs and injuries done them by the governors of towns and other officers, particularly when I was at Voronezh. But when I have promised to them that I would do my utmost and engage to obtain right for them, they have thereupon earnestly begged of me by no means to mention the things they have complained of, alleging that they would be ruined for their complaining of those in power over them.'

Another cause of misery was

'for those who were ingenious or better workmen than their neighbours for they have oftentimes more labour and work committed to their charge but have no encouragement given them for their ingenuity. . . . Notwithstanding all that I could do, I could never obtain so much as a single kopeck a day encouragement for any one person, it not being the manner of Russia on any such works as I was employed on, to pay any money or wages out of the Tsar's Treasure. All the common people or peasants are slaves, whether to the Tsar himself or to the boyars or monasteries. In fact the way of reckoning the value of an estate is according to the number of slaves upon it. When the Tsar wants workers he orders the governors to conscript them, and there is no precedent for the giving of money for men to do their duty and if they did not do their work they must be beaten to it. Upon these considerations it is no great wonder that the Russians are the most dull and heavy people to attain any art or science of any people in the world and the most apt to rebel. . . . The Tsar where he is present does indeed give encouragement to some who have the happiness to be under his eye, but his boyars are quite of another temper.'

Perry feared that if the Tsar should happen to die

'the generality of things wherein he has taken so much pains to reform his country will resolve into their old form, for it is believed that his son [the unfortunate Alexis] adheres to bigotry and superstition and will easily be prevailed upon to come into the old methods of Russia and lay aside many of those laudable things that have been begun by the present Tsar.'

One of the chief causes that make the nobility uneasy is

'that the Tsar obliges them to come and live at Petersburg with their wives and families, where they are obliged to build new houses for themselves and where all manner of provisions are usually three or four times as dear, or forage for their horses at least six or eight times as dear, as it is at Moscow. In Moscow all the lords and men of distinction have not only very large buildings within the city but also their country seats and villages, where they have their fish-ponds, their gardens with plenty of several sorts of fruit and places of pleasure. Besides, Moscow is the native place which the Russians are fond of and where they have their friends and acquaintance about them and their provision comes in easy and cheap, brought by their slaves.'

Perry declares that when he first saw Moscow with its steeples, cupolas and crosses at the tops of churches, gilded and painted over, he had thought it the most rich and beautiful city in the world, but inside it he was disappointed 'by the meanness of so many of the houses which, because of fires, had constantly to be rebuilt'.

At last, Captain Perry, in fear of the nobles he had offended, had to flee for his life. He knew that the Tsar, who loved to have skilful foreigners working for him, would never give him permission to leave. For fourteen years' work, of all the money promised him, he had been given barely one year's pay. The canal between the Volga and the Don was unfinished and destined to remain so until the twentieth century. He was a brilliant engineer and furious that he could not finish the work assigned to him. He guessed that the resources of Russia were immense, and grieved that they should not be exploited. He was maddened by the stupidity and ignorance of the ruling class and of the church which kept the people in darkness and induced them to oppose their enlightened Tsar.

Yet we read this book, not as a record of failure, but as we read *Robinson Crusoe;* the story of a man who sees everything with his own eyes, for whom facts are precious things, and who notes them down with the precision and loving care that make them vivid and unforgettable. Perry lived at the time when Defoe was writing his masterpiece. He has the same sense of reality, the same gift to tell the truth as he saw it, unadorned. His book deserves to be read still, like *Robinson Crusoe*. The two books please in much the same way, but Captain John Perry's narrative skill is at the service of history.

MRS VIGOR

Letters from a Lady in Russia

London 1775

MRS VIGOR is a valuable source of information about the court life of the Tsarina Anne. She was the daughter of Mr Goodwin, a Yorkshire clergyman, whose fortune she inherited when her brother died. She married, in 1728, Thomas Ward, the English Consul General, with whom she lived in Russia till his death in 1731. Soon after his death she married Claudius Rondeau, the English Resident in Russia. He explained the event in a letter to the Foreign Office.

'I have received many favours from the late consul Ward, with whom I have lived during his lifetime like a brother. I thought I could not do better than to marry his widow, who is a person of great worth. This is a miserable country for a single man that is willing to mind his business.'

Until Mr Rondeau's death in 1739, his wife's letters to a woman friend at home and his own despatches to the Foreign Office provided a running commentary on their lives at court. Hers are full of amusing gossip. She gives racy descriptions of the ceremonies she attended—christenings, marriages and funerals—and critical, though not malicious, analyses of the favourites and other powerful men at the Russian court. She did not share the contempt that so many of the English and Germans felt for the Russians. On the contrary she liked them. An English visitor described her as 'adorned with every perfection to be wished for in her sex; very tall and perfectly genteel'. She always behaved correctly and gave a ball every year on the day of the English king's birthday.

She gives a good example of her notable gentility in the letter in which she describes a favourite sport of the court ladies and gentlemen that she observed in 1735. A long wooden chute stretching from the top of a house to the courtyard below was covered with ice. The sport was to dash down it in a sleigh. Often the occupant tumbled head over heels. 'I was terrified out of my wits', Mrs Rondeau writes, 'for fear of being obliged to go down this shocking place, for I had not only the dread of breaking my neck but of being exposed to indecency too frightful to think of without horror.' One day the dreaded moment came. Someone said to her in public, 'You have never been down.' She was ready to die with horror, when the Tsarina Anne, who had always been kind to her, intervened. She was pregnant and not in a condition to go down. (The legend of English women's gentility and excessive prudishness persisted through Tsarist times and was fed by the numerous governesses and nurses who entered Russian upper-class families. It crops up again and again in novels and stories. One remembers the silent, buttoned-up woman who went fishing with her master in the Chekhov tale. After a moment of hesitation, he strips and jumps naked into the river for, after all, it is impossible to think of her as a woman or as having anything to do with sex. Turgenev's heroes, too, meet English women in Germany and turn away from their icy, disapproving looks.)

Perhaps because of her position at court, Mrs Rondeau writes in flattering terms of the Tsarina Anne who, according to other accounts, was a woman of vulgar mind, hard and unfeeling. She used to chat to Mrs Rondeau, who often beguiled weary hours at her embroidery frame, giving her the impression that she was affable and would have been 'a fine agreeable woman had she been a private person'. About Anne's sister, the Tsarevna Elizabeth, later to be Empress and a great patron of the arts, Mrs Rondeau was nearer the mark.

'The Princess Elizabeth who is, you know, the daughter of Peter the First, is very handsome. She is very fair with light brown hair, large sprightly blue eyes, fine teeth and a pretty mouth. She is inclinable to be fat but is very genteel and dances better than anyone I ever saw. She speaks German, French and Italian, is extremely gay and talks to everybody in a very proper manner but hates the ceremony of the court. . . . . I have a veneration for her and fondness in my heart, that makes the visit to her a thing of pleasure, not of ceremony. She has an affability and sweetness of behaviour that insensibly inspire love and respect. In public she has an unaffected gaiety, and a certain air of giddiness, that seem entirely to possess her whole mind; but in private I have heard her talk in such a strain of good sense and steady reasoning, that I am persuaded the other behaviour is a feint; but she seems easy; I say *seems*, for who knows the heart?'

Of Anne's detestable and extremely unpopular German favourites, the Duke and Duchess of Courland, Mrs Rondeau writes frankly and perspicaciously.

'They continue so much in favour, that it is by their frown or smile that the whole empire is happy or miserable. . . . They have the whole people at their command. He has a great share of pride and a great deal of passion and, when he is in one, vehement in his expressions. . . . He has a contempt of the Russians which he shows to the greatest of them so publicly, on all occasions, that I fancy it will one day be his ruin. His duchess is haughty and sour and has a harshness in her looks and manner that forbids the respect it would command, for as she is suddenly so much advanced in station, she is out of her sphere and thinks that to be haughty is to command respect.'

Of the Duke of Courland she wrote in another letter:

'When he shakes off the minister, he is a very entertaining companion. He has been very gallant but never cared for the trouble of a woman of distinction; so his amours have made no great noise, and now he seems to regard the sex in the light of mere gay and pretty toys (to unbend his mind when he has a leisure hour to fling away in trifles and chat).'

Of Russian friends, she speaks with the greatest enthusiasm of the cabinet minister Count Jyagosenki.

'His person is fine, he has a countenance, not of regular features but great majesty, vivacity and expression. He has a negligence and ease in his manner, so natural in him that everyone must think nothing else would become him. He has a fine understanding and judgment and the vivacity so strongly painted in his face runs through his whole character; for he dispatches more business in one day than most others do in a week. He always speaks his sentiments without flattery to those in high stations, which in this country is so dangerous that it makes his friends daily tremble for him. He loves to shake off the incumbrance of ceremonies that attend his station and to dine in a family way with a friend and is then the most delightful companion one can meet with.'

Of another member of the cabinet council Count Czerkaskoi, she says that his main title to fame is his great riches: 'he has thirty thousand heads of family who are his slaves and one only daughter to inherit them.'

Mrs Rondeau tells the story of the Polish ambassador's wife (invited to dine at Jyagosenki's) whose sledge falling into the river when the ice broke, was nearly drowned but managed to turn up 'new-dressed' in time for dessert and danced all night.

'Here have been two more Polish ladies of fashion as well as she; they are fine showy women; they all love dancing and singing and all manner of diversions and seem to be formed with bodies and spirits that can never tire. . . . They are very magnificent in their attendants and dress but have so much of national pride and martial manner that they lose the softness of our sex.'

When powerful favourites fall from power, Mrs Rondeau notes that no one ever mentions them.

'You will perhaps wonder at the banishing of women and children but here, when the master of a family is attacked, the whole family is involved in his ruin, all estates belonging to them are seized, they are sunk from nobles to the condition of the meanest people. Once in disgrace they are never mentioned.'

(This she wrote of the banishment of the Dolgorukis and Menshikovs on Anne's accession.)

Mrs Rondeau and her husband, like Jyagosenki, loved to shake off 'the incumbrance of ceremonies' and found ease and refreshment in their simple *dacha* outside Petersburg.

'The house is built of wood and has only a little hall, with two parlours on one side of it, and a kitchen and offices on the other, with four bed-chambers and closets above. It stands on a rising ground, that leads with a natural green slope to a fine meadow, which is terminated by the sea; behind it is a wood of many miles, of birch and fir. There is no art or cultivation about it, for the uncertainty of this country would make that expense ridiculous and as it is rural without, it is rustic within; the tables furnished with delft, and the beds with white calico, rush chairs and the rest in proportion. One parlour is furnished with books and maps; those and my frame for embroidery are the only things that make it differ from a farm. Here we spend three days in a week very agreeably. Mr R reads to me and I work, while our cows, sheep and poultry feed around us and are so tame they come close to the windows.'

Mrs Rondeau adds that her husband has two Englishmen friends and she wishes she had one of her own sex. 'But till that can be,

I have in him the confidence of friendship and tenderness of love.'

It was no wonder that Mrs Rondeau liked to escape from the life of Petersburg society. She describes court circles.

'The military have a rough savageness, a stalk in their gait and a fierceness in their looks and manners that raise the idea of the dreadful part of their profession too much to fancy them fit furniture for a drawing-room, though to do them justice they have it not in their conversation. The others are just such things as mere pretty fellows are everywhere, viz. nothing, dressed fine.'

About the Russian religion she had the usual Protestant reaction:

'It seems to consist in outward form and superstition. I have seen a christening and a wedding; the child was dipped three times in a tub of water; the gossips had everyone a wax candle in their hands; after the child had been dipped, the priest (who by the way was very drunk) put on the shirt and then exorcised it, and at the end of every sentence, he and the gossips spit to show they triumphed over the devil. The wedding was of one of my servants; the match was proposed to the girl's parents and they approving of it, came in form to ask my consent; when that was obtained the man sent her a present, consisting of a comb, some paint and patches; then he was permitted to see her for the first time; they gave each other a ring and a promise of marriage and the wedding was appointed for that day se'night. From that time to the day of her wedding, the girls of her acquaintance took turns to be with her night and day, continually singing songs to bemoan her loss out of their society; when the day came, they took a formal leave of her with many tears; and the man's relations came to fetch her and her fortune, which was a bed, and bedding, a table and a picture of her patron saint.'

Of the magnificent wedding of the wretched Princess Anne, niece of the Tsarina, of the masquerades, balls and jollifications that succeeded it, Mrs Rondeau gave a detailed description. When the Tsarina told Anne that she had given her consent to the marriage (to the Duke of Brunswick-Wolfenbüttel) she burst into 'an agony of tears'. The Duke looked rather silly standing by her. Mrs Rondeau, exhausted by the week's festivities, finished her recital of them:

'Thus ended this grand wedding from which I am not yet rested, and what is worse, all this rout has been made to tie two people together who, I believe, heartily hate one another; at least I think that is her case and she showed it throughout the week's feasting in a public shocking manner, and continues to treat him with the utmost contempt, when out of the Empress's sight.'

(Anne, banished with her husband to Riga in 1741, was the mother of the luckless Ivan VI, murdered in 1764.)

Out of prudery, Mrs Rondeau refused to witness the christening of some Tartar ladies because she thought that 'they should have had some other robe than that of righteousness', but she gave a detailed account of the burial of the youngest daughter of Prince Menshikov, wife of Count Biron, brother to the Duke of Courland. She, together with her baby, had died in childbed.

'The coffin was open; she was dressed in an undress as she died in that condition; in her left arm lay the child, dressed in silver tissue; in her right hand was a certificate from her confessor to St Peter. When all the company were ranged in her room, her servants came to take their leave of her, the inferiors first; they all kissed her and the child, asked her pardon for any crime they had committed, and made the most terrible noise imaginable, rather howling than crying.'

The upper servants and relatives followed all making a hideous noise. Then the husband, feeling that, though a German, he ought to follow the Russian custom tried to do the same, but, though fortified with hartshorn, he fainted and had to be carried away. 'When the corpse was buried, all the company returned to the house to a grand dinner, which had more an air of rejoicing than mourning.'

When, in 1739, Mr Rondeau died, his wife returned to England. Had she spent another year in Russia she would have been able to record the death of the Tsarina Anne and the accession to the throne (after a palace revolution) of the Princess Elizabeth, whom she so much admired. When her prophecy about Biron, the hated Duke of Courland was fulfilled and he was exiled to Siberia, she would have seen Russia, for the time being at least, shake off the influence of the Germans, whom they had come to loathe.

Mrs Rondeau, again did not remain long unmarried. Her third husband was William Vigor, a Quaker of Taplow, Buckinghamshire, whom she long survived. When, at the age of eighty-three, Mrs Vigor (as she now was) died in Windsor, the *Gentleman's Magazine* wrote:

'Her loss will be severely felt by the neighbouring poor, amongst whom she was constantly searching after proper objects for the exertion of her charity and benevolence. Together with great cheerfulness of mind and equality of temper, she retained an uncommon quickness of apprehension and vigour of understanding to the time of her death. Having lived much in the world and being well acquainted with books, her conversation was the delight of all who had the pleasure of knowing her; of the vivacity of her wit and her talent for observation the public have had a specimen in a volume of *Letters from a Lady in Russia*. At a time of life remarkable for apathy and indifference, she possessed a degree of sensibility and a tenderness of feeling approaching almost to weakness.'

JOHN COOK

Voyages and Travels through the
Russian Empire, Tartary and Part of Persia

IN TWO VOLUMES	Edinburgh 1770

D R JOHN COOK, a young Scots physician, tells us in his introduction how, unable to recover from attacks of 'intermittent fever', he decided that a change of air would do him good; and so, in July 1736, he took ship for Russia. Like Captain John Perry, he remained there in government service for fourteen years. Like him too he made a hasty exit with arrears unpaid, for, in spite of his affection for Russia and his many services to that country, he felt no longer safe from arbitrary arrest.

Cook's account of his experiences, working as a doctor both in Government hospitals and in private families, is instructive as well as being exceptionally lively and entertaining. He liked Russia and the Russians; he saw the best of them as well as the worst. He was a tough fellow, frank and forthright, able to stand up for himself and, when abused, to give as good as he got. (He returned insults in a telling way. When told by an impudent fellow that his rank was not high he replied: 'You are a mushroom sprung from froth.')

If one can believe his account of the many cures he made when other doctors had failed, he was an unusually skilful physician. In some ways he seems very modern. Like the Spanish doctor Trueta, he sees that open wounds when kept clean may be left to nature to cure: 'Nature when left to herself, sometimes makes incredible cures. . . . In the course of my practice I have known people lost by ignorant, daring surgeons.' He tells a beautiful Kalmuck princess who is under house arrest that her ailments are due to 'distress of mind': the only cure a 'free, serene mind'. He does not hesitate to tell a noble to whose bed he is called that he has nothing wrong with him and that he won't order drugs for him—only some harmless bitters.

Cook knew no one in Russia when he set out on his 'change of air' cure; nor had he any introductions, but at Cronstadt he called on his fellow Scot, Admiral Patrick Gordon, who gave him a letter to the Archiator, the President of the Chancery of Medicine, which had been created by Dr Erskine, a Scots surgeon invited by Peter the Great to be 'director of all physicians, surgeons, and apothecaries within his vast Empire'. No one could practise in Russia unless the Chancery certified that he had the necessary qualifications, 'which effectually prevents quackery of all kinds'. The Chancery was also in charge of all drugs.

Peter the Great had erected two hospitals in St Petersburg, one for the army and one for the navy. Each had an operating theatre and dissecting chamber. (Peter's introduction of dissection had caused great consternation among the pious and had contributed to the belief that he was anti-Christ, for how could St Peter recognize his own if their bodies were all in pieces?) Cook's qualifications were considered adequate by the Chancery (Latin was the language used in his examination) and he was appointed to the naval hospital which was in the charge of a Swedish prisoner of war. The professor of anatomy, a famous Swiss surgeon, persuaded him to teach anatomy to students. He was never short of bodies as there was a plentiful supply of criminals and suicides (although the latter were fewer than in Britain, Cook thought). When it was uncertain of what disease the patient had died, an autopsy was always performed. Here Cook worked for a year and then was appointed to an emergency hospital in the galley-haven.

Cook thought that the St Petersburg hospitals were well run and the students well trained. Records were kept, many successful operations made and diseases carefully diagnosed. In fact Cook makes the hospitals sound as if they had not much to learn from ours of today. Bells woke the surgeons at six; at seven they had to be in the wards, where the wounded were kept. Then came consultations about the more troublesome diseases. The medical assistants kept day-books for each patient, with his name, nature of ailment and doctor's prescriptions. The best of food was given and no ward was ever left unattended. Patients might make complaints but were severely whipped if these were groundless. (Dr Cook, good Scots Calvinist that he was, never believed in sparing the rod, although he did not approve of knouting, which often led to death.) Physicians attended the apothecaries' shops to give free advice and drugs to the poor at the Tsarina's expense—quite a Welfare State. If it seems that Cook gives too rosy an account of medicine in the Russian capital, it is clear that it had made enormous advances, owing to Peter the Great's reforms and the importation of so many skilled foreigners.

While in St Petersburg, Cook made friends with a Miss Hadderling, whose father was superintendent of sloop-builders and whose mother was the daughter of a captain in the Russian navy, both English. Cook 'contracted a great kindness for her' although he did not marry her for some years. He describes the city and its customs in some detail. He visited the Cadets' School, housed in the palace of Peter's favourite Menshikov, who had been disgraced by the Tsarina Anne. It gave lodging for 2,000 boys, from the age of seven to eighteen. They were not to be whipped with a birch, because they were gentlemen, but with a piece of fine steel, shaped like a sword, thin, long but not sharp. If they were 'not to be kept in order' they were whipped with these and might be made to serve as common soldiers. Otherwise they entered the army as officers. They bore a mortal hatred to their guards and their guards to them. Sometimes numbers were killed on both sides. One shudders to think of the suffering of these children, but at least they were taught more than eighteenth-century boys at Eton and Westminster, whose chastisements were probably just as severe. The cadets learned European languages, natural philosophy, mathematics, painting, dancing and fencing.

Cook noted, with surprising approval, that fornication was only punished with a few light penances. If a baby was born, the father had to buy his mistress a cow. Because of this, there was little child-murder. In Scotland the shame of public penance drove many women to kill their babies. Abolish that, Cook said, and nineteen out of twenty infants might be saved. Young women were some-times married to boys of ten but no one asked who was the father of their infants (often the father-in-law obliged). Children usually looked after their old people and did not 'let them pine in want'.

In 1737 Cook was ordered to march south to the neighbourhood of Azov, to look after the family of Prince Galitzin, the governor of the district, and his adherents. He was grieved to leave St Petersburg, where he had been very happy; his only 'incommodious' experience was being involved in two great fires which burnt down palaces and hundreds of houses. At the admiralty he was made to wait for a month for his papers: passport, orders for horses, etc., and all the certificates for his new appointment. Every day the secretary said '*savtra*' (tomorrow). Cook was told in secret that, although it was strictly forbidden, he ought to have offered a bribe. At last the minister intervened, and after Cook had threatened the secretary with his sword he got all that was required.

Cook gives a detailed description of his long and complicated journey and of all the towns which he passed. He went by road in carriages and later in sleighs, and often by boat along rivers. At first he joined a caravan of 300 sailors *en route* for Azov and driving carts like Jehu. From them he acquired an English boat-swain, of whose daily company, though not very refined, he was glad. The best part of his journey was his stay with the Don Cossacks, whom he much admired. When he was worried about his medicine chest and other possessions, they laughed at him telling him the Cossacks never stole from guests or from their own kind. He was impressed by their independence; they made their own laws, every man over twenty-one had a vote. Riches had no great weight with them. A poor man could become a magistrate as easily as a rich man. The steppe was free to all to pasture their beasts on. They thought it contrary to the design of the Supreme Being to buy or sell slaves (presumably those born amongst them). They were extremely hospitable and sent Cook more fish and game than he and his servants could eat, 'for the honour of their town' they said.

Cook arrived at last at Taverhov in the Azov district and made acquaintance with Prince Galitzin for whom he came to have a very great admiration. He was soon part of the Galitzin family. This is how he describes them.

'The Prince and the Princess were both of them the best of parents, extremely fond of their children, and had the art of bringing them up without any severe treatment, in the most agreeable manner. His sons had a governor and his daughters a governess. The sons slept together in one large room, each in a separate bed, and their sisters in another, with their governess, in the same manner. They rose at stated hours in the morning, paid their devotions, were dressed, took their meals, went to school and their daily diversions. They had four sons and three daughters at the Princess's arrival; and she was delivered of a fifth son in Taverhov, who was her last. This great and ancient family is derived from one of the most illustrious in Poland. Their first appearance in Russia was in the tyrant Ivan Vassilievitch's time. My Prince and Princess commanded respect from the greatest people, by their easy sweet deportment. I never knew a family that in the least could be compared to them.'

Cook was kept busy as soon as he arrived, as the Galitzin children all fell ill, but to his great satisfaction not one of them died.

'However in the year 1739 the good Prince was at once affected with a fever and a bloody flux. As I never loved a man equal to him, my constant attendance, without sleep for nine days and nights, except in an elbow-chair at his bed-side for half an hour at a time, had almost deprived me both of my appetite and strength.'

The Prince recovered slowly and lived, so Cook heard later, to be between eighty and ninety years old.

As illustrative of the ups and downs in the lives of Russian nobility, Cook mentions that because the Galitzins were relatives of Peter the Great, they fell into disfavour with the Tsarina Anne and her favourites. The Prince had been sent to be governor of this remote and turbulent district to get him out of the way. His elder brother was imprisoned. Taverhov was in fact practically in the war zone. Cook dedicates several chapters to a description of the Russian war against the Turks and Crim Tartars and their taking of Azov (lost in the subsequent peace). As this is no history book the details of the war find no place in it, but it is worth noting that the two great generals on the Russian side were both foreigners. Münnich was a German, 'an intrepid, bold man, who had no notion of sparing even his own men'. Count Lacy was an Irish gentleman who had followed King James VII (as Cook calls him) to France and had eventually come to Russia. He was the greatest possible contrast to Münich: he was a gallant officer who, though he never fought a battle which he did not win, always spared his men and was notably humane.

When peace was made with the Turks, Galitzin was made governor of Astrakhan. Cook, in spite of orders to return to St Petersburg, felt that he could not desert the Prince's family, several of whom were sick, and decided to go with them—to their great joy. In Astrakhan, the Prince had an enthusiastic reception. Merchants brought him costly presents 'some brought wines, fruits, sweetmeats of all kinds, others rich silks, satins, brocades, the produce of India and Persia'. The Prince returned them thanks in his homely way, but said that he was a simple man who never took presents and they must take them all back again. He forbade them to bring presents to the Princess (the poor woman was sad to see all the lovely silks taken away, but had to submit to her lord), or any of his family. All he wanted, he said, was to do justice amongst them to great and small alike. The merchants took their gifts back—much astonished as no governor had refused their presents before.

Cook gives intances of Galitzin's wise decisions and efforts to do justice. A Crim Tartar, given to him as a slave when he was nine years old, had met with his favour. He had educated him and eventually put him in charge, as his steward, of several villages on one of his estates. On finding it proved that he had robbed hundreds of the peasants, he made him restore the plunder and appointed another in his place. Cook found the unjust steward in irons near the Prince's house. The Prince would have been justified, according to Russian custom, if he had had the man hanged or sent to the galleys for life, but he decided (after a severe whipping, of course) that he could go back to the estate and work under the new steward. The Prince promised him eventual promotion if he did well.

Another example noted by Cook was his care to find out the truth of a charge of rape brought against a young officer, who swore that he had 'only fondled' the girl. Galitzin made Cook and other surgeons examine her. They found the charge false. The girl confessed, amidst sobs, that the young man had, in truth only fondled her. Her mother had egged her on to make the charge of rape, as the officer was well-born and very rich. Galitzin freed the girl, but the mother, Cook notes with satisfaction, was severely whipped.

On one occasion, Galitzin's compassion and desire to right a wrong had an unfortunate result. A Russian sentinel was told that if his third order to some passer-by to halt was ignored, he must fire, no matter on whom. The sentinel gaily replied that if it were the Tsar himself he would shoot him. For this indiscretion he was walled up in a tiny stone room, with only a slit for communication with the outside world and for his food. As the sentinel was a pious man and often heard praying, he gained the reputation of saint. Peasants came from far and wide to receive his blessing and listen to his preaching. This lasted for sixteen years. Galitzin, hearing his story, gave orders that he should be released.

Unfortunately his adherents gave the poor man so much to eat and drink that he died after four days.

Cook gives a description of Astrakhan and of the various races living in it and around it. It is amusing to note that this hard-headed Scot thought that the Armenians and Georgians were the Lost Ten Tribes, because they were as cunning and deceitful as their progenitors (the Jews). Of the Kalmucks and their religion he shows much greater understanding than other travellers. They were nomads, feeding their numerous flocks but tilling no land and with no fixed place of abode. Their tents were shaped like bee-hives, the better ones covered with felt. Each horde was subject to a prince they called Khan. The Russians pretended that they were subjects of their empire. This the Kalmucks denied, but said they were glad of Russian protection. 'They profess the religion of the Chinese [i.e. Buddhism]. . . . They worship idols but say this is their way of honouring saints, for they acknowledge only one God whom they praise by vocal and instrumental music, by no means disagreeable.' Cook noticed their prayer-wheels, their belief in a future state and their singular rejoicings in the time of the new moon. Cook considered their marriage customs reasonable though differing from those of all other countries. A young pair live as man and wife for a year. If a child is born the marriage is completed; if not

'they either make another year's trial or part. Nor is the woman in the least reflected upon; she is as greedily picked up for another trial by others as if she were a young virgin. Women, when married, are faithful to their husbands for a contrary practice is punishable with death. . . . Their priests never marry, but have the right to go into any man's wife for a night.'

Men consider this an honour. They have no possessions but can use anything belonging to the Kalmucks as 'their own property.' They make pilgrimages to China for instructions and benedictions from their lama or high priest.

Cook was appalled to find that the Kalmucks, although sometimes burying their dead, often threw them out to be devoured by dogs. In an effort to clean up Astrakhan and protect it from plague, he ordered the Kalmucks to bury their dead or throw them into the Volga. He insisted that all inhabitants should bury their dead deeply and tried to make them keep their houses clean. Plague was an ever-present threat. He remained on friendly terms with the Kalmucks and even on one occasion drank their disgusting tea, mixed with rancid butter and salt, and did not let them see him throw it up.

An unusual foreigner whom Cook met was M. Posset, a Huguenot, whose father had been broken on the wheel, when he was nine. He was put into a monastery, where he was cruelly treated. He escaped and, after innumerable adventures, came to Russia. In Astrakhan he was in charge of the imperial vineyards and became a very rich man. His house was robbed by a gang, but the commandant sent soldiers who captured the thieves. They, like his father, were broken on the wheel and his goods were recovered.

After spending a year and a half in Astrakhan (without receiving any salary) Cook went to St Petersburg. He passes over his journey to the capital briefly, noting only the terrible efforts of his oarsmen to row up the Volga, against wind and current. On arrival in the capital, his friends, even his own brother and the Hadderlings, did not recognize him, for he was 'as brown as a Spaniard, having been exposed to the weather for eighteen days'. By this time Cook's Russian was fluent and he did not need to communicate in Latin (which, incidentally, had for long been the language used by Galitzin in talking to him). He also knew some German, learned through studying the New Testament lent him by a Lutheran. At this point of his narrative he begins to talk of his wife, so that his suit to Miss Hadderling must have been successful. While waiting for the Medicine Chancery to decide on his new appointment, he looked round St Peterburg. He was surprised to see the number of ambassadors there. 'The Chinese ambassador was much esteemed. The Turkish was insolent, as was his numerous retinue, beyond all description. They entered into houses by force, and attempted to abuse women.' Most spectacular was the entry of the Persian ambassador with a train of elephants. An unruly elephant nearly crushed Cook and the English ambassador to death, but his rider controlled him. Later the Russians tried to goad two elephants to fight each other but 'they seemed to rejoice to meet'. When, goaded with squibs and fireworks, they ran off in two directions, one killed his rider, the other tossed a German baker into the air and 'pressed him with his foot to a mash'.

Cook was still in St Petersburg when the Tsarina Anne died. He gives a detailed account of the palace revolution of 1741, which

Above: Through the ice (p. 117).

Below: 'Judge of their condition' (p. 147).

VI

Above: 'Only a man I am having whipped' (p. 148).

Below: 'A violently emotional people' (p. 148).

put Elizabeth (daughter of Peter the Great) on the throne. In 1742 Cook returned to Astrakhan, this time accompanied by his wife. There he found a great change. There was a new governor in place of 'one of the best men the world had ever produced': Tatishev, a tyrant, in every respect the reverse of good Prince Galitzin. Tatishev was certainly a singular man. He was cruel and avaricious but very learned. He read Leibniz, Locke, Newton, Bacon and the *Spectator* and corresponded with the Bishop of Upsala and the most learned men of Europe. He was a freethinker; though, out of policy, he conformed to what the Church required of him. He even tried to persuade Cook to be baptized into the Orthodox Church as he would then be given estates and slaves and all sorts of honours. He flew into a passion when Cook said he would rather die than consent, out of interest, to abjure for himself and family the reformed faith he believed in.[1]

Cook was very busy at the naval hospital he had had built and of which he, because of Galitzin's recommendation, was put in charge over the head of all the other surgeons. At the same time he looked after Tatishev, although he hated him, as a man 'who laughed at all laws, human and divine, provided he could only keep himself in safety'. As an instance of his cunning and cruelty he tells of how he decoyed a Kalmuck princess to cross to the west side of the Volga, by showing her forged letters from the Tsarina Elizabeth assuring her that the Tsarina was appointing her ruler over a vast district, where lived not only Kalmucks but thousands of Christian Russians. Tatishev gave a great banquet for her, then surrounded his palace with grenadiers and informed

[1] Jonas Hanway who, in 1743, came on a trade mission to Russia and Persia, was, on his arrival in Astrakhan, at first well received by Tatishev. He writes of him: 'This old man had been a page to Peter the Great and, having long commanded in these parts, was greatly instrumental in reducing the Tartars; but his genius turned most to literature and commerce, nor was he at all deficient in the arts of gain. He mentioned that he had been about four and twenty years writing the history of Russia. This old man was remarkable for his socratical look, his emancipated body, which he preserved many years by his great temperance, and for keeping his mind continually employed. When he was not writing, reading or discoursing about business he played dice one hand against the other' (Cook had found him playing chess). Another time, Hanway writes, 'Tatishev speaking to his friends in my presence, "You are to consider", says he, "the English merchants in a different light from those of any other nation trading to this country; they are skilful, generous, humane, upright; they extend their commerce over the whole earth; and every country where they come is enriched by them. The commodities they deal in are necessary, substantial and of the greatest use to the community; and they take off more of the Russian commodities than all the other nations united." '

E

her that she was his prisoner. 'She was truly a stately, comely, beautiful woman. Her eyes were large, black and had a lustre which few can equal; and she had much sweetness in her countenance.' Cook who was so captivated by the beauty and sweetness of the Kalmuck princess was delighted that she had managed to smuggle her two sons to the other side of the Volga where they were guarded by a body of Kalmucks who swore that they would lose every drop of their blood in their defence. Tatishev was, maddened by their loss, for which he knew he would be much blamed, but all he could do was to keep their mother in his camp wherever he marched, under arrest in her own tent. (It was in this tent that Cook found her, lying ill on her couch, and, as already noted, diagnosed her ailment as proceeding 'from a distressed mind'—the only remedy 'a free, serene mind').

Cook stood up to Tatishev, when his conscience demanded, at the risk of his life. On one occasion Tatishev ordered him to prepare a strong poison, and flew into a furious passion when he refused. 'He beat his own hand with his cane, reeled about the hall raving like a madman.' He swore that he would report the disobedience to the Cabinet in St Petersburg and have Cook punished. Cook coolly demanded a court-martial. 'And thus', he writes, 'this weighty affair ended.'

At last Tatishev went too far. An Armenian merchant bringing priceless jewels came to Astrakhan. When Tatishev saw these he said that two of the most precious of them were only paste and that the Armenian had come to Russia to cheat the people. For this crime he had the poor stranger knouted so severely that he died. The Armenian community in Astrakhan did not suffer passively this injustice to one of their own race and religion. They sent a deputation to St Petersburg, which managed their matters so well that another governor was appointed to Astrakhan. Tatishev was ordered to come to Moscow for trial. Two years later Cook found him living under house arrest, seventy versts from Moscow. (Tatishev had sent him a message requiring his medical advice.) He writes:

'I was charmed by his way of living. He was employed in writing his history in a room adjoining his bed-chamber, in some disorder; for books and instruments were lying in confusion on the floor so that he had only a passage through them to the table where he wrote. In two years time he had built a house of timber and laid out a garden.'

He had made a lake which he had filled with fish and had built a mill. 'Of a country villa he had made a little paradise.' Cook visited him several times and was handsomely paid for his attendance. He begged him on each occasion not to rail against the government in his presence, as that put him in danger. Tatishev, he heard, died in 1750, 'worn out with care, chagrin, anger and age'.

But to return to 1745. In this year Cook was ordered to accompany Prince Galitzin as his medical attendant to Persia, where he had been appointed ambassador. Cook gives a detailed account of his journey to Persia and of his experiences there, of great interest but irrelevant to our enquiry. One incident may be recorded as throwing light on Cook's private life. He was obliged to leave his wife and baby son in Moscow. The Princess Galitzin gave them an appartment and promised to look after them, so Cook was leaving them without anxiety. But his wife clung to him when he was already in his carriage. He pushed her aside so that she should not be entangled in the wheels. At the next stop, overcome with remorse, he begged the Prince to let him return to see his wife again. Galitzin said that this would only prolong the agonies of farewell and advised him to write to his wife instead. This he did and, receiving an understanding note in reply, he felt that the advice had been good.

After his journey to Persia, Cook was sent to Moscow to await his next appointment. The Tsarina Elizabeth ordered him to the Ukraine, to look after Count Razumovsky's mother. He would have a good house, horses and carriages, men and women servants, all kinds of provisions and an increased salary. Cook replied to the Archiator of the Medical Chancery who transmitted the order, that after his distinguished services in hospitals he did not care to look after one old woman, however much a favourite of the Tsarina and however good the conditions. Beside, canny Scot that he was, he feared that he would be blamed if she died and that, if anything happened to him, his wife and children would be left destitute in a foreign country. (Cook knew of an Englishman baptized on his death-bed by a priest. His widow and children were then told that they belonged to the Russian church.) The Archiator, a Dutchman, induced the Tsarina to appoint Cook instead to be surgeon to Count Lacy's army.

Before leaving Moscow, Cook went with the Galitzin children to the Metropolitan Church in the Kremlin where thousands of

relics were exhibited. The priests shouted out what saint they belonged to, saying that they could heal all diseases. Cook, watching
the emotion of the devotees as they kissed the relics, reflected that
they must have had 'a good effect on people who implicitly believe
what their priests teach', especially when they saw one of the nails
that pierced Christ's hand and part of His vesture. He saw the tomb
of the Tsarevitch Demetrius, murdered when a child and now
considered a saint, but was scandalized that the sepulchre of Ivan
the Terrible should be covered with the richest silks in the church,
for was he not one of the most terrible tyrants that ever disgraced
humanity?

Cook went, with his family, from St Petersburg to Riga, where
he was graciously received by Field-Marshal Lacy, whom, as we
have seen, he greatly admired. The Baltic provinces had been
recently conquered, and Lacy was their Governor-General,
besides being in charge of the army. The Livonian nobility, Cook
writes, were not obliged like the Russians to serve in the army or
navy but had only the shadow of liberty left them. The peasants
were slaves and worse off than the Russian boors. Cook worked
in the army hospitals, where there were 'between five and six hundred to two or three thousand sick daily'. He had not been long
in Riga when he heard of the alarming fate of a German, who
had been physician to the army. Affronted by a noble, a favourite
of the Tsarina, he had dared to lampoon him and make him
ridiculous. Soon after this a captain of the guards arrived from
St Petersburg, requesting Lacy to send the German to attend a
relative of his who had fallen ill. No sooner was he outside Riga
than he was made prisoner by the captain and eventually conveyed
to Siberia. Here he managed to survive by telling the fortunes of
the superstitious inhabitants.

Cook liked the people of Riga, whom he found frank and kind
and very polite to strangers. The work in the army hospitals was
satisfactory although very fatiguing, but he was horrified by the
garrison hospitals, where men were dying of scurvy. Peter the
Great had allotted them gardens, where they could get fresh
vegetables, but these had been taken over by the officers and the
hospitals had not the smallest use of them. He appealed to Lacy,
who had the gardens restored to the hospitals. The officers were
furious with Cook who, remembering no doubt the fate of the
German doctor, began to feel very uneasy. He had now three sons:
what would happen to them and his wife, if he were no longer

there to protect them? Moreover, he wanted his children to be educated in a free country. Finally he had permission to send them to Scotland and petitioned for his own discharge from the service, asking at the same time for the support of Mr Dickens, the English ambassador. He received no help from this quarter, so, 'feeling no longer safety in Riga' he slipped away in a British ship and arrived safely in Dundee to his 'great satisfaction' and was soon reunited with his family, who 'were agreeably surprised' to see him.

He ends his long narrative, which he had privately printed in Edinburgh in 1770, by saying that if he were informed of any harm coming to Russia he would contribute all in his power to its safety, for he honoured it next to his own native country.

M. L'ABBÉ CHAPPE
D'AUTEROCHE

A Journey into Siberia
Translated from the French and published in London 1770

IN 1760, all European astronomers were in a ferment because Venus was due to pass across the sun on June 6th of the following year. The Academy in St Petersburg asked Louis XV to send an astronomer to Tobolsk in Siberia, where 'the Transit of Venus would be performed in less time than in any other part of the globe and could be viewed with more advantage than anywhere else'. The candidate was promised the company of Russian colleagues. (The observation of this transit would help astronomers to calculate the distance of the sun from the earth.) Louis XV chose the abbé Chappe d'Auteroche of the Royal Academy of Sciences for this mission.

He set off from Paris in November 1760, hoping that six months would be enough for his long journey, which he decided to make entirely by land. He arrived in Poland on January 16th. This country had not yet been partitioned by its neighbours, Prussia, Austria and Russia, and was still independent, although the astute abbé saw that, as the sovereign was without authority and the state without defence, it was open to every invader. Warsaw, he noted, was a very fine city, with elegant buildings, although without an inn (absence of these did not much matter in Poland because of the hospitality of the natives). The women were handsome and well read and, for all their love of pleasure and company, were strictly virtuous, rather, he thought, through superstition than religion. The land belonged to the nobles and the peasants were slaves, forced to work for them but allowed to keep the produce of the plots of land assigned to them.

By February the abbé was on Russian soil. He arrived at Riga, taken from the Swedes by Peter the Great. Here he encountered one of the great hazards of his journey, the vagaries of the climate, which made it impossible to know when a thaw would prevent further travel by sledge. Outside Riga there was no snow, so they had to fix the wheels to their carriages again and drag the sledges behind them. Soon they were in the middle of a violent storm 'whirlwinds of snow arose on all sides'. The postilion drove the horses and the carriage with their belongings into a hole, and they were two hours getting it out. Soon their own carriage 'disappeared all at once, so that the horses' heads could but just be seen and we were buried!'

They got out through a hole in the top of the carriage and spent all day trying to free the vehicle by harnessing to it all their horses. At the posting station they abandoned their carriages, bought four sledges, and experienced for the first time, the ease of this form of travel. 'We went on with the greatest velocity without meeting with any accident.' The drivers seldom used the lash on their horses but talked to them as though they were fellow humans, calling them father, mother, dearly beloved, whistling and singing to them. On February 13th they arrived at St Petersburg. 'We had met with such a variety of accidents every day that I despaired of reaching Siberia in time for the observation.'

Henceforth this was the abbé's constant preoccupation, and such is his narrative skill that the reader shares in his anxiety and suffers with him at his many mishaps and hold-ups.

In St Petersburg, the Tsarina Elizabeth gave him every help; he was under her protection throughout his journey. He had to procure the sort of things that had not been necessary until now, such as bedding. He needed, too, an interpreter and a clock-maker, in case his clock needed mending. Terrified that a thaw might strand him in the forests of Siberia, he set off with four sledges on March 10th. He himself was in a covered sledge drawn by five horses; his servant and the clock-maker were in a half-covered sledge; the guide was with the provisions; and his precious instruments were in the fourth. By the time he got to Moscow his sledges were all broken to pieces, because of the badness of the roads, and he had to buy new ones from the peasants. Count Vorontzov procured fresh provisions for him and he set off in haste down the River Oka. He was amazed at the smoothness of the frozen rivers in Russia. They had a surface like glass, so different from the Seine and, dedicated scientist as he was, he thought out various reasons for this—also for the holes, so often to be met with where the water never freezes. As one of his horses fell into a hole on the Oka he became aware of the danger and refused after this to travel at night on the rivers.

He found the Volga particularly beautiful at Nijni Novgorod, but did not dare to delay there longer than to get his sledges mended. At this time of year the shops were ill-stocked and the goods bad, but in the summer the hundreds of merchants who came for the fair made it one of the first cities of Russia. He noted that the lads of the town married at fourteen or fifteen and girls at thirteen (to prevent debauchery), and that women bred till they were fifty.

The abbé's most frightening adventure happened to him after he had left the Volga and entered the forest, through which, he said, he would have to travel almost all the way to Tobolsk. This was mainly of fir-trees and birches and very gloomy. He had gone only a few versts into the wood when he fell fast asleep. He awoke in the dark and realized that he had been abandoned.

'I called out to each person by his name but all was silent around me. . . . The horror of my situation will easily be conceived, when I found myself alone on one of the darkest nights, at the distance of fourteen hundred leagues from my native country, in the midst of the frosts and snow of Siberia, with the images of hunger and thirst before me. I was even ignorant whether I was in the beaten track or not; it did not seem probable.'

He seized his two pistols and got out of the sledge but soon sank up to his shoulders in the snow. After lying there for some time he roused himself and struggled back to his sledge but could not rest there. He went backwards and forwards a great part of the night in such agitation that, in spite of the extreme cold, he was in a profuse sweat. At last he walked far enough to see a glimmering light in a house, entering which he found all his men sleeping peacefully beside some young girls, for 'they seemed all to be in great want of rest'. (The abbé had realized already that his men did not care for the extreme haste with which he was travelling, only allowing them, now and then a short stop by a warm stove, nor did they see the reason for it.)

'I roused my servant and left the house as soon as I could for I was unwilling they should discover how rejoiced I was at finding them again. A light was soon brought and I found that they had left the other sledges at the bottom of the village. . . . It was evident that I was obliged to put up with this affair.'

The abbé found the passage through the Urals very heavy going. The mountains were small but the ascents very steep.

'The roads were dreadful, the nights so exceedingly dark that I was every instance liable to be swallowed up by the snow. Fir trees of the greatest height seemed to yield under the weight of the snow, which was everywhere more than seven feet thick on the ground. Even magpies and rooks which are met with in great numbers on the roads all over Russia, had quitted these deserts. The marks of the sledges were the only signs of these parts being inhabited. A melancholy gloom prevailed all round and the stillness was only interrupted by one of our company calling out for help, when his sledge was overturned. The inhabitants are shut up in their cottages nine months of the year, hardly ever going out as long as the winter lasts. . . . The snow does not entirely disappear until the end of May.'

The summer lasted only three months, but in that time rye, oats, barley and some peas were harvested. The abbé could not bear to spend more than a few hours in any of the *izbas* he passed, because of the unbearable smell. The windows were shut all the winter long; only a small valve in the ceiling was opened for a short time to let out the smoke from the stoves, which was so thick one couldn't see anything; the heat was unbearable and the people 'lived constantly in infected vapours'.

The abbé's most anxious moments were when he was only seventy leagues from Tobolsk, because the dreaded thaw began. At Tiumen he found that no one would cross the river because they were afraid that the ice was breaking. If this happened he would be stuck where he was; travel would become impossible, even in a boat, 'because with the thaw, the whole country is over-whelmed with torrents, pouring down on all sides'. By plying his men with brandy and promising them double pay he persuaded them to risk the passage and they crossed the river safely.

The abbé arrived in Tobolsk on April 10th, six days before the break-up of the ice and with plenty of time before him to set up his telescope outside the town.

The governor of Tobolsk received the abbé very politely and assigned him a sergeant and three grenadiers to guard him and his treasure. He had an observatory set up outside the town, but when the natives saw his quadrant, clocks and the telescope, 19 feet long, they decided that he was a magician and believed that he had caused the overflowing of the River Irtizh, which was worse than usual that year, carrying off many of the houses in the lower part of Tobolsk. Some people expected 'the instant end of the world' and longed for the magician to leave. He was advised always to have his guard in attendance and to sleep in his observatory, lest the mob should pull it down.[1]

He spent June 5th arranging his instruments. At night he was at first elated by the bright sky and then thrown into despair by a black cloud that overspread the hemisphere. He thought of how the whole learned world was in a state of expectancy. It was the first transit of Venus across the sun for a hundred years. The famous Halley, who had foretold it, had lamented on his death bed that he could not witness it. The abbé passed the whole night in dreadful agitation. His attendants were all asleep. No one cared. To think that he must return to France after a fruitless journey; that he was to be deprived of everything by a cloud!

The rising of the sun and an east wind that cleared the sky inspired the abbé, he says, with a kind of new life. The governor with his family, the archbishop (although he thought it all contrary to scripture) and archimandrites came along to share his joy. He was afraid of the people but they had fled in terror to the churches or shut themselves up in their huts. The clock-maker was keeping his eye on the clock. The interpreter was counting the time. When the moment of observation came, the abbé was seized with a violent shivering, but he collected himself and did not miss it. He reflected that his records would be useful to posterity, when he had quitted this life.

The abbé stayed another three months in Tobolsk, at the house of the proctor, who was next to the governor in rank, and was, he says, 'possessed of the most enlightened understanding, warmed with the love of truth and humanity'. He had brought from Moscow a select library, with books by the best French

---

[1] J. G. Korb notes that the Muscovites 'despise liberal arts as useless torments of youth, they prohibit philosophy and they have often outraged astronomy with the opprobrious name of magic'. They say that if astronomers 'may sometimes guess about the future what is beyond mortal ken', it is evil spirits that have instructed them. Korb notes that Peter I is trying to introduce arts and sciences into his kingdom but he is not sure how far he will succeed. Enlightenment had not penetrated as far as Tobolsk sixty years later, as the abbé found. (The archbishop told him that the Bible showed that the earth is flat and the sun went round it.)

writers. He had 'an uncommon politeness and gentleness of manners. Free from national prejudice, he could not consider his wife as his slave; she was his best friend; and by the goodness of her heart contributed to her husband's happiness.'

The abbé was shocked to find that this was rare outside St Petersburg and Moscow. Men jealous of their wives, keep them shut up, away from society; they are seldom seen together.

> 'That kind of delicate love which proceeds from sensibility, and against which the severest virtue cannot always guard itself, is here totally unknown' Here a lover never has the satisfaction of seeing the confusion and disorder of his mistress, endeavouring but unable to conceal her tenderness. . . . In these barbarous regions men tyrannize over their wives, whom they treat as their slaves, requiring of them the most servile offices' [as, for instance, bringing them rods and pulling off their boots]. 'The women are captivated merely by sensual pleasures, often giving themselves up to their slaves. . . . The manners of this people will never be improved, while the women are kept in a state of slavery. Although the men are remarkably severe to their wives, yet they are very indulgent to their daughters.'

They allow them a surprising amount of freedom, so that 'at twelve or thirteen they are frequently no strangers to the other sex'. Yet virginity before marriage is all-important. A jury of skilful women looks into the matter with an examination that in other countries would seem indecent. After the wedding night, the bride's linen is displayed to all the guests and this for several days. When the company is satisfied, the lady dances with her husband and everyone gets drunk.

The abbé found the many banquets he was invited to tedious and painful because of the coarse manners, the complicated toasts (often to unknown saints) and the shocking drunkenness. There were no women to talk to ('and company is nothing without them'); besides people were afraid of each other, for no one was safe. There was no friendship—'that sentiment which contributes to the happiness of our lives'.

The abbé decided to return to St Petersburg via Ekaterinburg, because he wanted to visit the mines there. His escort were horrified at the plan, as Russians had recently been murdered on that route by robber gangs of escaped convicts and deserters from the army. The abbé, as usual, had his way.

At Ekaterinburg he was exposed to the full blast of Russian
hospitality. When it was known that he needed provisions

> 'my little room, of ten feet square, was filled with two sheep continually
> bleating, with geese, ducks and fowls. These animals made so much
> noise that I was obliged to go out into the street to learn the names of
> the persons to whom I was indebted for this kindness. One of the
> soldiers immediately seized a sheep and carried it to a good old woman
> in the neighbourhood and in little better than an hour's time, he was
> killed, roasted and almost eaten up.'

The first counsellor of the chancery, a cheerful, intelligent man,
was exceedingly polite to the abbé, and his lady, a woman about
fifty, but still retaining marks of former beauty, told the abbé
she would be his mother while he was in their town. He was so
moved that he could not speak and readily acceded to her request
to show her the moon and Jupiter through his telescope. The
abbé now gave practical evidence of his Latin gallantry, not only
by giving a banquet for the lady and some forty other guests, but
also by deciding that the women should sit at the feast and the
men stand—an unheard-of thing. He startled the natives still
more by dancing with a country girl, after a banquet given in his
honour. He was told that no gentleman could dance with a slave—
but soon everyone was following his example. He was delighted
with the characteristic style of Russian dancing. It was like a pan-
tomime.

> 'This can only be danced by young people, who go through it with
> remarkable dexterity; they turn round on one foot when they are
> almost in a sitting posture; they then rise up in an instant and throw
> themselves into some fanciful or grotesque attitude which they vary
> every moment, in advancing, retiring or turning round the room.
> They often dance alone or with one woman who has very little to do.'

Their musical instruments were the balalaika and the violin.
The abbé was often visited by a schoolmaster, whose grandfather had been a Huguenot refugee from France after Louis
XIV revoked the Edict of Nantes.
The abbé inspected the mines very thoroughly. He was a man
of wide scientific interests and a great part of his book is given up
to a description of the minerals to be found in Russia and Siberia
and to geological data, as also to the geography of that great empire;

but his human observations are of greater interest to us now. He got back to St Petersburg in November and spent the winter and spring there, returning to Paris in August 1762.

The abbé had seen with his own eyes what life was really like for the convicts and political exiles in Siberia.[1]

> 'All criminals condemned to public labour [he writes] are treated in the same manner; they are shut up in prisons surrounded by a large piece of ground, enclosed with stakes. In bad weather they retire inside the prison, and when the season permits they walk about in the enclosure. They all have chains on their feet; and are kept for a very trifling expense, being generally allowed nothing but bread and water. . . . They are guarded by a certain number of soldiers, who lead them to the mines or other public labours, where they are treated with the utmost severity. . . . Persons condemned to banishment are not all treated in the same manner; some are shut up, others allowed a little liberty.'

The abbé describes the fate of Count Lestocq who had helped the Tsarina Elizabeth to the throne, and was exiled because he had made an enemy of her chief minister. For years he was kept a prisoner and not allowed to see his wife, who was suffering the same fate. Later they were allowed to live together, under house arrest. The Countess fetched water, brewed, baked, washed and worked in the garden. After fourteen years, they were recalled by Peter III on the death of Elizabeth. Count Lestocq told the abbé, who was then in St Petersburg, his whole story, although he knew he ran the risk of further exile for his frankness.

Not all political exiles were confined like the Lestocqs. The abbé once accidentally met a man who, with his untrimmed beard and ragged clothes, looked like a poor peasant. Surprised by his intent look and his 'singular countenance' the abbé addressed some re-

---

[1] Even in eighteenth-century England, exile to Siberia was noted by the poet John Dyer. In 1757 he published *The Fleece*, a long poem celebrating the benefits of our far-flung woollen trade. He notes that caravans taking our cloth, start in Petersburg, 'erewhile the watery seat of desolation wide' and crossing trackless deserts, white with continual frost, get to Tobolsk.

Tobol, the abode of those unfortunate
Exiles of angry state, and thralls of war;
Solemn fraternity! where carl and prince,
Soldier and statesman, and uncrested chief,
on the dark level of adversity
Converse familiar.

It will be remembered, too, that Robinson Crusoe passed through Siberia on his way home, and offered to take a political exile with him out to freedom, an offer which the exile had, sadly, to refuse but accepted for his son.

mark to him and was astonished to be answered in Latin. The man
discussed with him the sciences, government, the European powerss
he was extraordinarily learned. When a soldier appeared, the exile
turned pale and went away. Although the abbé sought him everywhere, he never found him again.

Such exiles are shunned, he writes, not for their crimes, but
for fear of offending the government. Those who are taken into
their service by Russians are better off, and treated like human
beings.

Nothing escaped the abbé's notice. Throughout Russia and
Siberia the peasant's babies were unswaddled. When very small
they were kept in a basket, fastened on a pole, easily moved by the
foot. The mothers rocked them while they were spinning hemp.
Later they rolled about naked and even played naked in the snow.
They were left to struggle by themselves and for this reason those
that did survive grew up much stronger than children in France,
and without deformities. The question was, how many did survive? About this the abbé made very gloomy calculations. Countless children died. Parents who had had sixteen or eighteen children had often only three or four left alive. He thought that half
died of smallpox, and that many were affected by the prevalence
of scurvy and syphilis, both endemic and venereal. There were
no doctors and old wive's remedies were ineffective. Probably
what surprised and interested the abbé's Western readers most
was his report on Russia's armed forces. (Algarotti's estimates are
several years before this.) As for their navy, it was negligible. Russians were afraid of the sea and depended on foreigners to man
their ships.

'The officers are but little acquainted with the theory of navigation
and still less with the practice, because they seldom go to sea. The ships,
surrounded with ice, and lying in fresh water, perish in the ports. A
great number of ships have been condemned before one sail has been
hoisted upon them.'

Russia, he adds, will never have good seamen 'till she carries on
trade by herself'.

Western fears of Russia were unfounded. In France people
expected her 'to overrun our little Europe', like the Scythians
and the Huns. Hamburg and Lübeck trembled at her name.
Poland and Germany 'considered Russia as one of the most formid-
able powers of Europe'. Russia had a large army (it was said to

consist of 330,000 men) because it cost them little. The soldier's pay was small—about a halfpenny a day—and the local population had to supply their garrisons with provisions. But the officers were ignorant. 'They are in general little acquainted with the art of war. . . . They have scarce any idea of tactics; they know not even the name of Xenophon, Herodotus, Polybius, etc.' They only knew the great generals of the present age from the report of their victories. Their engineers were so ignorant that they could not conduct a siege.

On his journey from Tobolsk back to St Petersburg, the abbé followed a detachment of soldiers and learned how Russians detested the army. 'The countenance of each soldier was clouded with despair; and the recruits appeared like a set of wretches condemned to the galleys.'

An officer told the abbé that there were a great number of desertions—that, in fact, Siberia was terrorized by deserters and escaped convicts. When on active service, large numbers died of sickness. They suffered through not having their twice-weekly baths on which they were dependent. It was true that they defended themselves with great courage and did not desert when they were in the field, 'either from the difficulty of getting away; or from religious motives; or because they are fond of slavery; or from imagining that happiness is nowhere to be found but in the midst of the snows of Russia'. (It was broadminded of the abbé to acknowledge the beneficial effect the baths had on the natives— they saved them, he said, from rheumatism and were their only cure for sickness. He himself had only tried one once and had found it unbearable: the extreme heat of the steam, the discomfort of being beaten with birch boughs, the cold douche afterwards— these things were not for him.)

The abbé's book might reassure the West, but could give no pleasure in Russia. In a brief chapter on its history, he emphasized the terror under which everyone lived. The nobles, themselves 'under the yoke of the most dreadful slavery', retaliate on their serfs, whom they sell 'as cattle is sold in other parts of the world'. They estimate their riches by the number of souls that belong to them. They impose what tax they please upon their slaves. If the lord does not get enough money from them, he allows them to hire themselves out to merchants or other persons and may give them passports for a few years, but only so that he may take a large part of their earnings.

The abbé ended his chapter on Russian history on a hopeful note. He rejoiced at the revolution that had ended the miserable rule of Peter III and given all power to the Tsarina Catherine, a woman of an extensive genius, who would certainly free her people. Happy the nation to be governed by such a prince!

The abbé hailed her, too, for her interest in the arts and sciences which she had shown by welcoming Diderot to her court. She had seen the importance of the Transit of Venus over the sun—what higher praise could be given her? The abbé did not agree with M. Rousseau of Geneva that it would have been better if Russia had never been civilized. He believed that under the Empress Catherine 'the general turn and spirit of the nation would undergo a total change'. It is pleasing to record that Catherine fulfilled the abbé's expectations of her, at least in one respect. In 1769, Venus was due to renew her walk across the sun. Catherine invited the learned German scientist Pallas to witness this phenomenon in Siberia. This he did and, like the abbé, he wrote a book about his experiences. (Captain Cook took Sir Joseph Banks to the opposite side of the world, namely the South Seas, to view this transit and, incidentally, on his way home, with the famous British absent-mindedness, stuck Union Jacks into New Zealand and Australia. It did not occur, either to the abbé or to Pallas, to take similar action in Siberia.)

WILLIAM RICHARDSON

Anecdotes of the Russian Empire

W. Strahan & Cadell, London 1784

WILLIAM RICHARDSON, scholar and humanist, was the most accomplished of the British visitors to Russia in the eighteenth century. True, as an impassioned hater of slavery and believer in liberty, he saw everything in Russia in the darkest light, but there was a social philosophy behind this view: he made a thoughtful analysis of the effect of despotism on the Russian character. The son of a Scots minister, he went at the age of fourteen to the University of Glasgow, where he distinguished himself in the study of language, philosophy and theology. He might have followed in his father's footsteps had he not, because of his exceptional brilliance, been appointed tutor to the two sons of Charles, Lord Cathcart. After two years at Eton he went, in 1768, to St Petersburg where Lord Cathcart had been appointed ambassador extraordinary to Catherine II, and wanted to have his sons and their young Scots tutor with him. After spending four years in Russia, Richardson returned to Glasgow, where for forty-one years he held the Chair of Humanity. It was during this period that he published the letters to friends which he had written while in St Petersburg. These have several picturesque and lively ancedotes but their originality is, in Richardson's point of view, in seeing man as the product of social forces. He saw despotism as degrading human beings, destroying the dignity which was their birthright. 'Those who treat their inferiors with contempt compel them to become worthless,' he wrote when analysing the 'character of many modern Jews'.

Richardson did not travel widely in Russia like Captain John Perry or Jonas Hanway. As secretary to Cathcart, he mostly kept to court circles. He expresses a certain guarded admiration of the

Great Catherine, but he was rightly sceptical about her vaunted
liberalism: her intention to reform the laws and emancipate the
peasants. This is how he describes the way the Tsarina spent her
day:

> Nov. 7, 1768. Her Majesty rises at five in the morning and is engaged
> in business till near ten. She then breakfasts and goes to prayers;
> dines at two; withdraws to her own apartments soon after dinner;
> drinks tea at five; sees company, plays cards or attends public places,
> the play, opera or masquerade till supper; and goes to sleep at ten.
> By eleven everything about the palace is still as midnight. Whist is her
> favourite game at cards. She usually plays for five imperials [ten
> guineas]; and as she plays with great clearness and attention, she is
> often successful; she sometimes plays too at picquet or cribbage.
> In the morning between prayers and dinner she frequently takes an
> airing in a coach or sledge. On these occasions she has sometimes no
> guards and very few attendants and does not choose to be known
> or saluted as Empress. . . . When she retires to her palaces in the
> country, especially to Tsarkoe Selo, she lays aside all state and lives
> with her ladies on the footing of as easy intimacy as possible. Any
> one of them who rises on her entering or going out of a room is fined
> a rouble and all forfeits of this sort are given to the poor. . . . The
> affability of her manners renders her much beloved.'

But was it, Richardson wondered, rather the desire for fame and
to be much spoken of than an urge to do good that actuated her?

It was difficult, he complains, to get information as to what was
going on. Nothing of a political nature could be gathered from the
newspapers. 'Half of Russia may be destroyed and the other half
know nothing about the matter.' How different from England
'enlightened by the radiance of Chroniclers, Advertisers and Gazet-
teers'.

Richardson was present at a meeting of the deputies, summoned
by the Tsarina from all the nations of her empire to consider the
making of a code of laws, but, magnificent as the idea was, he was
pessimistic about its success (quite rightly as it came to nothing).
'This assembly has no pretensions whatever to freedom of de-
bate . . . and may be dismissed at her pleasure.'

In July 1769, Catherine's wars were not going well.

> 'The people are beginning to murmur. Rumours of conspiracies
> are secretly propagated; several persons, I have heard, either guilty
> or suspected of treason, have disappeared; but these things are not
> noised abroad, they are only mentioned in confidential whispers. The

people are prohibited from speaking or writing about politics. The Empress tells them that as her maternal care for her dear people keeps her sleepless by night and busy by day they have no occasion to give themselves any further trouble about public affairs than to act implicitly as she directs. The spies are busy; the suspected great men are closely watched. Happy King of England who may go about with as much security after a defeat as after a victory and may allow his people to speak, write and think as they please.'

It will be seen from these extracts that Richardson realized that Russians, however rich and powerful, had no security, were in fact thralls to their sovereign, little better than slaves. 'They have no trials by jury, no Habeas Corpus Act. A person accused of crimes may be kept in prison for ever.' It was this insecurity he believed that made them careless in the education of their children.

'Their tutors are generally French or German into whose character they make but little enquiry. If their children learn to dance and if they can read, speak and write French and have a little geography, they desire no more . . . I do not wonder: why educate their children? They are to live and die in thraldom, they may be in glory today and tomorrow sent to Siberia. Why should they train their offspring for any expectations beyond those of the present moment? If, however, there was any possibility that by enlightening the minds of the Russians they should not only discern the abasement of their condition but contrive the means of emancipating I should heartily regret their present blindness.'

If Richardson felt that the upper classes in Russia were little better than slaves, what did he think of the serfs?

'Judge of their condition—From the hour of their birth, they are in the power of a rapacious chief, who may sell, scourge or employ them in any labour he pleases. They have no property, no home, nothing that their proud superior may not seize and claim as his own. The horse and the bull may choose their loves, a privilege not allowed the Russian. They no sonner arrive at the age of puberty, when they are often compelled to marry whatsoever female their proprietor chooses, in order, by a continued progeny of slaves, to preserve or augment his revenue. . . . The guile, the baseness and the rugged ferocity attributed to slaves are chiefly owing to their oppressors. . . They have no defence against oppression but deceit.'[1]

---

[1] Masson, who for ten years served in Catherine II's armies and had many friends in court circles, was shocked by the effect on women of having so many human beings in their power. In any case, he wrote, since Peter the Great had forced men to admit them into society, women had become dominant in

Richardson, seeing only the evils of slavery, did not realize with what kindliness the good landlord treated his serfs. But power corrupts, and good landlords were probably in a minority.

Richardson realized that the Russians were a violently emotional people.

'You may sometimes see persons of the highest rank, even before strangers, engage in violent disputes and treat one another at least with impetuosity In a few moments after, they are as calm as if nothng had happened, and seem to love one another more for this transient ebullition. . . . People of such irregular sensibility are occasionally very brave or very dastardly; and so are the Russians. Sometimes the slightest danger appals them; and sometimes you would imagine that they are incapable of fear or had no sense of danger. It is perfectly consistent with this, that slight enjoyments should raise them to the summit of happiness; and that slight losses or disappointments should cast them down in despair. Accordingly their happiness displays itself in infantine levity; and their despondency often terminates in suicide. . . . They are apt to be influenced by eloquence. Full of sensibility they enter easily into the feelings of others. Russians of all ranks are fond of music.

'The defects in the national character of the Russians seem to me to arise chiefly from want of culture. Were they taught to reflect on the

---

Russia, which was now a gynocracy. (He knew several examples in the army of generals who refused to take decisions until they had consulted their wives.) 'Always surrounded by slaves, ready to satisfy their slightest desires, they spend their time lying on sofas or playing cards. . . . It is revolting to see women presiding over the punishment of slaves, sometimes inflicting it themselves.' He cites the case of a lady who replied to her friends, to whom she was showing her jewels and furbelows and who were horrified by the cries they were hearing, 'That is nothing—only a man whom I am having whipped.' Serfs for sale were advertised in the papers. Masson quotes the following: 'Enquire at the laundry for a whole family or a man and girl separately. Ivan is twenty-one years old, very strong and can curl ladies' hair, Murpha aged fifteen is well made and healthy and can sew and embroider. They can be examined and bought at a moderate price.' The price for a girl Masson tells us, was between 50 and 200 roubles, for a man between 300 and 500. Sometimes they were exchanged for a dog or horse or wagered at cards. In the next century the price had gone up. The Frenchman, Jules Klaproth, Professor of Asiatic languages in Paris, travelling in Georgia in 1808, tells the story of a slave girl for whom a Jew offered Persian silks valued at 250 roubles. The bargain was concluded, but while the goods were being examined the girl said to some bystanders: 'I am a poor orphan whom everyone can insult with impunity. My guardian promised to marry me; now he has sold me for some silk garments; but he will never wear them.' Thereupon she ran into a neighbouring garden and hanged herself on a tree.

See C. F. P. Masson, *Mémoires Secrets sur la Russie* (Amsterdam, 1800 and 1802), and Jules Klaproth, *Voyage au Mont Caucase et en Georgie* (Paris, 1823).

past and anticipate the future, they would be led to form maxims and general rules for the direction of their conduct. But they will never either reflect or anticipate till they have entire security for their persons and possessions. Immortal would be the glory of that sovereign who would restore above twenty millions of men to the rights of intelligent and rational beings.'

If Richardson found little to praise in either the noble or the peasant he found still less in the priest. He saw little in their religion but formality and superstition. Yet, although scornful of the ignorant priests, Richardson found certain exceptions.

'Among the clergy there are some persons of learning and of great moderation. Some attempts have been made ... to disseminate among the people correct and enlarged sentiments of religion. Of this kind is a Catechism.'

This catechism was an enlarged edition of the Ten Commandments which 'not only breathes a liberal and pious spirit but is composed with much simplicity'.

The examples Richardson cites certainly manifest, for the times and indeed for all time, a remarkably liberal spirit. For instance, the catechism lists among those who disobey the sixth commandment (thou shalt not kill): those who let the poor die of cold or hunger: those who encourage hatred and anger to the destruction of mankind; and the unjust judge; all these are also guilty of murder. As for the eighth commandment (thou shalt not steal), those who exact from a workman more than he was engaged for or who take advantage of a dearth to raise the price of provisions are also guilty of theft.

Richardson mentions Ambrosius, Archbishop of Moscow as a man of 'great worth and liberality of sentiment'. Moscow was in the grip of plague and the superstitious people flocked round the ikon of the Virgin Mary, paying the priests huge sums for permission to come near it. The Archbishop, fearful of the spread of infection and hating to see the people robbed, removed the ikon but was torn to pieces for his pains.

Richardson also found examples of Russian kindness, for instance to their Turkish prisoners who were allowed considerable freedom. The Emir of Bender who had gallantly defended his city from the Russians

'had insisted on having a numerous attendance of Turks, including a part of his seraglio and a person of small stature, who displays the

antic gestures of a buffoon; his requisition was immediately granted.
. . . His buffoon appears often in parti-coloured garments in the
streets of the city and endeavours by his drolleries to amuse the
passengers. The Turks themselves appear so grave and solemn,
that it is really amusing to see a Turkish buffoon.'

Noticing the difference between Russians and West Europeans,
Richardson remarks that as they never had the judicial combat
in the Middle Ages so

'the duel of honour has never existed among them. But as the fashions
of Europe, and particularly those of France are making progress
among the natives of this country, some persons among them who
affect patriotism express their expectations, that they will soon have
the credit of blowing out one another's brains in the easiest and
politest manner.'

An expectation, alas, too soon fulfilled, costing the lives, amongst
others, of their great poets, Pushkin and Lermontov.

Richardson's most amusing anecdote is a description of the
blessing of the waters on January 6th, the day of Christ's baptism
—the ceremony described by Jenkinson in the sixteenth century
and that which had awakened the ridicule of Captain John Perry.
Richardson saw it performed on the Moika,

'a stream which enters the Neva between the Winter Palace and the
Admiralty. On the top [of the pavilion above the ice-hole] was a
gilded figure of St John; on the sides were pictures of our Saviour and
immediately over the hole that was cut through the ice into the
water was suspended the figure of a dove. The banks of the river
and adjoining streets were lined with soldiers. The procession then
advanced to the Jordan of the day with all their usual parade of tapers,
banners, lofty mitres and flowing robes. No parade of priests and
levites even in the days of Solomon and by the banks of Shiloh could
be more magnificent. After the rite was performed with the
customary prayers and hymns, all who were present had the
happiness of being sprinkled with the water thus consecrated and
rendered holy. The multitude when the ceremony was over, rushed,
with ungoverned tumult, to wash their hands and their faces in
the hallowed orifice. What pushing and brawling, scolding and
swearing—to get rid of their sins! . . . All infants who are baptised
with the water of the sacred orifice, are supposed to derive from it the
most peculiar advantages. I have heard that a priest in immersing a
child, let it slip through inattention into the water. The child was
drowned but the holy man suffered no consternation. "Give me

another," he said with the utmost composure, "for the Lord hath taken this to Himself." The Empress however, having other uses for her subjects, and not desiring that the Lord should have any more, at least in that way, gave orders that all children to be baptised in the Jordan, should henceforth be let down in a basket.'[1]

Yet, however ironic he was about the superstitions of the barbarous Russians, however indignant at the state of slavery in which their tyrannous rulers kept them, Richardson did believe that more education and an increase of liberty combined with the security, unknown to them under their present régime, might alter their national characteristics and make a happier and more prosperous country, although how the changes were to come about he did not dare to prophesy.

POSTSCRIPT TO RICHARDSON'S *Anecdotes of the Russian Empire*

Some years after Richardson had left St Petersburg, Radishschev published a little book, *Journey from St Petersburg to Moscow*, which, under the guise of simple travel sketches, was an outspoken attack on serf ownership and on absolutist, arbitrary rule. Radishschev's was the first Russian voice to make itself heard on these evils. He was a well-born young man who had been chosen by Catherine as one of twelve students to be educated in the West (in Leipzig). On his return he became chief of the St Petersburg Customs Office and, although it was known that he was 'infected' with Western ideals, he was supposed to be a pillar of the régime. Then, in 1790, his book, which he had had printed in his own home and which was being widely circulated, came to the notice of the police. Catherine read it, and was outraged by the only too obvious attacks on her and on Potemkin. Radishschev was banished to eastern Siberia and his book suppressed, though copies of it were made and circulated in secret, and even crossed the frontier. Merchants paid 25 roubles to be allowed to read it for an hour. Masson was the first foreigner to tell the West about the martyrdom of Radishschev and to salute his courage, but he had not read

---

[1] It is Casanova who tells this story in his memoirs and adds 'Imagine my surprise when I saw the father and mother transported with joy! They were sure that their infant had flown to Heaven. Blessed ignorance!' Jacques Casanova de Seingalt, *Histoire de Ma Vie*, 12 vols. bound in 6 (Wiesbaden, 1960–62), vol. X, Chap. 5, p. 111.

his book. Another foreigner, the Saxon, G. von Helbig, diplomat at the court of Catherine II, described it in a dispatch to the court at Dresden in 1799, and devoted a whole chapter of his book *Russische Günstlinge* to Radishschev. In his brochure, he says, he condemns many aspects of the present régime—above all serfdom. 'The book sold well because it was written in a vivid, racy style.'

The *Journey* is written like a folk-tale, a sort of secular *Pilgrims' Progress*. Radishschev gives a leisurely account of the people and things he saw as he walked through the countryside. He begins by telling how he passes a peasant ploughing his field on Sunday and asks him why he works on a day of rest. The peasant explains that for six days a week he must work for his master. He does not complain, for he can plough at night as well as on holidays and need not starve, although, he adds that he has seven mouths to feed while his master has a hundred hands for only one mouth. Radishschev watches the recruiting of serfs for the army and is shocked because three are being sold by their master who wants to buy himself a new carriage; another is sent off for some trifling offence. It was amazing that Radishschev dared to print his book but, a follower of Rousseau, he believed in the essential goodness of human beings and perhaps believed that if his countrymen realized the injustices of the system under which they lived they would reform them. Herzen, who greatly admired the book, re-published it in 1858. In the twentieth century its author was hailed as a forerunner of liberal Russians and even, though wrongly, of communism.

Because Alexander Vorontzov pleaded with Catherine II, Radishschev's fetters were removed. Otherwise he would probably have perished on his 6,000 mile journey to eastern Siberia. He was recalled by the Tsar Paul (because Paul hated his mother) and his estates restored by Alexander I but, fearing a second exile, he committed suicide.

See G. A. W. Helbig *Russische Günstlinge* (Tübingen, 1809); and D. M. Lang, *The First Russian Radical* (Allen & Unwin, London, 1959).

PART IV
1801–1825

THE REIGN OF ALEXANDER I

INTRODUCTION

For many people in Russia, the last years of the eighteenth century
had been a nightmare. No one had known what the mad Tsar
Paul might do next. Edmund Clarke, who travelled through the
country in 1799, wrote that honesty was found only in the victims
of tyranny, condemned for their love of truth to the mines of
Siberia or some dungeon of the empire. Now Paul was dead,
and liberals believed that Alexander, educated by his enlightened
Swiss tutor La Harpe, would bring reforms into the country.
Later, when he played a great part in the defeat of Napoleon, he
was represented as the new St George who had freed Europe from
its dragon and who, by his Holy Alliance, was going to free it from
all future strife. Travellers came and went for some years before
they realized how illusory these hopes had been.

Ker Porter's *Travelling Sketches* clearly show the new attitude
to the Scythian Bear. Hired originally to paint vast, romantic
pictures of the New Russia, he quickly came to believe in the
myth and fell in love not only with the princess whom he later
married, but with almost everything in her exotic country.

John Carr was another artist who travelled in Russia at this
time. He is worth quoting because he noticed things that had escaped the observation of other Western visitors.

The most entertaining accounts of this time are in the journals
of the two Irish girls, Martha and Catherine Wilmot, who lived
in the family of Princess Dashkov. It is to Martha that we owe
the *Memoirs* of the most remarkable Russian woman of her time.
She made Princess Dashkov write them, smuggled them out of
Russia and published them, Both girls wrote, often scathingly,
about the 'higher orders' whom they met. Unique are Martha's
stories of the serfs with whom she lived and of the day-to-day life
in Princess Dashkov's household. Catherine, more brilliant and
caustic than her sister, has amusing comments to make. Although
there were thousands of foreigners living in Russian families as
tutors, nurses or guests, throughout the nineteenth-century,
none have recorded their impressions as simply and as vividly as
these two girls have done.

Madame de Staël, although she spent only two months in Russia,
wrote a perceptive analysis of Russian character. She showed more
insight than other foreigners. True she was not altogether objec-

tive, for, as she saw Russians in their finest hour, when they were preparing to fight her arch-enemy, Napoleon, she was naturally prejudiced in their favour.

The memoirs of the romantic and flamboyant Brigadier-General Sir Robert Wilson, who fought side by side with Russians in 1812, 1813 and 1814, give vivid accounts of these terrible campaigns, but they are omitted as more particularly interesting to historians than the general reader. Xavier de Maistre is another foreigner who fought in the Tsar's army against Napoleon and writes, like Wilson, a harrowing account of the retreat of the Grande Armée. Xavier and his brother Joseph were the most brilliant writers among the numerous French émigrés who took refuge in Russia from the Revolution and from Napoleon. Xavier, who lived on and off in Russia from 1802 till his death in 1852, wrote many letters from St Petersburg to a friend in France, but they tell us little of day-to-day life there. In 1812, when he married one of the Tsarina's maids of honour, he adapted himself completely to Russian life, but he gives far more brilliant pictures of this in his fiction than in his letters. The most famous of these stories, *La Jeune Sibérienne,* used to be obligatory reading in French *pension-nats*. The *Histoire d'un Prisonnier Français* describes how an enlightened noblewoman ran her estate, and her attitude to her serfs, and it can be read with interest to this day. Xavier's brother Joseph will always be remembered, if only for his famous comment on Russia (in a letter of August 1811), 'Every nation has the Government it deserves'.

Dr Lyall, who practised medicine for some years in Russia after 1812, although an unattractive figure, made some unusual comments on customs and manners that are worth quoting, often for their unconscious humour.

The section ends with the letters and journals of two Quakers, Daniel Wheeler and Stephen Grellet. Wheeler, a Yorkshire farmer, spent many years draining the marshes near St Petersburg (Alexander I, who had visited a Friends' Meeting in London, had insisted on having a Quaker for this task). Grellet toured all over Russia, preaching 'as the Spirit moved him'. Although their writings are tainted with the repetitive pieties usual in their Society at that time, they are free from the scorn and condescension of other Protestants. The Quaker apologist Barclay had taught that even the Turk, the Jew and the pagan, by the holy light in their souls, might be united to God. They were eager to find spiritual depth in the Russians whom they met, not only in the mystical Tsar himself and many of the nobles, but even in the paid clergy, so much disapproved of by the Society of Friends. Russia had to wait for the visit of Liddon, Canon of St Paul's, in 1867, for a judgment as sympathetic.[1] Apart from the pieties, which we gladly omit, Wheeler, a practical man, wrote graphic descriptions of farming problems, floods, epidemics and his talks with the Tsar.

[1] 'The sense of God's presence—of the supernatural—seems to me to penetrate Russian life more completely than that of any of the Western nations.' (H. P. Liddon, Canon of St Paul's, after a visit to Russia in 1867.)

JOHN CARR

A Northern Summer of Travels round the Baltic

London 1805

JOHN CARR set out on his travels round the Baltic in May
1804. He was a painter and had already published a book,
A Stranger in France. He undertook his journey, partly, he
says, for his health's sake. He was prevented from going south,
because of the Napoleonic War, so decided on the less known
north, hoping that a description of his experiences might prove
not only amusing but of use to later travellers. He had no com-
punction about leaving his country, threatened with invasion,
because, in his home-town of Totnes, in Devon, he had offered
to command 'a spirited body of his fellow townsmen', but the
authorities, swamped with thousands of volunteers for their
militia, had turned him down. John Carr writes as a tourist, in the
inflated and would-be facetious style popular at the time, but he
was a genial, warm-hearted young man and, although he did not
penetrate deeply below the surface of Russian life, some of his
observations are acute and he relates things that escaped the notice
of our other travellers.

As an artist he was especially interested in architecture. All
the illustrations in his book are of cities, churches and monasteries. Petersburg, because of its vast space and areas, he thought
superior to every European capital. It was the result of one mighty
design, whereas our cities grow up haphazardly. Next to a fine
palace we may have a squalid tavern. There was obviously some
advantage in absolutism. 'Unbounded power presents the Emperor of Russia with the lamp of Aladdin. At Petersburg there is
no public to consult; the public buildings are therefore the result
of one man's will.' What death had prevented Peter the Great
from executing, the later rulers had accomplished with great

ПЕСНЯ

4 'No being surpasses him in gaiety of heart'.

taste, so that it seemed as though one mind had planned and executed the whole.

The first thing that struck Carr was the good-nature of the common people. A Russian might do a ferocious thing but not an ill-natured one. 'No being under heaven surpasses him in the gaiety of the heart. . . . There is nothing cold about him but his wintry climate; whenever he speaks, it is with good-humour and vivacity. Where a German would smoke for comfort, a Russian sings.' (Elsewhere Carr expresses great distaste for Russian singing, which he finds wild, harsh and barbaric.) This good-nature of the Russian he finds more remarkable because he is a slave 'never illumined by education, bruised with ignoble blows . . . excluded from the common privilege, which nature has bestowed on the birds of the air and the beasts of the wilderness, of choosing his mate, he must marry when and whom his master orders'.

Carr was charmed by the young Tsar, then twenty-nine years of age, 'tall, lusty and well-proportioned'. He was often seen

'wrapped up in his little regimental cloak, riding about the capital alone, upon a little common *droshki*. .. He is much attached to the English, numbers of whom have settled in the empire, and have formed under the auspices of the government, a sort of colony. .. The man within whose reach heaven has placed the greatest materials for making life happy was, in the Tsar's opinion, an English country gentleman.'

Carr met many of these English residents while he was in Russia. He paid several visits to the country houses of the English merchants on the Peterhof road, where they lived in great elegance. Carr even walked on English ground there, as his host had, at great expense, brought a quantity of ballast in British ships to cover his walks with.[1]

One of the most interesting of the Englishmen whom Carr met was Mr Gould who had laid out the pleasure grounds of the Taurida Palace for Prince Potemkin, and had amassed a tidy fortune as reward for his long services. Gould was a pupil of Capability Brown and had laid out very beautifully the small pleasure-grounds which he had created from a bog 'in the shade of which Potemkin, Catherine the Great and two succeeding emperors of Russia have sought tranquillity and repose from the oppressive weight of public duty'. From Gould, Carr heard many anecdotes about Potemkin, for whom the palace had been built, including a detailed account of the entertainment he had given in the vast hall of the palace in honour of the Tsarina, 'the most gorgeous and costly entertainment ever recorded since the days of Roman voluptuousness'. Gould showed him over the palace, and in the winter garden, amongst other statues, he was delighted to find the bust of Charles James Fox, which looked splendid with its background of huge orange-trees. He was grieved to hear that during his darkened hours Paul had ordered the bust into a cellar and had turned the palace into a garrison and a riding-school for his troops. Paul so hated the lover of his mother that he had the mausoleum she had had made for him in the Crimea destroyed and his body exposed to the birds.

Gould, as head gardener, had accompanied Potemkin on one of his journeys to the Crimea. They were preceded by hundreds of assistants who had surrounded his tent wherever it had been erected with an English garden of trees and shrubs. Gould admitted wryly that he had often suffered from the honour of sharing

[1] Ker Porter mentions the warm hospitality he received from these merchants, who were held in high esteem even by the Russian nobility. They lived during the hot, short-lived summer in little paradises on the road leading to Peterhof. Everything around him reminded him of dear England: 'The house embosomed in trees and furnished in the English style; gardens planted in the same taste; and the language and manners of the inmates; all would have persuaded me to forget I was in a strange land.' Even the aristocratic Lady Craven, who 'had no acquaintances in the world of commerce', was delighted to find in the quarter of St Petersburg where the merchants lived 'English grates, English coal and English hospitality to make me welcome and the fire-side cheerful'.

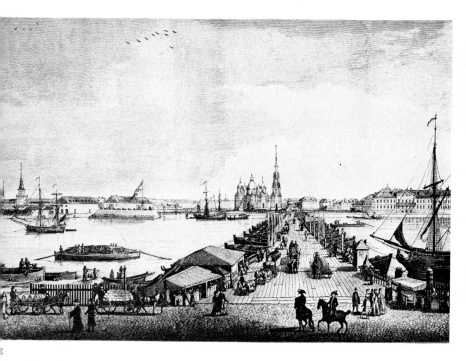

ove: The blessing of the waters (p. 150).

low: 'At Petersburg there is no public to consult; the public buildings are therefore the result
one man's will' (p. 158). The Admiralty Bridge.

VIII

Above: At the mouth of the Neva (p. 199).

Below: 'The poor wolves must be very hungry' (p. 203).

Potemkin's carriage as, while his followers were being sumptuously entertained, he would dine off a raw carrot or turnip and expect his guest to do the same.

Potemkin often refused to pay his tradesmen. He was fabulously
rich, owning estates worth nine million roubles, with 35,000 serfs,
and receiving, besides, enormous pensions, yet he was so prodigal
that he was often hard put to it to square his debts. A celebrated
French veterinary professor came from Vienna to Petersburg to
tend a horse, given Potemkin by Joseph II. He had built a special
stable for it and nursed it back to health, but never received a penny
in payment and was refused access to the prince.

Carr met several famous Scotsmen who had taken service with
the Tsars: Captain Elphinstone, whom Catherine had honoured
for his share in the defeat of the Swedish Navy, and Dr Matthew
Guthrie, personal physician of the Tsar. (Scots physicians were
apparently more trusted than any others from the time, in 1704,
when Robert Erskine had entered the Russian service and presided
over the Chancery of Medicine.[2]) Dr Guthrie was a philosopher
and scientist. Carr visited him in the wooden hut which, on a day
of tropical heat, he kept cool by keeping the windows shut and
having water poured over the branches of trees suspended over
his roof. He had a splendid collection of minerals and precious
stones from Siberia, and of stuffed water-birds from the Russian
archipelago. The Tsar Paul, in spite of his hatred of Britons, had
honoured him and made him a general.

Carr heard many stories of the wretched Tsar, who had been
assassinated only three years before he came to Russia. He
stresses the cruelty with which his mother Catherine had treated
him and hints that this was what caused the later derangement of
his mind. Catherine had ordered him abroad and then sent one of
his best friends to Siberia. Banished to Gatchina, he had seen his
mother's favourites constantly elevated to positions of power,
while he was kept in total ignorance of the affairs of the Empire.
Yet he was highly cultivated, generous and affectionate. He had
martial inclinations but was never allowed to exercise them. He
could never forget that his father had been murdered by one of his
mother's lovers, Alexis Orlov. Like Hamlet, 'the bleeding shade
whispered revenge to his morbid imagination'. Catherine 'pressed
and pierced the delicate and ardent mind of her son until she sub-

---

[2] Aksakov mentions that no Russian house was complete without Buchan's
Domestic Medicine, see *Years of Childhood* , chapter 1.

F

verted it'. The first act of his reign was to move the remains of his father to the sepulchre of Catherine II in the cathedral of St Peter and Paul. (He forced Alexis Orlov to be one of the pall-bearers.) Soon his mind showed 'the most fearful symptoms of distraction'. Yet, like Ivan the Terrible, he had accesses of remorse. After exiling Suvarov, who 'fell the broken-hearted victim of his madness', he raised a bronze statue to him and ordered his troops to march by facing 'one of the greatest and bravest generals of his or any other age'.

Carr was scandalized to see men and women bathing naked in a branch of the Neva, but admits that 'there was perfect innocence amongst all the parties'. He describes in detail a visit to the vapour baths and, although he was disgusted by the promiscuity, he admits that these baths, to be found in every village, prove that Russians are naturally clean. The Russians have a cure for every disease 'two glasses of brandy, a scourging and soaping in the vapour baths, and a roll in the Neva or snow'.

He visited the Academy of Arts, whose pupils were not only educated but clothed and maintained by the Crown, but deplored their lack of talent. 'Russia has never yet sent an illustrious painter into the world.' He was impressed by the Smolny Institute founded by Catherine II for the daughters of the nobility. Here 372 young ladies were educated in languages, drawing, music, dancing and every elegant pursuit, entirely at the expense of the Crown. It was especially patronized by the Empress Dowager. There was nothing like it in Europe. At the Institute of Marie, girls of humbler birth were educated and, at the age of eighteen, 'provided with respect-able situations in genteel families or married off with a small dowry'. Carr was not so impressed by the Foundling Hospital, where 2,500 abandoned infants had been received the previous year, of whom 500 had died. This was largely due to the wet-nurses, too often dirty and diseased.

Carr published his book in London in 1805. As Russia had be-come the ally of England on the death of the Tsar Paul (who had planned to invade India), a chatty book of this sort was timely.

MARTHA AND CATHERINE WILMOT

The Russian Journals, 1803–1808[1]

Edited by the Marchioness of Londonderry and H. M. Hyde

Macmillan, London 1934

IN the spring of 1803, Martha Wilmot set out from her home in Ireland for Russia. After four months she arrived at Troitskoe, Princess Dashkov's country estate, where for the next five years she was to live as a cherished guest. The Princess had long loved Ireland, where she had spent nearly a year of her six years' 'exile from Russia'. She had found in Dublin 'a society distinguished by its wit, elegance and good breeding and animated by a frankness of manner peculiar to the Irish character'.

The Princess had met Martha's father, Captain Wilmot, an Anglo-Irish landowner, and had become friends with Mrs Hamilton, a cousin of the Wilmots. It was on Mrs Hamilton's advice that Martha went to visit the Princess. This gentle, sensitive young woman was falling into a decline in her grief at her naval brother's early death of yellow fever in the West Indies. Her kind cousin, just returned from Russia herself, thought that the change of scene might bring her back to life.

Martha's brilliant sister Catherine followed her to Troitskoe in 1805. Both sisters kept diaries and wrote numerous letters. These remained unpublished until 1934. They are of great interest. Both young women were quick-witted, intelligent and, for the times, unusually well educated. They were warm-hearted (especially Martha) and responsive to experience. With their Irish back-

---

[1] We have decided to modernize the spelling of these journals, not to put in all their capitals, and to write 'dressed' and not 'dress'd', etc.—Editor.

ground they were more akin to Russians than were the English; they had the same spontaneity and frankness, not quite such uncontrollable emotions but something of the same temperament. They saw all sides of Russian life. The Princess Dashkov presented her guests at the Court of Alexander I but, besides mixing in the fashionable society of St Petersburg and Moscow, they also made friends of the household serfs and visited the peasants in their homes on the Princess's estate.

Before quoting from their diaries and letters, a word must be said about their illustrious hostess. During her six years' travels abroad, Princess Dashkov had met the most famous men of the times: Frederick the Great, Joseph II, Voltaire, Diderot, to name but a few, and many recorded their impressions of her, amongst them Horace Walpole. 'Who do you think has arrived?' he wrote to Sir Horace Mann. 'The famous Princess Dashkov, the Tsarina's favourite and accomplice, now in disgrace—and yet alive. She has put her son in to Westminster School. The devil is in it if the son of a conspiratress, with an English education, does not turn out a notable politician. . . . I am eager to see this amazon who had so great a share in a revolution when she was not above nineteen.' (The revolution referred to was the conspiracy which deposed the Tsar Peter III and made Catherine sole Empress. The Princess who idolized Catherine, had had an important share in this, although she had had nothing to do with the murder of the wretched Tsar.) When Walpole met Dashkova, he wrote:

> 'Her behaviour is extraordinarily frank and easy. She talks on all subjects, and not ill nor with striking pedantry, and is very quick and very animated. She puts herself above all attention to dress and everything feminine, and yet sings tenderly and agreeably with a pretty voice.'

Sir George Macartney, English minister to Catherine II, sized her up after her dismissal from the Court for her share in the anti-Peter III conspiracy. Everyone was delighted, he said, that she had retired to Moscow.

> 'She is woman of uncommon strength of mind, bold beyond the most manly courage and of a spirit capable of undertaking impossibilities—a character highly dangerous in a country like this, especially when joined to an engaging behaviour and a beautiful person. For, notwithstanding the general ferocity of the inhabitants, women here seem to have as much sway as among the most civilized nations.'

Catherine Wilmot described the Princess as she found her on her estate at Troitskoe in 1805. The Princess was now in her sixties and considered an old woman.

'In the midst of this immense establishment, and in the centre of riches and honour, I wish you were to see the Princess go out to take a walk or rather to look over her subjects. An old brown great-coat and a silk handkerchief about her neck, worn to rags, is her dress: she has worn it eighteen years because it belonged to her friend Mrs Hamilton. . . . She helps the masons to build walls, she assists with her own hands in making the roads, she feeds the cows, she composes music, she writes for the press, she talks out loud in the church and corrects the priest if he is not devout, she also talks out loud at her little theatre, and puts in the performers when they are out in their parts. She is a doctor, an apothecary, a surgeon, a farrier, a carpenter, a magistrate, a lawyer; corresponds with her brother who holds the first place in the Empire, with authors, with philosophers, with Jews, with poets, with her son, with all her relatives and yet appears as if she had her time a burden on her hands. She gives me continually the idea of being a fairy.'

Martha had dreaded meeting her hostess since she had been told by one of the Princess's enemies in St Petersburg that she was a cruel and vindictive person, that she 'lived in a castle, situated in a dreary solitude, far removed from the society of any civilized beings, where she was all-powerful, and so devoid of principle that she would invariably break open and read the letters that came to me'.

The Princess, however, received her so graciously that Martha soon forgot her fears. She began to chat with her 'about Kings and Empresses, and sometimes about wheat and rye'. The Princess received English papers and they fought English battles together (in the war with Napoleon) with the utmost valour, sitting under the British flag, for 'the Princess is a red-hot English woman'.

The Princess was at this time a very lonely woman. She had adored the Great Catherine. Though at times she had fallen into disgrace, the Tsarina had heaped her with honours in the periods when she was in favour, but all that was gone. She had been in disgrace during the reign of the mad Paul and, although she had returned to favour on his death, she was not an intimate of Alexander or of his wife. She had been devoted to her husband but he had died on campaign in Poland in 1764. She had had great hopes of her son, whom she had educated at Westminster and Edinburgh, but he had not had the brilliant career she had hoped for him and she had quarrelled with him because she disapproved of his marriage, which in fact turned out badly. Her daughter hated her mother and was cruel to her. The Princess was longing for someone to love. Martha came to her like a gift from heaven. She was soon completely dependent on her for her happiness. She loved her more dearly than she had ever loved her own children. She showered her with presents. Martha, a little embarrassed at first by so much kindness, soon reciprocated the Princess's love and felt a great responsibility for her. When Catherine Wilmot came to Troitskoe the Princess was charmed by her wit, her gaiety and beauty, but she never won her heart as Martha had done.

Martha was given her own serf-girl Sophia to attend to her wants. She was impressed by the social atmosphere in Russia so relaxed in comparison with the English. 'Tis by no means uncommon to see masters and slaves mingle in the same dance and, in visiting at a strange house, I have been more than once puzzled to find out which was the mistress and which the *femme de chambre*.' On October 1, 1803, Martha received a letter from her father. The whole household rejoiced.

'I do assure you [she wrote] I thought poor Katinka (the woman who brought your letter to my room) would have broke her bones running so fast with it; while, one by one, every creature in the house came to congratulate me. But I could not for my life help smiling at the joy of my own pretty little *femme de chambre* who did not arrive till after the others . . . loaded with a pie of such dimensions that I thought she must have sunk under the weight. She had also provided little baked cakes, and in a most artless and affectionate manner begged" *Mavra Romanovna* would *coucheet* (eat) and she was *Ochin harrasha* (very glad) *Mavra Romanovna* had heard from her *Batushka* (father) and truly, truly glad, my own *Batushka*, was I to receive your letter".'

Martha was amazed by the versatility of the serfs, all of whom belonged, body and soul, to the Princess.

'Her principles are noble and possessed of influence which extends to *absolute* dominion over the happiness and prosperity of some thousands of subjects. She invariably exerts for their welfare, entering into their circumstances; and by kindness as a landlord and forbearance, etc., etc., placing them in a situation of prosperity not universally known in this country.'

On October 19, 1803, Martha wrote to her mother:

'Think of our weather being fine enough for the Princess and me to
drive out in a *droshki*, a sort of jaunting car quite exposed to the air,
and I have just left her overseeing her labourers, who are sinking a
pond. Her servants are building a wall and no masons could perform
better. . . . I believe I have before now spoke of the versatility of the
Russians. It is really astonishing but the number of servants is dreadful.
Think of two, three and often four hundred servants to attend a small
family. A Russian lady scorns to use her own feet to go upstairs, and
I do not romance when I assure you that two powdered footmen
support her lily-white elbows and nearly lift her from the ground,
while a couple more follow with all manner of shawls, pelisses, etc.,
etc., etc. There is not a bell in Russia except to the churches, but if
a fair one gently calls, four or five footmen are ready in an ante-
chamber to obey her summons. Princess D, however, has no reproach
to make to herself on this subject—her servants work like labourers.
Order them to sing, and five or six will sing the airs of the country in
different parts, with a concord and medody which is delightful—
others will play on a variety of instruments with equal taste, indebted
only to nature. I have never yet seen a Russ man dance. The women
are very fond of dancing and do so in a style quite peculiar. We have
a little theatre here and our labourers, our cooks, our footmen, and
femmes de chambre turn into princes, princesses, shepherds and
shepherdesses, etc., etc., and perform with a degree of spirit that is
astonishing. 'tis droll enough to be attended at supper by the hero
of the piece who has been strutting before your eyes in gilded robes
etc., etc., for half the evening.'

In another letter Martha wrote:

'The Russians are very clever, quick as thought at catching an idea,
faithful copiers of any new invention, work or fashion; excellent
thieves, I am told, and possessed of various good qualities. I speak of
the lower orders; for French instruction has tinctured the manners
of the higher orders, without the polish which charms one into forget-
fulness of their want of sterling worth.'

The Princess had a house in Moscow and often took Martha
there during the winter season to attend balls and banquets and
meet people of the highest rank and most ancient families. Martha made many observations on these 'higher orders'. These are
much like those of other foreigners and not unusual like her artless
accounts of the serfs among whom she lived. (For more original

observations we must await the advent of her sister Catherine who had many caustic and amusing things to say about them.)

Martha was dazzled by Moscow.

'Thursday 11th (September 1805). Up at cock crow to drive to Sparrow Mount, from which spot Moscow is seen as a panorama and a most exquisite view it is indeed. The seven hundred churches or convents with their gilded spires and domes, the variety of their form, the groves of high trees which are in the town, its being built on a hilly spot and above all the Kremlin, that town walled round in the centre, produce an effect so unique that Kate, who has lately been visiting every part of the continent, was delighted with it and for my part I was really enchanted.'

Of unusual interest is Martha's account of her journey to Krouglo. This was the estate given by Catherine II to the Princess when she returned from her six years' travel abroad. She was then so high in the Tsarina's favour that she not only received this handsome present but was made Director of the Academy of Arts and Sciences founded in the reign of the Tsarina Elizabeth. Krouglo was near Mohileve in White Russia, and had been annexed by Russia in the First Partition of Poland. The Princess had been apprehensive about the gift. She admitted that she had been able to manage her children's estates to some advantage,

'but that I could ever flatter myself with similar success in the management of a people, half of them Poles and half of them Jews (ignorant as I am both of their manners and their language) is little to be expected, and in forgoing the hope of improving their condition I should lose half the pleasure of possession.'

Catherine had insisted and the Princess had accepted, although the journey from Troitskoe was so long and so complicated that she seldom visited her subjects.

Martha describes the caravan which set out (after the usual prayers in the church) on June 29, 1804, to visit Krouglo.

The kitchen cart, escorted by the butler,

'set forward an hour before the rest to find a shelter, light a fire to dress dinner which is afterwards served on silver dishes with plates, spoons, wine glassses, etc. . . . The service is large enough for six or seven people with all the elegance of a feast, the changes of plates, napkins, etc. After the cart follow two more with baggage of different kinds, amongst others a trunk which when open'd becomes a bedstead in which is found bed, pillows and every comfort to court sleep. Then follow three carriages. In short we were three ladies, five Abigails. fourteen men servants, twenty-seven horses and three dogs—such was the caravan that arrived at the peasant's house'

where they had spent the first night, finding all the family asleep on the stove and almost no furniture except the bench round the wall.

The journey of the next day was beautiful, 'the country so rich in wood and the fields waving with the most abundant crops of rye'. That night they spent at a gentleman's house, such was Russian hospitality that it did not matter that he was not at home.

'As the Princess was known to the servants, every room was thrown open and a splendid supper prepared and a desert of peaches, plums, melons, and strawberries. The next morning, after tea and coffee, we set forward, stopped to dine in a coach house, slept during the heat, and then went on. . . . One evening the village where we halted was so poor that shelter could not be obtained. Now don't suppose we were without a resource. The Princess desired a tent might be pitched and forwith a very elegant one was unfurled'.

Once they slept in the carriage but, the last night in Russia, a peasant's house was their shelter. Here poor Martha suffered martyrdom from the swarms of bugs.

The first people they saw when they entered 'poor conquered Poland' were Jews. She was amazed by the grand attire of the Jewesses.

'Only conceive, women very few degrees above Nelly your milk woman dressed in a sort of winkered cap of *pearls* which shades the face very becomingly; above this border is a turban. Their ear-rings, necklaces and rings sparkle in every direction, while a sort of waistcoat of one colour and petticoat of another finish their attire. The men look like monks; everyone of them wears a small cowl of black velvet and long robes with a broad girdle round their waists; their beards long, their faces pale and infinite intelligence in their countenances.'

One of the Jewish ladies visited the Princess. She noted that, wearing all her pearls and diamonds, 'she makes bread, sweet meats, cakes and what is more candles. In short she is never seen less magnificent.'

On one occasion they went to the synagogue of Krouglo. It was the Day of Atonement. The Jews were sinners in the Wilderness sorrowing for their transgressions. They had discarded their jewels and rich clothes and, clad in sackcloth and ashes, 'went with downcast eyes and penitent countenances to the synagogue. Most of the congregation had books, and read and wept for themselves, one in particular sobbed aloud. After they had prayed for several hours they returned home but not to the *inside* of their houses. Every one must sleep on the bare earth, and they do so most strictly, being tenacious to a degree of all their ceremonies.'

Martha describes all the religious ceremonies which she witnessed, whether Jewish or Russian Orthodox, coolly and objectively with none of the disparaging remarks usual in Protestant visitors. She does, however, notice that, on the Sabbath Day when it is a sin to carry anything, a rich Jewess, who consigned her infant to a Christian, kept the keys which 'unlocked untold treasures'. 'They would not eat with Christians for any bribe . . . although money is the grand touchstone with them, more than with any other people. . . . The Princess told me that in White Russia only 1,700 Jews pay the tax to the Crown, but that there are at least 100,000 in the country, their incessant journeying from place to place giving them the opportunity of evading payment.'

She remarked not only the 'infinite intelligence' of the faces of Jewish men but the beauty of many of their women. Yet the prejudice against them, among the Christians, was so great that even the penniless thought it a shame to serve them. As for the Poles, although they were as poor as the Catholics in Ireland, their dances were much gayer than the Russian, and the country (White Russia), where they lived, not only beautiful but rich with its 'sarrasin', corn, wheat, oats and rye, flax with blue flowers and 'peas so green'. They watched men taking honey from the wild bees and found it 'exquisite and in great abundance'. On September 19th, just before they left Krouglo, they witnessed the Feast of Tabernacles, a time of rejoicing, when the Jews wore their best clothes 'although their dirt was intolerable'. 'For six days they cannot eat or sleep in their houses. They have accordingly erected little huts like sties close to each other *without* a roof or nearly; and *without* a boarded floor, to imitate the huts in which they lived in Egypt [actually, in Sinai].'

When they returned to Troitskoe the Princess gave to Martha a little eleven-year-old girl, Pashinka, as 'her *own property* for ever'. But Pashinka cried so much, not even consoled by fine clothes and dolls, that Martha went to see her mother. She found to her surprise that 'far from considering the situation of lady's maid advantageous the Russ peasants usually look on it as a misfortune to have a child taken to the house of a noble'. Pashinka gradually got reconciled to her fate and Martha did not give her back to her mother for some time. Martha felt that the agricultural serfs were better off than the domestic ones.

'If they are slaves 'tis likewise the master's interest to treat them kindly. His population constitutes his riches; he who neglects or oppresses his subjects becomes their victim and sinks himself. Those indeed who class with servants are different. A master's caprice comes in contact with every act of his domestics, and as they cannot be discharged, corporal punishment must sometimes be inflicted. That's what we Islanders cannot bear to think of. Yet the greatest punishment that can be inflicted is "to be given for a soldier".'[1]

The Princess was once given an engaging pretty little Cossack boy, as she had been given Pashinka.

'She asked him whether he would quit her. He fired up instantly and said, "Oh yes." "What, you love me, are happy and yet you will go away from me!" "This because I left my poor Mammy in the woods." "Well, what could you do to help her? You are too little to be of any use!" "No, for my Daddy is gone away and when my Mammy cries *I help her to cry*." The P, was really affected by his answer but, alas, the excursion in which he was taken prisoner separated him for ever from his poor Mammy.'

But to return to Pashinka. On November 12th she was in floods of tears as her uncle had been taken as a recruit. The Princess was obliged to give to the army four men out of every five hundred of her serfs.

'The man who goes as a soldier is considered as *dead* to the family. This idea arises from the size of the Empire which (together with bad posts and little notion of reading or writing amongst that class) makes any news from a soldier a thing scarcely ever possible. His friends, therefore are inconsolable for a short time and when forget him entirely.'

Luckily Pashinka's uncle, though a fine handsome man, was returned, as his chest was half an inch too narrow.

[1] The sufferings of domestic slaves are told with infinite compassion by Turgenev in his *Mumu* and his records of his mother's cruelties to them. One she killed with her own hands. In another case she would not allow her lady's maid to have her children with her. These were hidden by the other serfs and never allowed to go out, lest the mistress should see them. See also Kropotkin's autobiography.

5 'A soldier is considered as dead to the family.'

'To be rejected is a great triumph. Happy he who is lame, deaf
blind or maimed (and, by the by, they often cut off the joint of a
finger as the time for recruiting approaches)'.

Because of her love of the Princess and her gentle, unpre-
judiced nature, Martha attended all the great Church festivals
and describes them respectfully. On Palm Sunday she got up
between four and five o'clock to attend matins at the church.

'A crowd of peasants were assembled; prayers were read and
chanted. The Gospel, which describes our Saviour's triumphal
entry into Jerusalem, was read. A tremendous bundle of branches
had been prepared, beforehand, which the priest blessed and
sprinkled with holy water. Immediately the people rushed forward to
snatch the boughs, and in five minutes every individual in the Church
stood, confessed with a green bough and a lighted taper. Most people
place the taper before a favourite image and reserve the bough to
flog one another, when they return home, for good luck. (My little
Sophia flogged me most devoutly.) The people were then anointed
on the forehead with the sign of the cross in holy oil, and dismissed.'

She allowed herself some caustic remarks on the superstitions
of the Russians. The Princess Galitzin went on a pilgrimage to ask
the saints whether she should marry a certain general. How convenient that the answer given was what she wanted! She thought

that both Catholics and Orthodox made religion more of a business than her fellow Protestants did. She hoped that there was more true feelings among Protestants.

But for really caustic criticism we must turn to Catherine Wilmot. She had some devastating remarks to make on Moscow society. On February 18, 1806, Catherine wrote to her sister Alicia that, after attending twenty-seven feasts,

'I feel a little tired with them. Their luxuries and magnificence soon lose their effect and the unnatural hours kept here totally destroy every species of pleasure once the gloss of novelty is at an end. The effect left on my imagination is that of having flitted amongst the ghosts of the Court of Catherine. Moscow is the Imperial, terrestrial, political Elysium of Russia. All those whose power existed in the reign of Catherine and Paul and all those who are discarded by Alexander hold an *ideal* consequence, awarded by courtesy alone in this lazy, idle magnificent and Asiatic town, for all their effective power has long since passed as an inheritance to their successors who rule the Imperial realm at Petersburg and flutter away their hours about the court.'

Catherine Wilmot goes onto describe some of the ghosts whom she had met: Prince Galitzin, Grand Chamberlain in the time of Catherine, Count Ostrowman, Grand Chancellor of the Empire in the reign of Catherine, a gaudy phantom of eight-three years with the orders of St George, of Alexander Nevsky, St Vladimir, etc., hanging round his neck, and Count Alexis Orlov;

'The hand that strangled Peter III is covered with its recompense of brilliants, beneath which the portrait of Catherine smiles in eternal gratitude. . . . Other conspirators of the year 1762 trundle about their paunches and patriotism, their swords and keys, and all the insignia of their former greatness. In short, the grandees—and in this circle, alas, we only move—are, as I said before, of another world. . . . I confess I am heartily sick of the name of *Great Catherine* from this group of displaced dotards. She is praised uniformly with a reference to their own services, and what is really doing in Russia in the political world, I don't know. As uniformly, Alexander is esteemed a driveller, a Frenchified innovator, a schoolboy and a tyrant in embryo. . . . One of the causes of Alexander's unpopularity in Moscow is his having called over the son of Arthur Young to examine the agricultural state of the country. He has been here these six months and receives £1,200 a year for this mission . . . his enquiries, it seems, lead to producing a spirit of discontent amongst the peasants which terrifies the nobles for fear of a rebellion.

These specimens of the Muscovites are mingled, to be sure, with wives and daughters and granddaughters beautifully dressed, sitting in gilded boudoirs with slaves dancing before them, burning perfumes and handing sweetmeats to their visitors. But though the French manner is universal, yet they are neither well-bred nor agreeable women but obvious imitators. . . . When the Moscow women eye you from head to foot, kiss you four or six times instead of twice, recommend themselves to your eternal friendship, tell you in a riotous tone and abrupt expression that you are charming, enquire the price of each article of your dress and speculate on the brilliancy of the next assembly of the nobles, there is no more to be hoped for.'

(The Wilmots obviously never met a family like the Rostovs of *War and Peace*, at this time living in Moscow, never saw Natasha or Pierre amongst the crowd of grandees, nor Prince Andrei, fresh from Austerlitz. After all they were outsiders.)

'In their comparison of the English and French, [Catherine continues] the Muscovites' prejudices are all in favour of the latter. For example everything is shocking for dinner that is not dressed by a French cook, every boy and girl awkward who are not educated by French people, every dress inelegant that is not Parisian and the French novels are exclusively *gobbled* by every boy and girl in Moscow, yet there is no one who does not blaspheme against Bonaparte lament Lord Nelson. The English Nation, abstractedly [sic], is respected, but its practices are unknown, its language rarely spoken, its fashions disliked and the individuals criticized in a manner absolutely different from any others.'[1]

---

[1] The French ambassador, the Comte de Ségur, wrote in 1789: 'You can find [in St Petersburg] a large number of elegant ladies, young girls remarkable for their accomplishments, speaking seven or eight languages equally well, playing several instruments and familiar with the works of the most famous French, English and Italian poets and novelists.'
In 1767 our ambassador, Sir George Macartney, wrote of the 'crowds of French adventurers who daily resort here, and are received into most families with open arms as secretaries, librarians, readers, preceptors and parasites; though the greatest part of these gentry are equally impudent and illiterate, vagabonds from indigence or fugitives for crimes.' '*An Account of Russia in the Year 1767*' in *Some Account of the Public Life of the Earl of Macartney*, ed. John Barrow, Vol. II.
In 1790 an English traveller, A. Swinton, wrote: 'Russia resembles an heir newly come to his estate. She is only beginning to learn and seems struck at her own importance. The young heir has got his different masters to attend him: the English master is teaching him the art of navigation and commerce; the French, as usual, to dance and to dress; the Italian is drawing plans for his house and teaching him to sing; the German makes him wheel to the right and left and teaches him all the other arts of war.' Andrew Swinton, *Travels into Norway, Denmark and Russia in 1788, 1789, 1790 and 1791* (London, 1792).

Catherine relates some Moscow scandals:

'A nephew of Princess Dashkov has married the daughter of a French Tutor. Signor Tonce, a man of sixty (an Italian painter) has turned Princess Gagarin's head at twentynine by professing himself an atheist and a believer in Berkeley's Visionary System of Shadows. Every one thought him an inspired genius and threw open their palaces to him. I saw him once and took him for a quack mountebank doctor. On being asked what religion he was of he laughed and said, "Any or none." This produced a growl amongst the bears. However he turned Greek the next morning and was accordingly married. Four different large, fat princes cried to me in relating the disgrace.'

Yet Catherine was sorry to leave Moscow.

'It is warmer than Troitskoe and scarcely a day has passed that Matty and I have not trudged round the house in the snow for an hour to the amazement of the Russians, who literally never put their feet to the ground.'

Before she left Moscow the Princess took the Wilmots to a famous tavern where there were no grandees but only merchants and

'everything was in the Russian style, every dish peculiar to the country—and I suppose there were at least a hundred of them! To make the matter complete, *la Maîtresse d'Hôtel*, dressed in gold embroidery and diamonds, sat at the head of the table with her face, neck and arms painted like a doll. This painting is not from necessity but national usage ever since Russia was in existence. Our attendants, to the number of forty, were bearded men dressed in yellow, purple and various coloured shirts.'

After coffee, gipsies were brought in and danced beautifully. 'Their vivacity bordered on frenzy. . . . It was impossible to imagine them the inhabitants of this drowsy planet.'

Catherine Wilmot found the journey back to Troitskoe in the middle of March almost intolerable as the roads, 'because of the constant passage of merchandize were ploughed up into rocks of frozen and refrozen snow'. The horses were continually falling into holes from which dozens of people had to pull them. They needed nine equipages to convey them and their luggage. 'When they were all drawn up in a half-moon before the door at Moscow, we wanted only a few elephants to give us the appearance of an Indian army.' She found Martha, who had arrived before, stretched on a sofa with a sore throat 'and scarcely a moment has that excellent Princess stirred an inch from her side except when she helped to smooth the bed with her own hands, to mix her drink, and to apply cataplasms to her feet'. One of her expressions was "Ecoutez, ma chère Kaity, dis day my Jews in Poland m'ont envoyé deir rents, two thousand guinea; and I would fling it in de bottom of de river if dat would make well my little angel!" Another time Matty told her not to forget that her illness was infectious: ' "Well, and what id dat to me? Only un motive plus fort, for I might take it off upon my own self. I have asked God Almighty dat prayer already." Her adoration of her surpasses anything I ever saw.'

Catherine was sorry to have left Moscow, but the Princess was in heaven. She was certain her guest had never seen anything so beautiful as her park, which she had laid out in the English manner. "Tell me out true, is it not un vrai paradis? Et pourquoi, mon enfant? I did make it myself, I did work with de mason at de walls, I put in de little trees in dier holes; 'twas my own hands done dat. I draw de plans, and tousands of my peasants helped with their hatchet."

In 1807 Catherine decided to return home. What impressions did she take back with her? She wrote:

'Russia is but in the twelfth century! Yes! I know all about the luxury of Moscow and the civilization of Petersburg, but have you ever seen a clumsy, romping, ignorant girl of twelve years old with a fine Parisian cap upon her head? The cloister's ignorance not only of the twelfth but of the eleventh century is the groundwork of this colossal region, and five or six centuries will no doubt produce the same effects here they have in other parts of Europe. [Some prophets were nearer the mark than Miss Wilmot.] But what business have I to shake my ears over the world? . . . I will take you down stairs into the hall where dozens of slaves are waiting with bread and salt to greet the Princess [After her return from Moscow]. When she appears they fall down before her and kiss the ground with that senseless obeisance that stupefaction feels at the approach of a superior power. Her lenity makes their lot better perhaps than that of others, but that's saying very little for the system. Each noble is omnipotent. He may be either an angel or a devil. The chance is on the latter side and it must be almost an angel indeed who is not ruined by the possession of uncontrolled authority. . . . 'tis impossible to be in their company without recollecting that they are subjects under a despotism, for in their judgments *bad and good*, literally, appears to be synonymous with *favour and disgrace*.'

But there were things that Catherine enjoyed: 'The dryness of the climate, the elasticity of the air, the extraordinary diversion of the ice mountains, the *traineau* courses [sledging], the stoves, the baths, the warmth of clothing, and the habit of breakfasting in one's own room'.

Catherine was rather shocked than impressed that every woman in Russia had 'right over her own fortune, totally independent of her husband', so that a wife might be living in luxury while her husband languished in jail for debt. 'This to a meek English woman appears prodigious independence in the midst of a despotic government.' (Not till the Married Woman's Property Act in the 1880s did the meek English-woman have the same rights.)

Catherine Wilmot left Russia just before diplomatic relations between that country and England were severed, owing to the Peace of Tilsit. She managed to smuggle out in her luggage a copy of the Princess Dashkov's memoirs, which Martha had induced her to write and later translated from the French. This was important for posterity, as it was the only copy which survived abroad. (In Russia a copy preserved in the Vorontzov archives was published in 1881. Private copies had circulated before this.)

In 1808, when the Peace of Tilsit, concluded in July 1807, led to open hostilities between England and France, Martha felt that she must follow her sister and return home. In St Petersburg the difficulties of getting an exit permit seemed almost insuperable. The authorities had been warned that she might be taking important papers out of the country. Martha burned the Princess's memoirs and all the letters entrusted to her, including a love letter from the Princess Scherbatov to Ker Porter. When the police informed her that they had found something so dangerous that they must lay it before the government, Martha trembled but screamed with laughter when she was shown some music script (supposed to be cypher) and a French exercise about a mouse. Her ship was held up until its dangerous passenger was 'screened'. At last the all-clear was given and Martha left Russia for ever. Her adventures were not over. She was shipwrecked on an island off the Finnish coast and spent weeks in the cottage of the local Mamma who became a Mamma to her almost as devoted as the Russian one she had left behind.

To finish Martha's story briefly. She did at last get back to her home in Ireland. She married the Reverend William Bradford, Rector of Storrington in Sussex and later chaplain to the British

Embassy in Vienna. She died in 1873, aged ninety-eight. She did not publish Princess Dashkov's *Memoirs* till 1840 as the Princess's brother, Simon Vorontzov, formerly Russian ambassador in London, and still living there, objected. After his death it became possible.

As for the Princess, left behind in Troitskoe, she survived the loss of her beloved Mavra Romanovna for little more than a year.

> 'Now all is changed at Troitskoe' [she wrote]. 'The theatre is closed. I have not had a single performance. The piano is silent—the servant girls no longer sing. Everything paints your absence and my sorrow. But why should I talk to you like this? You are surrounded by relatives who delight in you and whom you love. . . . Whilst I know that you are happy I will not complain.'

The Princess made plans to rejoin her darling in Ireland if 'the stupid war' between their two countries should end. 'My life is a torture', she wrote in one of her last letters, 'from the first instant of your departure, and will continue to be so till God grant me the bliss of our reunion.'

The reunion was not to be. The Princess died in Moscow in January 1810, and was buried without pomp in the village church of Troitskoe. At the time she seemed forgotten, but the memoirs which Martha had induced her to write were a monument to her.

> 'What a woman!' the revolutionary Herzen exclaimed on reading them, 'What a rich and vigorous life! . . . In Princess Dashkov the personality of the Russian woman . . . emerges from her seclusion, displays her capacity, demands her share in politics, in science, in the reformation of Russia and boldly takes her stand beside Catherine the Great. Catherine II, in making her the President of the Academy, recognized the political equality of the sexes, which is perfectly consistent in a country which has accepted the civic equality of women before the law, while in Western Europe they still remain bound to their husbands or in perpetual nonage.'

Of the Princess' love for Martha Wilmot, Herzen wrote:

> 'She loved her passionately as she had once loved Catherine. Such freshness of feeling, such feminine tenderness, such craving for love, such youthfulness of heart, are astounding at sixty. The solicitude of a mother, a sister, a lover are what Miss Mary [Martha] found at Troitskoe.'

ROBERT KER PORTER

Travelling Sketches in Russia and Sweden

Philadelphia 1809

R OBERT KER PORTER is a refreshing change from our other visitors to Muscovy. In 1804 he was invited by Alexander I to illustrate by historical paintings the glorious past of Russia. He was already a well-known artist. His European fame had begun when, at nineteen, he had startled London by his huge canvass of *The Taking of Seringapatam*, Sir Thomas Lawrence had called it 'the Wonder of the World, a picture of two hundred feet dimensions, painted by the boy Ker Porter in six weeks!'

Robert Ker Porter came from a family distinguished by its intelligence as well as by its high connections. His father, a surgeon in the Enniskillen Guards, had died when Robert was a baby. His mother was Scots and, after her husband's death, she moved with her children to Edinburgh, then at the height of its fame as the 'Athens of the North'. It was a richer cultural centre than anywhere in England at the time. Here Robert and his two sisters (later famous for their romantic novels) listened to tales of Scots heroes told them by their servants. (Later on, in Russia, Robert felt he was back in the feudal world of barons and serfs, whose legends had so delighted his childhood.)

In 1790 the Porters moved to London, and Robert studied historical painting under Benjamin West at the Academy of Arts. In 1804, when the Tsar Alexander's invitation to him came, the climate was favourable for his visit. England and Russia were allies in their struggle against Napoleon. Moreover Western Europe had great hopes of the young Tsar, so different in every way from his father, the monstrous and mad Tsar Paul. He was reputed to agree with advanced liberal opinions and even to want to free the serfs. Robert stayed in Russia from 1805 until the Treaty of Tilsit had broken diplomatic relations between London and Petersburg and he was most reluctantly obliged to leave (in December 1807). During his stay he wrote many leters to a fellow-officer and extracts from them were published in England and America in 1809.

Robert Ker Porter was an aesthete and a romantic. He saw Russia with an artist's eye. He did not criticize it or want to change it. He was enchanted by its difference from the rest of Europe. Its landscape had for him the spaciousness and charm which we find in the landscapes of Tolstoy and Turgenev. He made many friends among the aristocracy and fell madly in love with the beautiful Princess Scherbatov who, four years after he had left, followed him to England and became his wife. (And what better way to become intimate with a foreign country than to fall in love with one of its natives?)

Robert's love for his Princess, his knowledge of being on the same side in the war, his admiration for his patron, the Tsar, all helped him to see Russia from the inside rather than as a superior and hostile stranger let loose among barbarians. Yet he had little understanding of the peasant, whom too often he dismissed as *canaille*. He was perhaps influenced in this attitude by the many French emigrés who had taken refuge in Russia from the Revolution. It was characteristic that all he saw in the peasants was that groups of them, 'often engaged in useless labour', added to 'the picturesque of the scene'.

Robert found that winter changed St Petersburg, not only in aspect, but in gaiety.

'The natives have suddenly changed their woollen kaftans, for the greasy and unseemly skins of sheep but the freezing power which has turned every inanimate object into ice, seems to have thawed their hearts: they sing, they laugh, they wrestle; tumbling about like great bears amongst the furrows of the surrounding snow. In fact this season with them seems more congenial with their natures than their short but vivid summer. Petersburg at this moment presents a prospect of much greater warmth and bustle than during the warmer months. The additional multitudes, spread in busy swarms throughout ever quarter, are inconceivable: sledges, carriages and other *traineau* vehicles, cross and pass each other with incredible velocity. . . . The sledges which succeed the *droshki* are generally very neat but always gaudy, being decorated with red, green gold and silver with strange carved work and uncouth whirligigs of iron. The sledge of a prince is uncommonly handsome. All its appointments

are magnificent and never out of harmony. In it we behold the
genuine, uncontaminated taste of the country: no bad imitation of
German or English coach work. The horses attached to this con-
veyance are the pride of the opulent. The harness of these creatures
is curiously picturesque, being studded with polished brass or silver,
hundreds of tassells intermixed with embossed leather and scarlet
cloth.

'[On the frozen Neva] your astonished sight is arrested by a vast
open square, containing the bodies of animals piled in pyramidal
heaps in all sides. Cows, sheep, hogs, fowls, butter, eggs, fish are
all stiffened into granite. . . . Their hardness is so extreme that the
natives chop them up for the purchaser, like wood; and the chips of
their carcasses fly off in the same way as splinters do from masses of
timber or coal. A hatchet, the favourite instrument of the country,
is used in the operation; as indeed it is generally applied to every
other act of ingenuity or strength. If the boors were taught to write
I have little doubt but their pens would be repaired with it. At
certain hours every day the market is a fashionable lounge. There
you may meet all the beauty and gaiety of St Petersburg; even from
the Imperial family down to the Russ merchant's wife. Affecting scenes
often occur. Whenever a new levy is taken for the army, a given
number is taken from every hundred slaves capable of bearing arms.
Most of the villages have been thus deprived of some of their inhabitants; and it is with the affectionate hope of again seeing their relatives, that many very aged men accompany these frozen caravans.
Ignorant of any particular corps and only conscious that it is a *soldier*
that they seek, they look for the blessing of again embracing a son,
a brother or some other near and beloved kinsman. Hundreds of soldiers are seen going from group to group, searching for their own
parents among these patriarchal strangers. . . . Nothing can be more
affecting than to witness their joyful meetings; fathers embracing
their sons, brothers their brothers. But the heart saddens while listening to the impatient enquiries of many, by the information that
another country contains their offspring; perhaps another world.'

Robert Ker Porter enjoyed his mid-winter journey from
St Petersburg to Moscow. He was in a comfortable sleigh ('a
kibitka, a well contrived and snug machine') in which he could lie
full length on straw and pillows and covered with furs. He found
more beauty and variety in the landscape than many of our
travellers and more colour. The shutters of the windows of the rude
peasant huts were often painted with 'flowers, stars and strange
devices' and there was sculpture and painting on their façades.
'In some of their wild carvings' he saw 'the germs of real talent'.

But he was horrified when he went into these peasant huts. He described (and painted) the post-master's dwelling. This consisted of one room only. It was

'rendered insufferably stifling by the stove, the breaths and other fumigations. Here were not only the postmaster and several other men but his wife, mother, wife's mother and baby all lying almost in a state of nature on top of the stove. A bed with dirty curtains [an unusual object] filled one corner of the room; a few benches and a table completed the furniture. The walls were not quite so barren, being covered with uncouth prints and innumerable daubings. In one spot was placed a picture of our Saviour and the Virgin, decorated with silver plates.'

Robert was glad to get back into his sleigh. On the immense snowy plains, he felt he might be at sea, out of sight of land and then suddenly, perhaps emerging from a dark forest, he would see an immense caravan of sleighs, seldom fewer than 'a hundred and fifty in a string, having a driver to every seventh horse', all laden with the wares they were carrying to every part of the vast empire of Russia.

'The effect of this cavalcade at a distance is very curious; and in a morning as they advance towards you, the scene is as beautiful as striking. The sun then rising throws his rays across the snow, transforming it into a surface of diamonds. From the cold of the night every man and horse is encrusted with these frosty particles. The manes of the horses and the long beards of the men have a particularly glittering effect.'

In Moscow, Robert was dazzled not only by the lavish hospitality he was shown but 'by the general polish of manners'. He was invited to the English Club to a dinner given in honour of Prince Bagration and 'conducted with the nicest decorum'. He was, however, shocked by the horn music. Here, forty serfs had been trained to play a single note on long horns. 'The performers are in general thin and pale,' destined, Robert felt, to a life shortened by these unnatural exertions. 'What a difference! A great warrior on whom all eyes were fixed with admiration; and a set of mechanized wretches, reduced to the level of a child's whistle.' Shocking, too, were the dwarfs that nearly every nobleman possessed who, 'at almost all entertainments, stand for hours by their lord's chair, holding his snuff-box, or awaiting his commands'. There was usually also a fool or two, 'like the motleys of our court in the days of Elizabeth', though not in wit, for they were usually over-fed and sleepy.

'What with the dwarf pages, fools, numerous attendants and customs of hospitality practised here, I cannot but be struck with its resemblance to the establishments of our old English barons.'

Yet, though pleasure was the order of the day—'a continual carnival of balls, private theatres, masquerades and assemblies of all sorts'—Robert felt, that contrary to his expectation, the moral tone of society was high.

'I never saw married people more happy or apparently more affectionate towards each other: I never met with young women more amiable and virtuous. . . . For a city whose sole object is pleasure, Moscow possesses less of what is called fashionable vice than may be found in countries where more seeming austerity is practised.'

Fortunately for their health the Muscovites

'are particularly fond of pleasure out of doors. Their favourite amusement is what they call the *promenade*. It consists of all the carriages of the city perhaps to the number of seven thousand, trailing after each other in regal procession, filled with all the beauty and splendour of Moscow; and in my life I never beheld so many lovely women at one time.'

In the beauty of its women Moscow was beyond comparison, superior to St Petersburg, perhaps because of the intermarriage of the nobility with Circassians, Georgians and Poles. The merchants' wives were in strong contrast. They were dressed richly but in a fashion 'hot, stiff and discordant with their figures. Their faces were disfigured with white and red paint, their teeth stained with black.'

Delightful as was winter in Russia, one longed after so many months of it, that it should end; but the much desired spring brought intolerable inconveniences and even dangers, not only in the countryside, where villages are isolated for weeks from market towns by floods and the breaking up of wooden bridges, but also even in Moscow, although 'thousands of boors' hastened the thaw by breaking up the ice of the streets with their hatchets and carrying it to the river. Walking is intolerable; leather boots are like blotting paper. If you walk near the sides of houses, you risk being crushed to pieces by the immense weight of the falling icicles and of the snow and ice from the roofs. On the River Moskva, you see not only floating masses of ice but fragments of cottages rolling down its current. Sometimes, higher up, whole villages have been swept away. Then, suddenly, what a fortnight ago was a plain of ice is now robed in green and everywhere there are budding trees and shrubs and flowers!

Robert found the return journey to St Petersburg, in mid-summer, in no way as enjoyable as his winter one. All was flat and uninteresting. There were no gardens round the cottages as in England—no honey-suckle or roses climbing round their doors. The burning sun and intolerable dust scorched his soul.

St Petersburg he found less brilliant and festive than Moscow, although he did attend a brilliant fête, given in honour of the name-day of the Empress-Dowager, in the gardens of Peterhof. Walks of five and six miles, bordered with fine trees, were hung with millions of lamps. Fountains played in every part of the garden, throwing up their waters to an amazing height. The reflections of the lamps in the numerous lakes 'bewildered the sight'.

At last the terrible news of the Russian defeat at Friedland came through and, to Robert, the not less terrible news of the Treaty of Tilsit. The British were leaving, although in the tolerant manner of those days, they were not forced to do so, even though diplomatic relations had been broken off and French interests had become paramount. Robert longed to stay where his beloved Princess Scherbatov lived, yet felt it his patriotic duty as 'a loyal Briton' to return to his homeland. He had accomplished what he had been invited by the Tsar to do. He left behind him a set of large canvasses, idealizing the achievements of Peter the Great, hung in the new Admiralty building in St Petersburg. He took home with him some more intimate sketches of Russian life. With the tears of his princess still wet on his cheek he left Russia on December 10, 1807, at five in the morning, on a day 'the most fearful in his life'.

MADAME DE STAËL

My Ten Years' Exile[1]

Paris 1821

WHEN Madame de Staël arrived in Russia, on July 14, 1812, it seemed on the face of it an inauspicious moment. She was fleeing from Napoleon, her arch-enemy, and on June 24th, at the head of half a million men, he had crossed the *Niemen* and started his invasion of Russia. But the country is vast and, though often afraid of falling into his hands, Madame de Staël evaded capture. For her and for us who read her it was the best moment possible for her Russian visit. You get to know a people best, she said, when you are sharing their sufferings. Compared to Europe, forced into uniformity by Napoleon, Russia seemed to her a land of freedom. Unlike so many visitors she was predisposed to see the best. She shared the feelings of the people; they had the same cause at heart. She was a woman of strong emotions and was not afraid of enthusiasm. This did not mean that she was sentimental. Her observations, her analyses of Russian characteristics, are among the most acute made by a foreigner. Not for nothing had Madame de Staël become the most famous woman in Europe. This 'whirlwind in petticoats' as Heine called her, had not only a brilliant, almost masculine, intellect but also subtle feminine intuition.

Madame de Staël's fame had preceded her. She was received like the commanding general of an allied power. At Kiev she was the guest of the governor. Rostopchin, governor of Moscow, gave a dinner in her honour. Society flocked back from their summer *dachas* into Moscow to catch a glimpse of her. On the whole they were disappointed. 'They saw a hefty woman of fifty whose clothes

---

[1] *Dix Années d'Exil*. The extracts are translated by the Editor.

were inappropriate for her age', one of them reported. 'Her manner was not liked; her speeches seemed too long and sleeves too short.' At dinner she sat with her elbows on the table, rolling and unrolling little tubes of paper. Little did the Muscovite ladies realize how astutely this clumsy, unfashionable French woman was sizeing them up and committing them to posterity. She wrote:

'They are much more hospitable than the French but society does not, with them, as with us, consist of a circle of clever people of both sexes, who take pleasure in talking together. They meet as they go to a fête, to see a great deal of company, to hear music, to play; it is external objects that excite them. They are in general very ignorant; find little pleasure in serious conversation and do not pique themselves on wit.'

But although Madame de Staël was bored by the society chatter of the Muscovites, she was amazed by their patriotism and the lavishness of the gifts which they made to help the war effort. 'A young Count Momonov raised a regiment for the state and refused to serve in it except as second-lieutenant; a Countess Orlov, rich as an Asiatic, gave a quarter of her income.' One noble, she heard (and the expression shocked her), had given a thousand peasants to the state, another two hundred but it seemed that such was the universal desire to free the country from the invader, that the serfs were as eager to fight as their masters.[1]

Madame de Staël was amazed by the hardihood of the nobles.

'When necessary, they live the lives of the people. The lords in whose houses are found luxuries gathered from every quarter of the globe, feed, when they are on a journey, much worse than our French peasants. They put up with miserable physical conditions not only in war-time but on many occasions of their life. The harshness of the climate, the bogs, the forests, the deserts of which so much of their country is composed, mean that men are in continual fight

---

[1] Sir Robert Wilson who, after campaigning against Napoleon in Portugal and Spain, was appointed by the Tsar as brigadier-general to continue the fight in Russia, noted the same spirit and the lavishness of the gifts made by the nobles and, indeed, by all classes of the population. 'The reinforcement and provisioning of the assembling army was one of the most extraordinary efforts of national zeal ever made. No Russian who possessed any article which could be rendered serviceable to the state withheld it: horses, arms, equipment, provisions and, in brief, everything that can be imagined poured into the camps. Old and young flocked to the standards and would not be refused service. Fathers of families, many seventy years of age and upwards, placed themselves in the ranks, and encountered every fatigue as well as peril with all the ardour of youth. . . . The camp resembled a bee-hive in the activity of its swarming hosts. The whole nation was solicitous to fill it with stores and useful largesses.'

with nature. . . . When they can't have luxury, they go without even essentials. You don't find what the English call comfort in Russia. Nothing is perfect enough to satisfy the imagination of the great Russian lords; when the poetry of riches is lacking, they drink mead, lie on a board, travel night and day in an open cart without regretting the luxury to which they are accustomed. It is magnificence they want, not day-to-day ease. This is one of the reasons which explains the fine courage with which the Russians have born the ruin caused by the firing of Moscow.'

Madame de Staël was writing this after she had left the country, but she had already noted the unpossessiveness of Russians—one of their most attractive characteristics. Not that they do not want possessions. The peasants, she noted at the whim of the moment, are adept at stealing objects, but they give them away with as great a pleasure as they acquire them.

The Russian landscape did not enchant Madame de Staël. The endless steppes did not exhilarate her as they did Gogol and Chekhov. She found the drive over the 900 versts from Kiev to Moscow almost unbearably monotonous. Her Russian drivers drove her like lightning, singing encouragements to their horses. There was nothing barbarous about them—on the contrary they were gentle, always saluting women of whatever age as they passed and crossing themselves when they passed a church but, although driven with great speed, she felt as though she were stuck in the same place, so monotonous was the country. She wearied of the birch-trees. Nature was not inventive enough for her in Russia. Nor was man. The wooden houses in the rare villages were all made on the same model. The only thing that delighted her on the journey, which seemed like crossing infinite space in an eternity of days, was when Cossacks dashed past her to join the army. They came singly, without order and without uniform, a long lance in their hands and dressed in a grey garment part of which made a huge hood over their heads. She had imagined them quite differently, but felt that in their sombre colours they might terrify their enemies like ghosts.

Madame de Staël regretted the lack in Russia of a middle class, so necessary for the enouragement of literature and the arts. At the same time this meant that there was less distance between the nobles and peasants, and a greater mutual sympathy. The feeling between master and serf made her think of the Romans and their affection for their slaves. But like all enlightened people she regretted serfdom and liked to believe that Alexander would abolish it. Madame de Staël knew no Russian but was charmed by *la docueur et l'éclat* of its sound. She hoped that their writers would draw their poetry out of their own wells and not imitate the West. (She did not know how soon their greatest poet Pushkin was to do this very thing.) Russians should study Greek rather than Latin. Not only was their script like the Greek but, in times past, they had had intercourse with the Byzantine Empire and had taken their Church ritual from them. She was moved by their services, finding much that was poetic and beautiful in them, although, brought up in Calvinist Switzerland as she was, she remarked that religion in Russia affected the imagination rather than conduct. (When, later, she arrived in Finland she noted the decency and honesty of the peasants of a Protestant country.) The magnificence of the priest emerging in a blaze of light from the sanctuary where he had been celebrating mass, his garments shining with jewels, reminded her of sun worship. Indeed she felt that Russia was near the Orient from which so many religions have come and, as she put it, 'still holds in its bosom incredible treasures of perseverance and depth of mind'.

On her journey to Moscow, Madame de Staël heard Ukrainian peasants singing their folk-songs. They sang of love and liberty with melancholy and wistfulness. She begged them to dance for her and was struck by their grace and the mixture of indolence and vivacity in their movements. Their passion and dreaminess had not been curbed by civilization. She was almost the first European to appreciate the folk-songs and dances of the Russian peasants and to realize that education might deprive them of something of value, that barbarism, the primitive, had its merits.

She sensed what was elemental in the Russians.

'In every way there is something gigantic about this people: ordinary dimensions have no application to them. . . . Their boldness, their imaginativeness know no bounds. With them everything is colossal rather than well-proportioned, audacious rather than well considered, and if they do not attain their goals it is because they exceed them.'

They unite the violence of opposite extremes, the vitality of the south, the melancholy of the north, the religious spirit of the east. If she knew them for ten years would she ever be intimate with them? They seemed more capable of passion than of friendship, they were so impetuous and yet so reserved.

Madame de Staël arrived in St Petersburg when Napoleon was

already nearing Moscow, but everything there went on as usual: fêtes, balls, banquets, as though the country were not at war.

She was charmed by Alexander, who received her cordially and talked to her very frankly, acknowledging that he was carried away by Napoleon's charm at Tilsit, as his grandfather (the miserable Peter III) had been by Frederick the Great's.

One thing she reproached the Russians with was their lack of frankness about the war. No one knew how things were going. In England, people were told the truth—disasters were not concealed.

In St Petersburg she went to a succession of parties, visited all the sights, admired the mammoth that had been unearthed in Siberia, presented herself at the various embassies, discussed the future of Europe with Baron von Stein and with the English ambassador[1]. At the Naryshkins she drank a toast to the victory of Russia and England but declared with emotion that, much as she desired the defeat of Napoleon, she could not rejoice at the defeat of the French. The true French will triumph, she said, when their tyrant is removed. Her audience seemed to agree with her. When she visited the Dowager Empress in the Taurida Palace, she passed through a room built by Potemkin, a room of incomparable grandeur. That made her think of the character of the great men of Russia, such as Potemkin, Menshikov, Suvarov, Peter the Geat and, in older times, Ivan the Terrible. Generosity, barbarity, unbridled passion, superstition, all met in the same character. It was the same today, for civilization had not penetrated deeply even among the great lords. That made their strength and originality.

In mid-September she left Russia. She had only been eight weeks in the country but gave the world, in her memoirs, one of the most perceptive and original accounts of its people which we have from a foreigner.

[1] Quincy Adams, the American ambassador to Petersburg, relates in his *Memoirs* that he received a note from Madame de Staël asking him to call on her. He found her 'in very animated conversation with Lord Cathcart (the newly arrived British Ambassador) expressing in warm terms her admiration of the English nation as the preservers of social order and the saviours of Europe. She also complimented his lordship very highly upon his exploit at Copenhagen. My Lord looked a little awkward at the size and frankness of the lady's applause: to the personal tribute offered to himself, he made no answer but [remarked] that his nation felt itself bound by moral obligations which it would always fulfil. I thought of the moral obligations of the Copenhagen expedition and of the American Revolutionary War. Lord Cathcart had his share in both. The English talk much about their honour and national morality, generally with a mixture of hypocrisy and self-delusion in about equal portions'.

ROBERT LYALL

The Character of the Russians and a Detailed
History of Moscow

London 1823

D R LYALL spent several years in Russia after 1812. He married a Russian woman who bore him, he says, numerous offspring. He became a member of the Agricultural and Physico-Medical Societies of Moscow. He dedicated his book to the Tsar Alexander I, whom at first he much admired. This admiration was tempered with criticism by the time he had finished his book, which took him eight years to write, for he disliked the part Alexander was playing in the Holy Alliance, the chief instrument in suppressing liberty in Europe. He also thought it dangerous that Russia had gained so much territory by the Congress of Vienna. 'It is not by conquest, and extending dominions already too great, that the rapid civilization of Russia is to be accomplished' he had admonished the Tsar in his original dedication, afterwards suppressed.

Lyall declares that his object was truth: 'I have sought to unshackle myself from prejudice, and to keep clear of malevolence.' Even while living in Russia he recorded facts and expressed opinions with perfect freedom, he says. His book is agreeably illustrated by the coloured drawings of a Russian artist, Mr. Lavrov.

A great part of Lyall's section on the character of the Russians is taken up with quotations from the books of other travellers and his criticisms of them. Some, he says, have given an account of Russia which is too favourable. Noblemen and titled gentlemen arriving in Russia, introduced to the first families in Petersburg and Moscow, 'everywhere find open tables, cheerful and pleasant society, all kinds of amusements, evening parties, *conversaziones*, balls, masquerades. The same round of pleasures meets them wherever they sojourn.'

They have no idea of the general state of society in Russia.[1]

'Other travellers, without rank or introductions, find everything gloomy and are startled with difficulties and disagreeables at every step. At length they get introduced to the secondary circles of the nobility and are disgusted with their customs and manners.'

Many compare Russia with European countries which 'have been civilized and polished for centuries'. This is unfair. Russia should be compared with what it was before Peter the Great 'opened the flood-gates of civilization', and later in the century, when Catherine II encouraged arts and sciences and foreign commerce. 'The just discrimination of national character', writes Mr James in his *Journal of a Tour in Germany, etc.* (1816), 'is denied to the native from prejudice, to the resident from too great familiarity, to the visitor from too little means of observation.'

Lyall begins with an attempt to characterize the nobles. They are too often servile to superiors and haughty to inferiors but, in his experience, they were not generally cruel to their slaves; in fact there was a familiarity between lord and vassal which no other state of society would admit.

The Russians are insinuating and cunning . . . fond of novelty and improvident; when cash abounds they are generous, ostentatious and improvident . . . they are disposed to indolence, to a sedentary mode of life, and to much sleep . . . yet when urged by affairs or necessity they are excessively active and withstand extraordinary hardships and fatigues. What noble but a Russian could exchange his comfortable carriage for a *telega* and travel by night and by day thousands of versts in that dreadfully jolting, uncovered equipage and with a celerity which is astonishing.'

Lyall quotes James on the nobles' love of display.

'They are as yet a young nation and better pleased by show than by reality. Generally they are accused of too great fondness for osten-

---

[1] 'The foreigner and above all the Frenchman, after having passed through the inhospitable wastes of Prussia and the savage fields of Livonia, is amazed and enchanted to find, in the middle of a vast desert, a city [St Petersburg] immense and glorious and societies, amusements, arts and tastes which he thought only existed in Paris.' Masson, *Mémoires Secrets sur la Russie* (Amsterdam, 1800 and 1801).

tation, but we must confess that it is always the splendour of an hospitable and liberal mind which they exhibit. The pride of display is regulated in each branch with taste and elegance.'

About religion, Lyall makes the comments usual to Protestants. Although he admits that the ritual of their church captivates the imagination, it has little influence on moral conduct. Later in his book he describes with enthusiasm the work of the Bible Society in Russia and the Tsar's support of its activities. Lyall has nothing but praise for the religious tolerance of the Russians; the 'charity in religious belief prevalent among all ranks of society'. He quotes Clarke on the superstition of their Church.

'The wild, untutored savage of South America, who prostrates himself before the sun, exercises more natural devotion than the Russian who is all day crossing himself before his Hat, and sticking farthing candles before a picture of St Alexander Nevski.'[2]

Discussing morals, Lyall notes with disfavour marriages of convenience, arranged by the parents, the frequent separation of husbands and wives and the tolerance of each other's infidelities by married couples. He was titillated by the account by two Frenchmen of a highly select Physical Club, which was a nobleman's brothel, but as this was suppressed by Catherine II (who might have been expected to sympathize with it), the detailed account he gives of it seems irrelevant.

Noting the primitive habits of the aristocracy, Lyall remarks on the absence of bedrooms. He was present at a fête, given by one of the gentry in central Russia.

'Throughout Saturday, carriages filled with nobles continued to arrive, some of them with large bags filled with beds; others followed in *telegas* loaded with beds and pillows. Conversation and cards were the evening amusements and at 11 o'clock an elegant supper was served up and at its conclusion a scene of bustle and confusion followed. The dining-room, drawing-room, hall and the whole suite of apartments in which we had passed the evening were converted into bedrooms. Scores of servants were now running backwards and forwards, with beds and mattresses, *shubas* and baggage; beds were arranged on the floor, some upon chairs, others upon the stoves.'

Servants, he notes, lie about anywhere in their lord's house; he even stumbled against them on the stairs, when he rose early.

---

[2] E. D. Clarke, *Travels in Various Countries in Europe and Africa* (London, 1811), Vol. I.

Above: Transporting iceblocks for the cellar (p. 258).

Below: 'The most fervent prayer of the beggar is for brandy' (p. 232).

x

Above: It meant a great deal to the common people (p. 239).

Below: 'The view of Moscow is truly grandiose' (p. 243).

This, he thinks, partly accounts for the vermin found in the best houses and on the most exalted people. But at least they get rid of a good deal by their weekly visits to the baths. He quotes unsavoury stories of Potemkin taking lice (which Lyall is too prudish to name) from his head and killing them on the bottom of his plate at dinner, and he laments the habit of spitting.

About the famous hospitality of the Russians, Lyall did not agree with the *Deux Français* (who, incidentally, belonged to the least hospitable country in Europe) that it was something they have in common with savages and was a relic of barbarism. Some foreigners thought it due to their love of display, but even the critical Clarke had to acknowledge that during the reign of Paul, when it was dangerous to be kind to Englishmen, the nobles entertained them 'notwithstanding the risk incurred'. Sir Robert Wilson noted the disinterested, generous help given by high and low to prisoners on their trek to Siberia. When in the Russian army, he experienced the liberal hospitality of the officers. 'Whatever one of them possesses is alike the property of friend or stranger; and the banquet or the solitary loaf is equally partaken by the invited or uninvited guest.'[3]

'The openness [he writes] with which even unmarried females speak of pregnancy, of confinement, of the diseases of child-birth, and even of those changes which are peculiar to the sex, in the presence of males, has often astonished and disgusted me. As a medical man, I soon found that delicacy of expression, and of allusion, used in Britain when examining patients, altogether unnecessary in Russia. . . . They talk of diseases and their symptoms with the greatest indifference. This practice is peculiarly disgusting during meals.'

Lyall was outraged that, in a lake famous for curing 'the curse of barrenness', only eight or nine miles from Moscow, you could, after attending church on Sunday, watch men and women bathing 'as in the days of primeval innocence'. (This had also shocked the more indulgent artist Ker Porter.[4]) He admits that Russians and other continentals often talk of 'the cautious, cold, prim and even repulsive manners of the English ladies' but he prefers

[3] R. T. Wilson, *Private Diary of Travels, etc., in the Campaigns of 1812, 1813, 1814* (London, 1860).

[4] The Austrian Korb, Secretary to the Imperial Envoy in 1698, was shocked by the sight of men and women bathing naked together, not only in Russia but also in Poland. Count MacDonnell, translating his book into English in 1863, leaves this passage in the decent obscurity of Latin.
See J. G. Korb, *Diary of an Austrian Secretary* (London, 1863).

G

'their charming modesty, the result of moral and religious principles, to licentious frankness'.

Lyall was also incensed by the curiosity of the Russians.

> 'With as much ease as they say, "How do you do?", the nobles
> ask the most impertinent questions, with respect to your connections
> and family, your property and revenues, and your secret affairs
> and private opinions. An evasive answer only prompts their curiosity.
> But they do not content themselves merely in making enquiries of
> yourself; they will apply to your servant-women or servant-men,
> to your lackey or your coachman. If you are living in their families,
> the master or mistress is generally acquainted with everything you
> do, through enquiries made of your servants.'

Lyall was hurt by the way his cures were laughed at when he
was physician in Count Orlov's family. As treatment of intermittent fever, beside Peruvian bark, he used 'that renowned
remedy the arsenical solution' and advised the shaving of the head,
unaware that, because recruits' heads were shaved, it was considered degrading. Dinner-party guests were told that he used
'killing cures'.

Lyall was on firm ground when he refused to sign a certificate
of illness for a steward whose mistress, a general's wife, wanted to
keep him although his passport had run out and officials demanded
his presence in St Petersburg. '*Vous ne risquez rien du tout,*'
she said. 'Such things are done every day! It would be a Christian action.' When Lyall said that physicians in England did not
do such things, the lady replied, 'In Russia, you should do as
Russians do.' The lady, he adds, soon after became a nun.

Lyall joyfully records that, in 1818, Alexander gave to the Bible
Society the building which formerly had housed the office of Secret Affairs, called by foreigners the Inquisition. This had been
founded in 1658. He quotes Levesque on the Secret Chancery,
a kind of State Inquisition by which the most respectable
citizen could be arrested when accused by the most miserable
wretch.

> 'What a contrast [writes Lyall] from being an Inquisition to be
> come, in a mild reign, the depository of thousands of Bibles, New
> Testaments and Gospels, in about twenty languages; a central depot
> of Christianity, in which secret inquisition is unknown; a focus from
> which the divine doctrines of the way, the truth and the life, are
> scattered over the Russian Empire.'

Lyall does not tell us in what building the Tsar re-established his Secret Police. Probably, good man, he thought it was abolished. He was convinced (for he did not foresee the terrible fate of the Decembrists) that the Russian officers who had lived in the west after the defeat of Napoleon, would bring back to their country the gospel of liberty, which they had learned there, and introduce into their country gradual reforms, including the freeing of the serfs. On these notes of piety and hope, we may leave Dr Lyall and his pompous, long-winded but informative book.

POSTSCRIPT TO R. LYALL'S *Character of the Russians*

More than half of Lyall's book is dedicated to a detailed description of Moscow. He describes, often with drawings, many of its innumerable churches (Jonas Hanway says there were 1,800 when he visited it in 1736), its monasteries, foundling homes and many of its palaces and great houses. He recounts its history from the Middle Ages until 1820 when he last visited it. He quotes foreigners who had visited it before the fire of 1812 had destroyed it.

Coxe on Moscow in 1784

'I was all astonishment on the immensity and variety of Moscow. Wretched hovels are blended with large palaces; cottages of one storey stand next to the most superb and stately mansions. . . . Churches presented themselves, some with domes of copper, others of tin, gilt or painted green and many roofed with wood. Moscow may be considered a town built on the Asiatic model, but gradually becoming more and more European.'

E. D. Clarke on Moscow in 1800

'Moscow is in everything extraordinary. . . . when [entering the gate into the city] you ask "How far is it to Moscow?" they will tell you, "This is Moscow", and you behold nothing but a wide and scattered suburb: huts, gardens, walls, pig-sties, brick walls, churches, dung-hills, palaces, timber-yards, warehouses and a refuse of materials sufficient to stock an empire with miserable towns and miserable villages. One might expect that all the states of Europe and Asia had sent a building. . . . mosques from Constantinople; Tartar temples from Bucharia; pagodas, pavilions and verandas from China; cabarets from Spain; dungeons, prisons and public offices from France; architectural ruins from Rome; terraces and trellises from Naples and warehouses from Wapping. Having heard accounts of its immense population, you wander through deserted streets. Passing suddenly to the quarter where shops are situated [you find] Greeks, Turks, Cossacks, Chinese, Muscovites, English, French, Italians, Poles, Germans all parading in the habits of their respective countries.'

Mr James, who saw Moscow soon after the fire of 1812 which destroyed nearly three-quarters of the city, describes 'the universal scene of desolation', but Lyall describes its miraculously quick rebuilding.

'In the summer of 1815, in every suburb, in every street, in every lane, crowds of workmen were employed. In 1816 on the return of the spring, thousands of artisans and labourers were seen in every quarter of the city, and it being known that the Emperor would visit the ancient capital, the nobles and merchants vied with each other in building and repairing. The Emperor on his first visit after the destruction of Moscow was highly pleased to see her, like the phoenix, rapidly rising from her ashes. . . . By the burning of innumerable small sombre wooden houses and hovels, and by the superior and tasteful manner in which most of the city is rebuilt, Moscow has greatly changed its appearance. . . . She is daily losing her Asiatic appearance. From this observation the Kremlin must be exempted; its ancient singularity and grandeur are preserved completely. It ought to be held sacred to posterity. To the honour of the Emperor, of the government and of the Russians such sentiments have had due influence on their conduct. The renovation of the Kremlin is the most splendid monument of the present reign.'

DANIEL WHEELER

Memoirs

London 1842

D ANIEL WHEELER was the first Quaker to spend several
years in Russia. He went there at the invitation of Alexander I, who wanted the marshes near St Petersburg
drained and turned into arable land. He asked the English to send
him an expert capable of this, insisting that he should be a Quaker.

To understand why the Tsar asked for a Quaker needs explana-
tion.

On his visit to England in 1814, Alexander I had been impressed
by Quakers. He knew of them by repute, as his ancestor, Peter
the Great had often attended Quaker meetings at Deptford when
he was working in the dockyards there. The urbane William Penn
had interviewed him, explaining in German the principles of the
sect and giving him a copy, in German, of *Barclay's Apology*.
In a paradoxical way this sect, entirely opposed to war and slavery,
interested the rulers of Russia, the most ruthless autocrats of
Europe. Catherine the Great had her whole family inoculated
against smallpox by the Quaker doctor Dimsdale. (It was said
that the Tsarina kept a carriage and post-horses ready for the doctor to escape in, if anything went wrong. Fortunately it did not.)

Alexander, knowing about Quakers from his ancestors, was eager
to meet them but, in the first instance, it was the Quakers themselves who sought him out. Stephen Grellet had 'a concern' to
plead with him to be a peacemaker. Grellet, a French aristocrat
and émigré who had joined Friends (as the Quakers called themselves) in America, had seen for himself, on a tour of France and
Germany in 1813 and 1814, the horrors of war: hospitals full of
wounded and dying, towns and villages laid waste and the misery

of the homeless. He had come away with a renewed conviction of the rightness of pacifism. Alexander I was at the height of his prestige; no Tsar had ever had such influence in Western Europe. More than anyone he had helped to defeat Napoleon and he was now believed to be an angel of peace, with plans for the settlement of European disputes by negotiation instead of war. With the approval of the Quakers, William Allen asked the Russian ambassador if he and Grellet might meet the Tsar. (William Allen was a distinguished man, a chemist and Fellow of the Royal Society.)

Alexander was as eager as the Friends and, one Sunday in June, he and his suite poured into the Friends' Meeting for Worship in St Martin's Lane. The Tsar was impressed by the meditations and especially by a prayer that broke the silence of the meeting. He asked his ambassador to arrange for an interview.

William Allen and Stephen Grellet were delighted by the Tsar's talk of the guidance of the Holy Spirit, of worship as a spiritual exercise and at his apparent response to their pleas against slavery and for the opening of schools for poor children. The Tsar invited them to come and see him in Russia. Alexander was also affected by this interview for, when driving towards Dover, he stopped his carriage on seeing a couple in Quaker dress and asked permission to enter their home. The couple showed him over their house and farm, which so deeply impressed Alexander by its orderliness and efficiency that, when he wanted an Englishman to drain the marshes, he insisted that the man should be a Quaker.

Daniel Wheeler accepted the assignment. Who was he? His history and character illustrate the mettle of the Quakers the Russians met.

Wheeler had had a swashbuckling, violent and most un-Quaker like youth. The son of a prosperous City wine merchant, he was early left an orphan, went to sea at fourteen and spent six years in the Royal Navy at the time of our wars with revolutionary France. He distinguished himself by his courage and initiative and gained promotion. Afterwards he said that the navy had been a school of vice and immorality and he confessed that he had joined in all the riotous pastimes of his companions afloat or ashore. When he left his ship he squandered his money and was tempted to commit suicide but, instead, enlisted in the army, where he was given a commission. He saw action in the Low Countries and narrowly escaped death when sailing with his regiment to the West Indies. A hurricane sprang up when they were in sight of shore. Many of the crew and his fellow officers were drowned. In the midst of the storm, with death all around him, Daniel Wheeler experienced a 'new birth', nothing he said, to do with his own will or human agency but 'the immediate work of the Holy Spirit in the heart'. Convinced of the wickedness of war he left the army, returned to England and settled near Sheffield in the family of his eldest sister, who had recently joined Friends. Their beliefs and way of life 'spoke to his condition' and he too joined them. Daniel Wheeler married a Quakeress, had children, and built up a prosperous business as seed-merchant. But the Conviction came to him that he was serving Mammon. He gave up his business and started farming outside Sheffield. Here he could find time to meditate daily in his meadows and to work in the Quaker ministry, but, almost in spite of himself, his farm prospered and became famous as a model. Wheeler was convinced that his life was too comfortable; he must give it up and take the Quaker message to foreign lands. When a Sheffield Friend told him of the Tsar's invitation, he felt that he was the man. It came as no surprise to him; two years earlier something had told him that he was to go to St Petersburg. He often had these intuitions.

Although Daniel Wheeler aspired to be a Quietist—his spiritual experiences were deep and real—he was a man of action and he set about the complicated task assigned him with practical good sense and scientific skill. In June 1817 he went alone to St Petersburg, made a preliminary survey of the marshes and obtained a promise from Alexander to undertake the expenses of transport of the Wheeler family—his wife and six children—and their assistants from England to Russia, and their support there. In June 1818 the Wheeler family sailed from Hull to St Petersburg, accompanied by two other farmers and their dependants and by George Edmundson, a Quaker schoolmaster of nineteen, their children's tutor. They had with them a good supply of agricultural tools, seeds and cattle.

Wheeler's first task was a pioneer scheme covering about a thousand acres at Ochta, a few miles outside St Petersburg. Here the Wheelers were given a house on the Neva, almost opposite the Smolny Institute.

Young George Edmondson was invaluable in this work at Ochta. He had been trained in surveying and in the making of maps. His letters to friends at home give the best account of the problems Wheeler faced and the methods adopted to combat

them. The land was not as bad as they had been led to expect.
'No part of it is so wet as to be called a swamp. . . . Most of it is
good solid ground except here and there [where] there is a good
turf moss likely to answer very well' The trouble was massive old
tree-roots and dead trees. These had all to be dragged out.
The Tsar had assigned 180 soldiers and a few crown serfs to help
in the work. The soldiers were paid 30 kopecks a day (about 3d).
Wheeler, much to their surprise, offered them extra for overtime.
The main problem was drainage. To get rid of the surface water,
a wide and deep drain was dug round the boundary of the land,
with outfall into the River Ochta. Smaller drains ran across the
whole plot. Severe frosts crumbled the sides of these drains, so
that every year a large part of the work had to be done again.
Edmondson wrote, in July 1823, after five years of work:

'After the frost has broken the soil, it is ploughed, manured and
sown in the following spring with oats, then fallowed and sown with
rye in the autumn. The first crops are always thin and poor and it
takes a few years manuring to get decent results. Lime is far too
dear. Manure is cheap. Nightsoil is next in my estimation . . . mixed
with decayed moss. I have got not less than 2,000 loads of nightsoil
this winter and, . . . upwards of 3,000 loads of horse manure, besides
what our own fold will yield. Part of it (moss and nightsoil mixed)
I have used for turnips and it answers well. [These, a valuable
delicacy, sold well in the Petersburg markets.] It is now the middle
of hay-time with us and so far we have had a very favourable time.
I shall have abundance of produce this year, both of hay and corn.
My stack yard already begins to look rich. The land William Wheeler
had under care last year paid 12½ per cent . . . and they expect this
year a much greater return.'

That the land was actually making a profit must have been satisfying to the pioneers who, during the first year, had received no
money from the Tsar and had had to live on credit. These financial embarrassments make it pardonable, perhaps, that Edmondson in his letters home often mentions ways of making money on
the side. He sends for a recipe for ginger-beer! A Friend in Leeds had
made a lot by it. He could make a profit in Russia on worsted
stockings, and so on.

George Edmondson was a down-to-earth young man, uncommonly capable for his years, and his letters are refreshingly free
from the tiresome pieties that ruin so many Quaker letters of the
period. A few more may be quoted.

To his parents:

'All the peasantry, in speaking to each other, use the word "thou" and address each other by the term "brother" or, to an old man, "father". . . . The most respectful title for the Emperor is Alexander the son of Paul. I am called George the son of John.'

'Every person is obliged to have the street opposite his house clean swept and the dirt taken away every morning before six o'clock, by which means the city is kept much sweeter and more wholesome.'

'The workers live chiefly off rye bread and salt and sometimes a little soup. They [at Ochta] are fed and clothed by the Emperor and also have 3d a day. They consider this a great acquisition.'

To William Singleton:

8.9.18. 'One day a poor sweep called at the Bible office, as it is called [Alexander I had admitted the Bible Society into Russia and given it an office], and begged he might be permitted to sweep the chimneys gratis. His mite was accepted. And he has not only continued to sweep the chimneys gratis, for it is a large building, but he is a subscriber of 50 roubles a year. The construction of the fireplaces here will not admit of climbing boys.'[1]

'The owners of large estates formerly cared nothing about the cultivation of the land. If the peasantry paid their yearly tributes they were indifferent to everything else. But now vassalage is much on the decline and the ground becomes more the object of attention. Many noblemen have given liberty to all their slaves. The Emperor is continually giving a number their liberty. He is very desirous to have the feudal system abolished entirely.'

'In speaking of slaves we immediately attach the idea of misery and labour to the situation. Here the state of slaves is this; he is considered as belonging to a certain nobleman to whom he must pay a small sum, perhaps 20 shillings yearly. This money he obtains either by working for others or at their several trades, chiefly in carpentry, but they are more commonly employed as labourers. We have twenty-one of this class who receive 50 shillings a month and upon this they live comfortably during winter. Many of them come several hundred miles out of the interior.'

To his parents:

'9.2.19. An improvement in the arts and manufactures is a favourite object with the government. There are several arts which would meet with great encouragement: a good locksmith is much wanted, a brush-

---

[1] This is a topical reference, in a letter to Sheffield, where James Montgomery was beginning the protest against the use of climbing boys.

maker too I think would do well, a tanner and currier and woollen
cloth manufacturer would meet with great encouragement.'[1]

About the cold, Edmondson of Yorkshire thinks Russians make
too much fuss.

To his parents:

'9.2.19. We, are often reminded of the line 'Imperial Mistress of
the fur-clad Russ' [Cowper]. We see so many muffled up, some in
bear-skins, some in wolf, others in sable, etc. The Russians take
great care in keeping themselves warm both when abroad and at
home. The houses are heated to an uncomfortable degree, at least to
us uncomfortable, and when in the open air, with a large bearskin
wrapped round him, a pair of large boots lined with fur and a cap
wadded to a thickness of two inches with cotton wool and frequently
covered with fur, he is well equipped for braving a little cold.'

In the summer of 1819 a change came for George Edmondson.
He had done so well at Ochta that Wheeler put him in charge of
the much larger site at Volkova (about 50,000 acres), which the
Dowager Empress, to whom it belonged, wanted to have turned
into arable land. Volkova was on the south side of the city and about
ten miles from Ochta. It was a lonely life for a lad scarcely out of
his teens. He lodged with an old peasant, cooking his own meals.
He rose at 4 o'clock and swept out his room before starting work.
He was in charge of 200 men and had to supervise them in the
making of ten miles of drainage, two miles of road and the digging
up of sixty-four acres of tree roots. He acquitted himself so well
that Wheeler took over Volkova from him and transferred him back
to Ochta, putting him in charge there with an increased salary
and the use of one of the many houses that he had been building.
Edmondson now asked the Tsar's permission to return home. He
wished to marry Agnes Singleton, who had long been his sweetheart. 'Bring the lady here,' the Tsar said, when he gave permission, 'I do not like to lose honest men out of my Empire.' (About
honesty he was right. All the farm profits were put into the Government Bank. The Quakers were supported but did not grow rich
through their hard work.) In 1821 Agnes returned with her hus-

---

[1] Alexander I on his visit to England in 1814 had been impressed by its
manufactures and made aware of Russia's lack of them. Fifty years later, Leskov
in his *Lefty of Tula* makes a point of this. Edmondson notes that the Tsar, since
his visit, had introduced raised pavements for pedestrians, a thing almost
unknown on the Continent except in Switzerland.

band and soon a daughter was born to them. Unfortunately Russian life proved too hard for mother and child. They fell ill, and in 1825 the Edmondsons returned to England. George was not sorry to leave. He was noticing a great change in the atmosphere at court.

To his sister:

'5.2.24. There seems great alteration in the state of things here. . . . The minds of the clergy seem to be in a very irritated state against everything that exposes their superstitious practices and their power over the Emperor is on the increase. . . . Neither schools, the distribution of Bibles, tracts or anything of the kind is now encouraged. When the right time comes we shall have no objections to leave this unprincipled land.'

Daniel Wheeler wrote vivid letters to his friends at home. He often mentions the Tsar. Alexander, to the end, treated Wheeler with great informality. He would leave his carriage and leap over a ditch to talk to him, would enter his house unceremoniously, discuss his problems for an hour or two and always kneel in prayer before leaving. As in all reports from Russia there is a good deal about the cold and about wolves. Wheeler expresses a half-ashamed sympathy for these beasts, which is as endearing as it is unusual.

To David Mallinson:

'Feb. 1820. We don't go out at night for fear of the wolves, of which we have great abundance. They are driven from the severity of the weather nearer than usual to the abodes of man. When the frost is very great the poor little birds fall to the ground. I have seen several of them. Sometimes I think it is permitted, as the poor wolves must be very hungry—and they find the dead birds no doubt. One man has had his face torn by a wolf, close by our house, but he succeeded in killing the wolf. We all saw him but it is a terrible animal to encounter, I can assure thee.'

The flood of November 1824 was the worst in living memory. (It is celebrated in Pushkin's *Bronze Horseman*.)

'2.11.1824 (old style). A dreadful tempest came on during the night of the 6th, from the southwest, and continued to rage with unabated fury nearly the whole of the next day. Two days previously an unusual roaring of the sea had been noticed about the head of the Gulf of Finland and at Cronstadt. On the morning of the 7th the

6   St Petersburg under flood.

sea began to rise and shortly afterwards to push the waves into the
heart of the city. The people at first . . . manifested no particular
alarm; but before noon they became convinced of the necessity of
flying for their lives. The road we live on exhibited a scene of terror
and dismay not easy to describe; every one anxious to save himself
and his cattle. As our situation is somewhat higher than the city itself
we had many applications for food for the cattle and for shelter,
which of course we were glad to comply with. From the upper part
of the house we could see the city standing as it were, in the open
sea.'

Wheeler tried to get into the city when the waters subsided,
but could not as the bridges were carried away. There had been
12 feet of water in many streets—one-storey houses were completely swamped, the survivors had to cling to the roofs.

'Our land is covered over with timber, boats, dead horses, cows,
barrels of fish, crosses from the graveyards and other articles and, I
regret to add, many human bodies, drowned by this disastrous flood;
one is a female with a child beneath each arm which she was endea-
vouring to save. . . . I fear the number of lives lost will amount to
ten thousand and the loss of cattle and property is estimated at 20

million roubles. Whole squadrons of cavalry horses were drowned in their stables, and many saved by being led upstairs. One Englishman, a horse-dealer, has lost all his horses.

'When the water began to rise above its usual height in floods, the Emperor went in person and ordered the sentinels away from the different posts. When the palace was surrounded by water many feet deep, he appeared with the Empress on the balconies, encouraging the people to exertion and offering rewards to those who would endeavour to save life; by this many were saved. A subscription has been begun today for the benefit of the sufferers, to which the Emperor has given a million roubles (£40,000 sterling) and he has ordered the military governor to take care that the poor people are furnished with food.'

Wheeler's last graphic letter may be quoted here, although not written till 1831. It concerns the cholera epidemic. Even in 'civilized' England there were many outbreaks—not only in barbarous Bethnal Green but even in Westminster. Wheeler describes a peculiarly horrible aspect of the outbreak in St Petersburg in 1831. He wrote to a friend in October. He had just returned from a visit to England and after arriving in Cronstadt he saw an open lighter full of men and horses, fleeing from the infection. 'I think I never saw such a closely stowed cargo of men and beasts in all the course of my pilgrimage.'

Petersburg was in the grips of a panic which had savage consequences. The people were ignorant of the cause of the malady and they found a scapegoat: the rumour spread that the victims of the epidemic were being poisoned by the Poles.

'The doctors were implicated in this suspicion and I believe that at least one was killed by the rabble [who] broke into some of the hospitals and speedily liberated the patients. The confusion was at one time so great that some people are said to have died of fear. . . . The police very improperly took up every man whom they suspected of having the complaint and carried him off to hospital where, in spite of all he could say, he was immediately treated as a patient, and many such never came out again alive. The treatment exasperated the people to such a degree that they broke through all bounds. One of our men was taken up, charged with having the disease; in vain he declared that he was in perfect health. [He] was released from his perilous position by the multitude getting possession of the hospital, when he availed himself of the opportunity of escape and returned to work. To prevent the disease from spreading, the dead were hastily put into the coffins. Some were detected with living bodies in them.

Wheeler adds that the total loss throughout the Empire was put at 52,000—certainly an underestimate.

(Within six months of this letter arriving in south Yorkshire, cholera followed and Wheeler's friends and relations in Sheffield saw for themselves the ravages of the epidemic. All other measures failing, August 22, 1832 was declared a day of public humiliation and prayer. Perhaps owing to this, the mortality rate was much less than in St Petersburg, where nine out of ten infected people died: in Sheffield, one out of three.)

To the end of Alexander I's life, Wheeler felt a deep affection for him, although he was disillusioned in him. Because of his extraordinary friendliness and apparent response to them, the Quakers had had great hopes of Alexander, but they had seen him grow more and more reactionary. William Allen had been especially aware of this and, like the Old Testament prophets who had boldly rebuked their kings, he had taken the Tsar to task for his failures. (Allen met the Tsar at Vienna and in Verona in 1822.) Alexander did not resent this, although it had no effect on his conduct. His admiration of William Allen and Stephen Grellet was genuine. In October 1821, after an absence from Russia, he visited Wheeler at Ochta. 'There has not been one day, not one day,' the Tsar told Wheeler, 'but I have thought of you and of Messrs Allen and Grellet and always felt united to you three in spirit'.

Allen and Grellet made a great impression on the Russians and their visit was an immense encouragement to Wheeler. Before starting on their journey through the Russian provinces, they had often attended the little Quaker meeting which Wheeler held twice a week at Ochta. Wheeler wrote in March 1819:

> 'I saw them set off from the city, just at the edge of dark, in a covered sledge, in the midst of a very heavy snowstorm. They are furnished with letters and documents, sufficient to open the way wherever they go; they have also a document called a *podorojni* which obliges the post-masters to furnish them with horses as soon as they arrive at a station. Their luggage is put in the bottom of the sledge; over it is a bed covered with black morocco leather, on which they can either sit or lie; they have also provisions with them; and a servant who can speak French, German and Russian.'

Wheeler adds that he had felt 'much poverty and strippedness since their departure'.

The journey of the two Quakers, as recorded in Stephen Grellet's *Journal*, was a triumphal procession. Everywhere they went, people flocked to hear them. They addressed schools for the sons of soldiers and the sons of clergy; they had long talks with archimandrites and monks, finding many of them 'open to the truth'. Grellet was extremely eloquent and French was everywhere understood by the educated. He found spiritual depth in many Russians. The Quaker call to a more personal, less formal religion awoke response in many of their hearers. They were naturally eager to meet the dissenters, who they knew had suffered much persecution from the Orthodox Church. They felt great fellowship with the Molokani, whose principles were so much like their own (Like Quakers they had no paid clergy, no baptism, no rites, no ikons, nor ornaments, and refused to take oaths. Those who could, read passages from the Bible to the rest of the flock.)

They made an especial effort to meet the Doukhobors, as Alexander I, passing through one of their settlements in 1818, had been much impressed by its order and prosperity and wanted a report on them. They were shocked to find that they denied the divinity of Christ. It left them much saddened. They believed erroneously that this was a splinter group and that other Doukhobors had the same beliefs as the Molokani. Doukhobors had been so much persecuted that it was not easy for foreigners to find out their exact beliefs.

Few people read Stephen Grellet's *Journal* now. The taste for Quaker 'holy boastings' has faded. But, if we can inure ourselves to a religious idiom that is not ours, we may find in it points of great interest. The two Friends made considerable discoveries on their pious journey. Unknown to the West, there had been a revival in the Russian Church at the turn of the century. It was the age of the *staretz* or elder, not made widely known in Europe until Dostoievsky's portrait of Father Zosima in *The Brothers Karamazov*. These *startzi*, dedicated to poverty themselves, were helpers of the poor and gave advice to the simple people who flocked in their thousands to consult them. Grellet and Allen, visiting the *staretz* Macarius in his monastery cell, were convinced of his saintliness. He told the two Friends that he was led in paths that few around him could follow and that he no longer prepared his sermons, as then they were dry and lifeless, but waited instead 'for the quickening influence of the Spirit'. This struck an answering chord in Quaker breasts. Where other visitors noticed only drunken popes, gabbled services, moppings and mowing and tiresome fasts, the Friends found a revival of true religion in many unexpected places. In Tula they discovered a ninety-year old priest living in poverty himself but supporting sixty poor men in a home he had founded with the gifts entrusted to him.

A few years previously, John Howard, the English reformer, had died of gaol fever after visiting a prison in the Crimea. Well aware of the risk, the two Friends refused to leave the same district until the governor had taken them to inspect a local prison where typhus was raging—a new experience for the man responsible!

Their journey throws incidental light, too, on something not always noticed by Westerners: the extraordinary tolerance of the Russian people. Nothing could have been more eccentric than the Quakers, not so much because of their strange garb as because of their refusal to remove their hats, not only to their superiors, including the Tsar himself, but even to the holy ikons. Yet everywhere they were met with respect, no one expressing ridicule or any sense of outrage. This tolerance seems inbred in unspoiled Russians. What has always been unnatural is a conformity forced upon them from above, whether in Tsarist times or nowadays. The Russian is not by nature a sheep.

The Quakers had affecting interviews with all the royal family. They admired the simplicity of the Tsarina's dress ('a *friendly* coloured pelisse') and manner. She told them that she envied the maidens who carried the milk about St Petersburg. She even apologized for troubling them to come to her and ended the interview in tears. But whether their protests against the state of the prisons and the Foundling Hospitals, with their shocking death-rolls, had any lasting effect they never knew.

Daniel Wheeler—to finish very briefly his story—felt, in 1824, just as young Edmondson had done, that the atmosphere was thickening. The priestly hierarchy in St Petersburg was showing its jealousy of the favour shown by the Tsar to the Quakers. Wheeler stuck it out. He had a real affection for Alexander, a deep love of the Russians and a great sense of duty and desire to see a work well done. The news of the death of the Tsar at Taganrog afflicted him deeply, but so well did he understand Alexander's weakness, his inner conflicts and the burdens thrust upon him by his intolerable position and the influence of his evil advisers, that he felt glad that he had been removed 'so peacefully from this scene of conflict and trouble'. (Many Russian princes, including Alexander's own father had not died peacefully in their own beds, with their family around them.)

Wheeler stayed until 1832, in spite of all frustrations and difficulties and the periodic illnesses of his family. Nicholas I supported Wheeler as enthusiastically as his brother had done. He saw that he was on to a good thing. The new farms were a model to the neighbourhood and bringing in a handsome revenue. For Wheeler, the prolonged stay in Russia with its cruel climate, its loneliness (especially after Grellet and Allen had left it) and its extremely strenuous work brought pains and sorrows. 'I am a sparrow on the housetops, or an owl in the desert', he wrote. His subsequent history is beyond our scope. Of importance to Russia was that he brought up his children in the way they should go. His sons were all well trained in the management of the Russian farms. When Daniel Wheeler, believing that he had a call to take the Quaker message to the South Sea Islands, sailed away from Russia, in 1832, he left his eldest son William in charge. Later, the youngest son, Daniel Junior, came out from England to help him and, when William died in 1837, he took over the management of the whole estate, only leaving in 1840 when he had trained a German to look after it. By this time 100,000 acres of waste land and marshes had been drained, at least 5,000 acres brought into cultivation, and fifteen farmhouses built and occupied, although not, as Wheeler had hoped, by freed serfs.

The experiment had been successful, although costly in health to the Wheelers. Jane Wheeler died in Russia in 1832 and her daughter 'Janinka' five years later. Nicholas I, knowing that Quakers refused all decorations or other honours or gifts assigned them a burial ground in his private domains in the Tsarskoe Selo district. There the Wheeler graves were found by Richenda Scott in 1962.

POSTSCRIPT TO DANIEL WHEELER'S *Memoirs*

Throughout the nineteenth century, Quakers continued to visit Russia with a 'concern' to plead with the Tsar for liberty of worship for the Dissenters. Several of them visited the Molokani, the Stundists and Doukhobors. They were always received politely, if not by the Tsar, at least by high officials, but their pleas were unsuccessful.

The most daring was the mission of Joseph Sturge and two

others who in January 1854 pleaded with the dread Nicholas I
to take measures to prevent the outbreak of war with the West.
They left him in tears, and it was thought that he believed the
Quakers to represent official opinion. The Russian phobia that
led to the Crimean War was so fierce in England that the Quakers
on their return were branded as traitors and madmen. Their
first relief for distressed civilians was for the Finns who, because
at that time they belonged to Russia, had been wantonly bom-
barded by our Navy (in 1855). In 1891 they raised £40,000 for the
relief of sufferers from famine in the Volga area. The Quaker
envoys sent out to supervise the purchase of food visited Tolstoy
who, with his son, had opened 270 soup kitchens in Samara.
Quakers came into touch with the old Count because of their
help to the Doukhobors, in whom he took great interest.[3]

This relief work for Russians in the nineteenth century was a
foretaste of the work on a much vaster scale undertaken by
American and British Friends in the Buzuluk area during the
devastating famine of 1921 and 1922.

[3] See footnote [2], p. 248.

PART V
1825–1900

THE LATER NINETEENTH CENTURY

INTRODUCTION

In this period a great many foreigners wrote their impressions of
Russia. As early as 1839 Robert Bremner gave as an excuse for
publishing his book, *Excursions in the Interior of Russia*, the
'overwhelming interest' which existed in regard to Russia. But,
except for Mrs Smith, who wrote vividly, if naïvely, of day-to-day
life in St Petersburg, English accounts written before the last
quarter of the century have been excluded. They are too prejudiced. This is true not only of George Sala, whose cheap journal-
ism had once a considerable vogue, but of the more serious Laurence Oliphant and Charles Henry Scott. These Englishmen,
travelling on the eve of the Crimean War, wanted only to whip
up hatred of Russia. They laid stress on her dangerous ambitions
and gloried in her weaknesses. If these are discarded, why choose
the equally prejudiced Marquis de Custine? He opens this section in an atmosphere of unrelieved gloom. But his book is in a
different category from theirs; though repetitive and diffuse it is
better written and of all the works on Russia this book had the
greatest influence on Western opinion in the nineteenth century.
It is still read. It has been recently republished. Although Custine
was so prejudiced that even Russian hospitality seemed to him to
have sinister motives, yet he saw, with startling clarity, the effects
of a police state on a whole people.

It is a relief to turn from the gloomy Marquis to two Germans
writing of Russia at the same period. The genial Kohl, who lived
for six years in Russia and learned its language, responded to the
warmth of its people. Haxthausen, a lover of the primitive, studied
the life and social organization of the peasantry. He was the first
to describe the *mir* to Western readers; the first evangelist of that
mystique of the 'wisdom' of the illiterate Russian peasant, which
was, in part, the origin of the later cult of the 'Slav soul'.

It is a relief, too, to turn to two of the Marquis' compatriots,
who boasted that, in spite of the Crimean War, the French had
always been friends of the Russians: the flamboyant Dumas, seeking colour and copy in the Caucasus: the poet Gautier, looking for
beauty in landscapes and cities; the journalist Tissot, finding, in
the Ukraine, song, dance, colour and a yearning for the freedom
to express their own culture. Tissot stressed the growing hatred

and fear of the Germans who, for so long, had been the most numerous and—because they pervaded every walk of life—the most influential of all foreigners in Russia, and who were considered the embodiment of efficiency and culture.

That very superior person, George Nathaniel Curzon, noticed the same in 1888, *en route* for Samarkand. He commented on the 'overwhelming antithesis between the German and Russian character, the one vigilant, uncompromising, stiff, precise; the other sleepy, nonchalant, wasteful and lax'. He was pleased with Alexander III's anti-German policy; German language forbidden in the schools of the Baltic provinces, German fashions proscribed at court. He found much in common between the Russian and Briton, 'qualities that make for greatness; self-reliance, pride, a desperate resolve, adventurousness and a genius for discipline'. The Russians admired the English, he said, for 'their silent fury and aristocratic impassivity'. They despised France 'for its music-hall statemanship and epicene civilization'. Altogether fairly satisfactory; though Curzon was taking no chances and was going to see what Russia was up to in Asia and what designs she had on India.

In the last quarter of the nineteenth century, the English writers redeemed their sorry performance of the 1850s. The intelligent, sensitive Scottish journalist E. D. Noble lived a long time in Russia and knew its language and literature. The great Russian novels were beginning to be known in the West; Turgenev's greatest work *Fathers and Sons*, was translated into English in 1867, Tolstoy's *Childhood* in 1862. The celebrated Danish critic, Georg Brandes, wrote at length and with enthusiasm about the new Russian literature in his *Impressions of Russia* (1888); but in England and America, Noble's writings were more influential. At a time when there was general horror at the assassination of the Tsar Liberator, Alexander II, Noble insisted that there were only a few hundred terrorists among the revolutionaries of Russia; the majority were peace-loving, dedicated young men and women, like the Narodniks who were trying to educate the peasants. He tried to dispel the myth that absolutism was inherent in Russia; on the contrary, revolt was a recurring theme in her history. Their old heroic lays sang of their love of freedom. The millions of dissenters showed their rebellion against authority. The great Razkolnik revolt in the seventeenth century had not been over a trifling question of how to make the sign of the cross; it was a protest against authority, a refusal to obey the dictates of the all-powerful hierarchy.

In the 1880s, Mackenzie Wallace, a distinguished writer and *Times* correspondent, published his monumental study of Russia. This is too vast and serious a work to represent by brief extracts. But we do include his account of a meeting of a *mir*. His record of the discussions he overheard gives a better understanding of how this peasant commune managed its affairs than any abstract accounts of its constitution. His conversations with a member of the Molokani give an insight into the beliefs and way of life of this interesting Russian sect.

Noble, Brandes and Mackenzie Wallace certainly improved understanding of Russia in the West but, as soon as Constance Garnett and other translators had introduced Russia's own voice in her great writers, their importance diminished. Herzen makes us realize, in human terms, what the tyranny of Nicholas I meant to his people. Bazarov, in Turgenev's *Fathers and Sons*, embodies all Nihilists; Marianna, in his *Virgin Soil*, all Narodniks; Yelena, in his *On the Eve*, all pan-Slavs. Dostoievsky's *Devils* leads us into the revolutionary cells of the seventies. Why read of these phenomena in Mackenzie Wallace? Tolstoy takes us to the Caucasus in his *Cossacks* and *Hadji Murad*, and shows us daily life, dramatic, complex and warm, in his great novels.

It might be objected, too, that because of Dostoievsky's personal account of penal servitude in Siberia, in his *From the House of the Dead* (translated in 1881) we need no account of it by a stranger. But this is not so. No native could have been given the chance of visiting the prisons, hospitals, transport columns and barges that George Kennan was given, nor of holding conversations with political prisoners, even with police and governors. Only Kennan could give the overall picture we have in his magnificent *Siberia and the Exile System*. Perhaps no-one at that time but an American would have combined such scrupulousness in fact-finding and such a passion for accurate figures with such humanity and understanding.

Kennan is the only American to appear in this book, although there were several in the nineteenth century who wrote of Russia. Of these perhaps the most important was Isabel Hapgood, who lived in Russia towards the close of the 1880s, translating the epic songs and Gogol and Turgenev. She told her countrymen that Russians were not as complicated as they thought, and that 'all classes from the peasant up possess a naturally simple, sympathetic disposition and manner. . . . for the rest, characters vary quite as much as they do elsewhere'.

Her articles in the *Atlantic Monthly*, for instance, 'Count Tolstoy at Home' and 'A Journey on the Volga', were eagerly read, and she induced literary conferences in America to discuss Russian history and literature. In 1867, Mark Twain and his 'Innocents' had visited Yalta, where they were charmingly entertained by Alexander II, 'a determined-looking man, though a very pleasant-looking one. . . . It is easy to see that he is kind and affectionate. There is something very noble in his expression when his cap is off. There is none of that cunning in his eye that we noticed in Louis Napoleon's.' (After the publication of Kennan's book on Siberia, Mark Twain's attitude to Russian tsars changed and he wondered loudly why nobody assassinated the monsters.)

Henry Adams, visiting Russia in 1897 and 1899, spoke of Russia and America as 'the two future centres of power; and, of the two, America must get there first! Some day, perhaps a century hence, Russia may swallow even her.' He suggested, too, that Siberia could, with advantage, be Americanized.

Finally we leave airy theories and prophecies and return to the direct experience of the Scotsman Hume, who introduced reaping-machines onto the steppes of the Ukraine. He shared the life of the peasants, often toiling and sleeping with them and he writes of them with understanding and sympathy. He ended with a hope which history has made pathetically comic, that the country would liberalize itself and become a United States of Russia, like America.

MARQUIS DE CUSTINE

Russia in 1839[1]

Paris 1843

THE Marquis de Custine was one of the travellers in Russia who went there especially to write a book about it. He made his journey in 1839. Since early youth he had been a great traveller. Wherever he went, he tells us, he had two ruling passions: love of France and love of humanity. Love of France made him severe in his judgments of other countries; he was not mild in his judgment of France. The book on Russia consists of the letters which he wrote to friends abroad, and which he either smuggled out or kept carefully concealed till he could take them out himself. That they would offend his Russian friends he knew but honesty forced him to write as he did.

The Marquis was profoundly religious. He hoped that one day Christianity would be triumphant and the world united not by force, but by persuasion and example, into one Catholic Church. His Roman Catholicism naturally made him regard the Orthodox Church as schismatic.

Custine was by birth, education and taste an aristocrat, but he was not illiberal. His grandfather and his father had both perished on the guillotine. His father had welcomed the French revolution at its beginning and was a friend of the Girondins and, like them, was condemned to death. He was detested as much by his own caste as by the Jacobins. His mother, a beautiful young woman living in the country with her little son, had come to Paris to try to save her father-in-law and her husband. She was imprisoned for her efforts, then, after eight months, miraculously released

---

[1] *La Russie en 1839.* The extracts are translated by the Editor.

after the fall of Robespierre. She went into exile with her son and although they returned when Napoleon took power, they were, so outraged by the murder of the Duc D'Enghien that they again went to live abroad.

These circumstances perhaps explain Custine's very strong reactions to the despotism he found in Russia. He was exceptionally well treated there; fêted everywhere, presented at court, singled out for attention by both the Tsar and the Tsarina, and invited to balls at the Winter Palace, and at St Michael's Palace by the Grand-Duchess Helena. In spite of all this, no notable book ever written on Tsarist Russia gives such an unredeemedly black picture of it as this favoured guest's. No book did such harm to Russia's reputation, and not only in France—it was read in translation in England.

Unfortunately he had the innate French belief in the superiority of *la civilisation française* and it did not occur to him to learn any Russian. The aristocrats with whom he mixed all spoke French but none of them belonged to the intelligentsia, although this already existed in St Petersburg and in Moscow. When Pushkin was mentioned as a great poet, Custine, reading him in translation, saw in him merely an imitator of the new poetic school of Western Europe. Custine thought of Russians as without a literature, without art and as merely vapid copiers of the West, absolute slaves of their absolute monarch, not daring to have a thought of their own. Yet in spite of this blind error, he is worth studying because much of what he says was true, and was soon to be much more strongly put, and more violently and more brilliantly by Russian writers themselves.

Custine had not only this *idée fixe*, namely that Russians were without originality and would produce nothing of their own in the arts or sciences, he had another: that Russia threatened the West, that it was one great military machine, that would not be satisfied by going East and dominating Asia, but would send its barbarian hordes against our gates, too. 'I think', he wrote, 'that it is destined to chastise our miserable civilizations; we are for ever threatened by this eternal oriental tyranny.'

When Custine arrived in St Petersburg, he was already prejudiced against Russia by talks he had had on the boat with an elderly prince who, taking him out of the hearing of his compatriots, told him what he thought of his backward country.

Russia, said the prince, had never had the age of the Crusades and of chivalry. They were not formed in that brilliant school.[2] The notion of honour, of the *parole d'honneur* was unknown to them. They had received their Christianity, their arts and manners, their politics with their tradition of cunning and fraud, from the Byzantine Empire.

'Russia [said the prince] is scarcely four hundred years away from the barbarian invasions [of the Mongols], while the West has these fourteen hundred years behind them: a civilization a thousand years older puts an immeasurable distance between nations'.

'The Slavs who had been amongst the freest people of the world, became with the Mongol invasion, first the slaves of their conquerors and later of their own princes.'

'Our Government lives by lies, for truth terrifies the tyrant as such as the slave. . . . At the time when Western monarchs were emancipating their people, Russian princes were degrading them into serfdom.'

Custine's first letters from St Petersburg are full of his sufferings at the hands of the customs and the immigration authorities. These interrogated the foreign visitors as though they thought them a menace to the country. 'I realised', Custine writes, 'that I was entering the empire of fear. Every foreigner is treated like a criminal on arrival at the Russian frontier.' When at last he was through the formalities at Cronstadt, he took a small boat to the quay. He was shocked by the sailors who manned these boats, at their filthy clothes, their sickly look, their expressionless eyes and their silence.. He compared them in his mind with Mediterranean men who pass their lives half naked in the air or water. His disillusionment increased when, exhausted by the irritations incident on his arrival, he took a nap on the sofa on his hotel room, only to find himself devoured by bugs. These unlike the prudish English he calls by their names and describes in detail. Henceforward he depended on a camp bed.

His first letters are full of descriptions of St Petersburg. Unlike most foreigners he is not impressed by it, feels that the classical

---

[2] Oddly enough, Trotsky in one of his early writings was also to lament that Russia had escaped the age of chivalry, not because of the loss to the aristocracy, but because of the loss to the bourgeoisie who had given to Western citizens a gay pageantry of processions and fêtes, arts and skills, and Gothic cathedrals. What had the bourgeoisie ever done for Russia, that miserable pettyminded class of merchants and *tchinovniks* that had arisen in the nineteenth century? Both Custine and Trotsky ignored the brilliant Kievan period.

Roman style, borrowed from Italy does not suit Russia. He is critical of Peter the Great, who had dragged it out of the mud into which he believes it will one day disappear. (The Englishman Sala prophesied the same thing in 1856.) 'The Neva, the bridges and the quays are the real glory of Petersburg, but Venice and Amsterdam are better defended against the sea than it is. Here water will sooner or later triumph over the pride of man.' He admits the grandeur of its conception. He is shown the cabin where Peter the Great lived while his city was being built. No carpenter nowadays would dare to put his apprentice into such a hovel.

'This splendid austerity is typical of the country, not only of Peter the Great's time; Russia sacrifices everything to the future.' They were building for the glory and power of their great-grand-children and not for themselves. 'Not since the temple of the Jews did the faith of a people in its destiny ever tear from the soil anything more marvellous than St Petersburg.' But, although against his will, Custine admires the force and genius of Peter the Great, he hates him; he cannot forget that the city is built on the lives of a hundred thousand men, conscripted to build it, who perished in its bogs. Moreover he feels it a false trail. Russians should never have attempted to mimic the West nor have this window into it. Moscow should have remained their capital.

Occasionally Custine pays a grudging tribute to the beauty of the city at twilight, or as the dawn struggles through soon after midnight, but he is not dazzled by it.[3] He was worried by the in-

---

[3] Joseph de Maistre, in his *Soirées de St Petersbourg*, gives a far more brilliant impression of that city than Custine does in all his wordy pages. Joseph de Maistre and his brother Xavier were amongst the most distinguished of the many émigrés from the French Revolution, and later from Napoleon, who took refuge in Russia. (Joseph was Minister in St Petersburg to Louis XVIII, dispossessed and in exile in Mittau.) At the beginning of his book, he is being rowed up the Neva, at the end of a hot day in July 1809: 'Nothing is rarer, nothing is more enchanting than a fine summer's night in St Petersburg. . . . The Neva flows through the heart of a magnificent city; its limpid waters lap the lawns of its islands and it is contained for the whole length of the city by two granite quays, unequalled in splendour. A thousand boats cross each other and furrow the water in every direction; one sees afar foreign ships hauling sail and anchoring. They bring to this sub-polar region tropical fruits and all the products of the universe. The brilliant birds of America float over the Neva in groves of orange trees; they find on arrival the coconuts, pineapples, lemons and all the fruits of their native land. . . . We met at times elegant boats drifting with shipped oars along the peaceful currents of these beautiful waters. The rowers were singing a folk song, while their masters were enjoying in silence the beauty of the sights and the stillness of the night. Near us a huge ship was bearing rapidly along the wedding party of some rich merchant. The sound of

tolerable heat of July. One of his first impressions was the emptiness of the streets. Crowds were discouraged. Fear ruled.

'In their movements people seem stiff and constrained. No one seems to be going where he wants to but appears to be carrying out some order. An officer gallops past to carry an order to some commandant, a *feldj¨ger* to the governor of a province.

'There are few women in the streets, which are not brightened by pretty faces or girls' voices; everything is gloomy, as disciplined as in a barracks or camp; it is war without its enthusiasm and life. Military discipline dominates Russia. The look of the country makes me nostalgic for Spain. It is not heat that is lacking, for it is stifling; it is light and joy. Unknown here are for the heart, love and liberty; for the eye, brilliance and variety of colour. . . . I think I see the shadow of death hover over this part of the world. . . . Officers, coachmen, Cossacks, serfs, courtiers are all servants of the same master, with different grades, all blindly obey a thought which they don't understand.'

Custine deplores the lack of a middle class. Nearly all the merchants and factory-owners are foreigners, mostly Germans. If a Russian middleclass grew up it would have an alienating impact on serfdom.

He was shocked by the frivolity of the aristocracy, Only futile amusements are permitted in Russia. In the theatre you see Vaudeville, in the salons you read Paul de Kock. The women get up late, having passed their night playing cards. They spend a long time over their toilette and pay a few visits in the evening. There is no conversation, for to converse is to conspire; thought is a crime. Fear of the truth is universal. The oppressor escapes criticism only through terror and mystery. One can't discuss people here, nor even things, nor the past; how the tsars died, for instance. Peter the Great pointed the way by remaking the past. When he wanted to marry his washerwoman, he gave orders that noble ancestors should be discovered for her in Lithuania. (In his fur-

---

horn-blowing was carried afar. This music belongs to Russia alone. . . . The equestrian statue of Peter I rises on the edge of the Neva. All that the ear hears or the eye sees of this superb spectacle exists only through a thought in that powerful head which called out of the swamp these splendid monuments. On these desolate shores from which nature seemed to have banished life, Peter placed his capital and created his subjects. His terrible hand is still stretched over their posterity, who press around his imposing effigy; one looks and wonders—does this bronze hand protect or threaten?'

See Joseph de Maistre, *Les Soirées de St Petersburg* (Paris, 1888).

ther travels Custine finds the past being remade at every turn—usually by imperial decree.)

As Custine was so acutely aware of the terror reigning in Russia and had such a horror of despotism, it is strange that he speaks so kindly of the Arch Despot and Terrorist, the Tsar Nicholas. The fact is the Tsar paid him great attention and Custine fell under his spell; he was, he said, the prisoner of a system which he had inherited and for which he was more to be pitied than blamed.

The first time he saw the Tsar, he was impressed by the sternness and uneasiness of his expression. He was tall, had Greek features, a high forehead, a straight nose, a beautiful mouth, a noble face, a military air, German rather than Slav. (He had in fact more German than Russian blood.) He had not the natural grace and charm of his brother Alexander I whom Custine had seen in Paris and at the Congress of Vienna, but he looked stronger, a man who wished to be obeyed. Custine was invited to be present at the marriage of the Grand Duchess Marie, the Tsar's daughter, to the Duke of Leuchtemberg. He describes the long and complicated ceremonies of the Orthodox wedding. He found Marie charming but the Duke repellent. He notes with genuine enthusiasm the exquisite singing of the unaccompanied choir of boys' and men's voices: 'I was moved. Music helps one to forget for a moment even despotism.'

Later he was presented at court and invited to a ball at the Winter Palace. The Tsar greeted him, and the other distinguished foreigners present, with exquisite politeness. He told Custine that he should go to Moscow and Novgorod, for 'St Petersburg, though Russian, is not Russia'.

The Tsarina showed him exceptional friendship. Custine was alarmed by her look of extreme delicacy. She appeared to adore the Tsar and to sacrifice her health for him. When she was ill it was said that he looked after her with great tenderness; in fact he was, like so many tyrants, an excellent family man. The Winter Palace had been rebuilt in a year after a fire and filled everyone, even Custine, with astonishment. Such magnificence he had never seen. It was brilliantly illuminated by candles. The ambassadors of all Europe had been invited to admire the terrific feat of the government—the rebuilding of one of the largest palaces in the world in one year. The polonaise was danced and later supper was served to a thousand people.

What finally seduced Custine was the conversation he had with the Tsar about the mutiny he had suppressed in 1825 (i.e. of the Decembrists). He immensely admired the Tsar's courage and failed to admire the courage and idealism of Russia's first revolutionaries. The only one who had spoken to him frankly in Russia, he said, was Nicholas himself. Strange that Custine who saw with such clarity the horrors of the terror that reigned in Russia did not realize that under Nicholas it had become a hundred times worse than before.

It is true that Custine blamed the cowardly aristocracy for the terrorism of their régime. Two years before, the all-powerful minister Repnin had fallen from power. No one ever dared to mention him, nor knew if he were alive or dead.

'What is the Russian noblesse doing? It adores the Tsar and makes itself an accomplice of the abuse of sovereign power so that it can itself continue to oppress the people whom it will chastise as long as the god it serves leaves the whip in its hands. (Note that it is the noblesse which has created this god.) Is that the part reserved to it by Providence in the economy of this vast empire? It occupies all the posts of honour. What has it done to deserve them? The exorbitant and ever increasing power of the master is the only too just punishment for the weakness of the aristocrats. In the history of Russia no one except the Tsar has done his job; the noblesse, the clergy, every class of society has failed. The oppressed have always merited their sufferings; tyranny is the work of nations. Either the civilized world will, in less than fifty years fall under the yoke of the barbarians or Russia will have a revolution more terrible than the revolution of which Western Europe is still feeling the effects.'

It took eighty years, not fifty, to fulfil Custine's prophecy.

When Custine fell ill, he could not find a doctor. The only doctors he heard of were Germans and mostly attached to princes.

Another thing that irritated the Marquis was that he could see nothing without a guide. 'They do not want you to make your own observations and judgments,' he said.

Custine's letters have their contradictions. In the letter he wrote on the eve of leaving St Petersburg for Moscow, he gives an instance of the implacable cruelty of the Tsar. Someone had shown him a letter from Princess Trubetzkoi to the Tsar. He relates her story. Prince Trubetzkoi, one of the Decembrists, had been condemned to fourteen years' hard labour in the Ural mines. His wife with extraordinary courage and devotion, had made the

terrible journey across Russia, in order to share his exile and had
there given him five children. Her petition to the Tsar to send her
children to Petersburg to be educated had been refused. The fourteen years were now up and the Trubetzkois had been sent to a
more remote part of Siberia. Now all that the Princess dared to
ask was that they should be allowed to live nearer some town like
Tobolsk or Irkutsk where she could get medicines for her children
when they were ill. The answer of the Tsar to the relative who
presented this petition was: 'I am surprised that you dare to speak
to me twice in fifteen years of a family whose head conspired
against me.'

After this, Custine is glad that he will never see the Tsar again.
He had at last, recognized his Janus character. The face presented
to him had dignity and beauty but on the face turned away there
was 'violence, oppression, exile: Siberia'. And he had seen, in imagination, all the roads of Asia covered with Polish exiles, torn from
their homes, 'Poles who, had their rebellion [in 1831] succeeded,
would have been recognised as heroes, the noblest and bravest
of all the children of old Europe. . . . Nicholas may be a great
sovereign; he is not a great man; he lacks mercy.'

Custine describes in detail his journey to Moscow on what the
Russians called 'the finest road in Europe'. Like all travellers he is
amazed by the skill of the Russian coachmen (although these are
often boys of ten) and the furious speeds to which they urge their
horses. He is impressed by their grace, the vivacity of their movements, the lightness of their walk when they put their foot on the
ground. They recall the most naturally elegant people in the world:
the gipsies of Spain. The villages he passes depress him by their
monotony and gloom; two lines of log cabins placed along a road
which seems unnaturally wide. The people, though not gay,
seem less unhappy than those in the capital, for work in the fields
induces patience and is not against their natural inclinations.
But he is horrified by the houses they live in—dark and airless
with only benches to lie on (and the stove in winter) for there are
never any beds.

The songs the coachmen sing to their horses, like a long-drawn-
out conversation, he finds lugubrious but reflects that they are
talking to the only friends they need not fear.

The first sight of Moscow is unforgettable.

'You have in front of you a landscape, sad, but as vast as the ocean

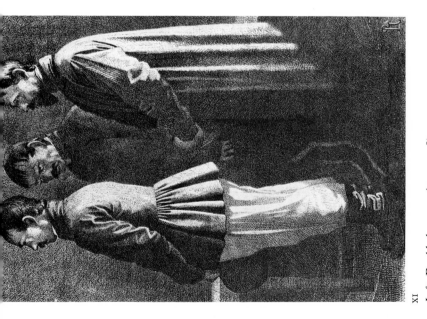

XI

Left: Doukhobor men (pp. 247–8).
Right: Doukhobor women.

XII

Above: The weekly bath was a sacred duty (p. 255).

Below: 'On horseback and under arms' (p. 266).

and then suddenly on this void, a poetic city, whose architecture is indescribable for it is unlike anything else.'

It is unnecessary to repeat his descriptions of the innumerable churches of Moscow, Basil the Blissful and the Kremlin 'the work of Russian genius'. This, he feels, is the real capital of Russia and not St Petersburg. Istanbul should be their door of communication with the world; the Bosphorus was awaiting them. For this remark the Russians would have forgiven Custine much. Indeed the Slavophils would have been in agreement with his emphasis on what was Muscovite in their civilization.

The Frenchman was an uncompromising critic of the Orthodox Church. Peter the Great had taken away its life by abolishing the Patriarchate and making himself spiritual head. Custine was strengthened in his approval of the celibacy of clergy imposed by his faith: the innumerable sons of the priests, who become petty officials are the scourge of the people, hated alike by the aristocrats and by the serfs whom they tyrannize. (Later travellers noted that they filled the ranks of the police.) Custine found Moscow society agreeable:

'The mixture of patriarchal traditions of the old world with the easy manners of modern Europe produces something original. The hospitable customs of antique Asia and the elegant language of civilized Europe here have their rendezvous. . . . Only Moscow possesses the seeds of Russian independence and originality.'

He admired the dachas built of wood, best suited to the climate.

Custine stood on the Sparrow Hills and thought of that week in 1812 in Russian history, when the Muscovites resisted Napoleon, that monster of egotism and vanity, and set fire to their city, 'the most astonishing event of modern times'. But he couldn't get Russians to talk of it. It seemed as though they wanted to forget their history.

A characteristic he stresses several times is the refusal of the Russian to recognize difficulties.

'With his axe, which never leaves him, the Russian peasant triumphs over a crowd of obstacles. He is hard-working. If you get lost in a forest, you will have a shelter in a few hours and can spend the night more comfortably and certainly more cleanly than in an old village.'

From Moscow Custine drove to Yaroslavl on the Volga, north of Moscow, and noted that it was the most important centre for

H

the interior trade of Russia, connecting St Petersburg, through rivers and canals, with the Caspian and all Asia. He complains again of the climate. He walks along the Volga in the teeth of the north wind, which for three months sweeps dust in your eyes, and for the rest of the year snow. But he finds some kind things to say. The Russians are a handsome people and their voices beautiful. He praises the hospitality of the governor of Yaroslavl (by this time he suspects what he calls the much vaunted hospitality of the Russians, whom he accuses of using it to fulfil their lust for spying). He was given a dinner which was '*bon et bien servi*', not only with the usual delicious *zakuski* (hors d'oeuvres) but with sturgeon from the Volga, 'one of the most delicate fishes in the world'. As a rule he didn't care for Russian food; mince made into rissoles, cold consommé and 'soups made with sweet vinegar'. In the evening the music delighted him, the singing of national folk-songs and above all the talk of the ladies. They were more honest, more frank and more independent in judgment than the men. 'They are better educated, less servile, more energetic in feeling and thought and often heroic.'

So many, like Princess Troubetzkoi, have followed their husbands into exile in Siberia. He is astonished by the piety of the governor's brother-in-law, a former aide-de-camp of Alexander I, who, taking him over the Monastery of the Transfiguration, the residence of the Archbishop, kissed twenty ikons and relics and made at least fifty signs of the cross and genuflexions. He is amazed by the beauty of Russian singing—without training, the peasant sings in parts in complicated harmonies, but their songs are full of sorrow, of complaint of their hard lot; the Tsar would be wise to forbid them. But the country was monotonous and induced melancholy. A line of convicts among whom he discovered some Poles, escorted by Cossacks on horseback, deepened his gloom, especially as he felt that his courier was spying on him to see if his face registered pity for the criminals.

From Yaroslavl he went to the fair at Nijni Novgorod, always a magnet for travellers and tourists. He then sums up his impressions of Russia repeating the criticisms he has made before. He reaffirms his belief in the superiority of the Roman Catholic Church over the Orthodox 'schism' and tells the story of a Russian, noble in birth and character but, unfortunately for him, devoured by love of truth. This man had dared to write in defence of Catholicism, and of the superiority of its priests over the

Russian 'popes'. His book, miraculously escaping the censor, had aroused cries of rage and alarm. The Tsar, in his mercy, had declared that the writer was not a criminal but a madman and had sent him to a lunatic asylum. Now set at liberty after three years of torment, he had confessed that the Tsar had been right, that he had been mad to have written as he did.

Custine does, now and then, have a good word to say for Russians but it is usually barbed. 'The Russians are the gentlest wild beasts on earth. Their well-concealed claws, unfortunately, divest them of none of their charms.'

In his last paragraph Custine gives final advice to his compatriots.

'If your son is discontented with France—send him to Russia.'

POSTSCRIPT TO CUSTINE'S *Russia in 1839*

A Reply to Custines's 'Russia in 1839' by Labensky, with a Preface by the editor, Henry J. Bradfield, was published in London in 1844. It is amusing to glance at Labensky's indignant reply to Custine, warmly supported by its English editor, Bradfield. Custine's book had 'become celebrated and caused much excitement'. Many of Labensky's criticisms of it arouse one's sympathy. After four months of travel, Custine had made all sorts of hasty generalizations, seen all Russians as 'knaves, liars, flatterers, boasters, vile slaves happy in our chains, vaunting our hospitality [of which he so liberally partook], apes without invention, spies for the love of espionage, etc.' More particularly he ridiculed Custine's obsessive fear of Russia attacking the West. Russia had looked on calmly enough while France conquered Algeria, and England made war in China and annexed Scinde. As for the Trubetzkoi story which had so much affected Custine's readers, what other country would have spared the life of a traitor conspiring for the overthrow of his government? And how much worse was banishment to Devil's Island than to Siberia, where exiles so often settled down with their wives and children to become excellent colonists!

If Custine so hated flat countries, why had he not explored the Crimea and the Caucasus? He despises St Petersburg because its architecture is Italianate and imitative, but do not all nations learn from each other; Rome from Greece, France from Italy and so on? Did the French invent the compass, or printing, or electricity? If Russia is such a miserable country, why did so few Russians remain in France and Germany after 1815 and so many deserters from the Napoleonic armies stay in Russia and

'why, now, do so many English, French, German and American merchants flock to our shores, together with hosts of professors, teachers of languages, artists, mechanics, workmen, not counting all the sectarians, Moravians, etc., who travel to the south, peopling the wilderness and colonizing the desert.'

Custine often quotes Karamzin's accounts of the bloodstained passages of Russian history. Labensky could do the same for French history. As for the diatribes against corrupt officials, why has he not read Gogol and seen these characters held up to ridicule on the Russian stage in his *Inspector-General*? How dared Custine, who had passed his life in agreeable travel, in pleasure and amusement, how dared he 'asperse with reproach' a warrior like Peter the Great, who had made the world tremble with terror and admiration? Would he have liked Russia to remain for ever in obscurity and weakness?

J. G. KOHL

Russia

Chapman & Hall, London, 1842

IN the 1830s, J. G. Kohl spent several years in Russia. Kohl was a German who had studied law at Göttingen, Munich and Heidelberg and then, for six years, had tutored the sons of a Baltic baron in Courland. He left the baron, to travel in Russia, and the volumes he wrote on the 'general features and popular manners of a large portion of the Russian Empire' are amusing and instructive—more so than any other works by foreign visitors of the period. It is odd to reflect that Kohl was travelling about Russia at the same time as the Marquis de Custine—so many of their impressions contrast so greatly. Kohl was warm-hearted, lively, tolerant and observant. He took the trouble to learn Russian; he talked in their own language to every one he met: to the *izvoztchiks* who drove him about, to the small shopkeepers with whom he bargained for food or souvenirs, to the peasants and innkeepers in whose houses he dossed down, to the monks and priests who showed him round their churches, to schoolmasters and professors, and everywhere to the Germans whom he found in every walk of life all over the vast Russian Empire. He did not, like the Marquis, mix only with the French-speaking aristocracy, indeed he seems scarcely to have met them. He was not received by the Tsar and Tsarina, nor invited to court balls and banquets but, like the Marquis, he was critical of much that he did see. He was aware of the horrors of Siberia, of the effect of tyranny on the life of the people but, because of his sympathy, response and understanding, he saw beneath the surface; he came to have a real affection for the Russians, especially for the common people.

There are, as in all travellers' accounts, many pages of descrip-

tions of the cities, market-towns, villages, rivers and the tundras
and steppes of this vast but little-known empire. These we can,
in general, skip, quoting only what is more original in Kohl's
observations.

St Petersburg, with its broad streets, its vast open spaces,
mighty river and immense houses, seemed to Kohl the 'offspring
of an enlightened age' and to compare favourably with German
towns with their narrow tortuous lanes and gabled, inconvenient
houses 'crystallized during the barbarism [sic] of the Middle
Ages'. The streets in winter were badly lit (with oil lamps) but,
in spite of the dimness, they were not wanting in life, because of
the sledges dashing out of the shadows with the shrill cries from
the *izvoztchiks* of '*beregissa*' (take care). But it is above all the
Neva that impresses. Its water from Lake Ladoga is so pure that,
when the ice melts in spring, the Tsar drinks the health of his
citizens in it. The Neva is as daily a topic to Russians as the Nile
to the Egyptians. From the interior of the Empire it brings, in its
barges, what is needed for food, clothing and to build and warm
their houses; at its mouth it receives the luxuries of foreign regions. It yields fish for their banquets, washes their bodies and
their linen and carries away their impurities. But the Neva is the
source not only of delight but of constant anxiety and, at times, of
terror. And here, like Custine, Kohl expresses his fear that St
Petersburg will not endure. When a gale blows from the west,
the waters of the Gulf are blown into the Neva and dam up those
that come down from the lake. As the palaces and houses have
been built only 12 or 14 feet above sea level, a rise of 15 feet would
put the whole city under water, a rise of 40 feet be enough to drown
the whole population. This, of course, could happen only if a
storm from the west met the breaking ice at a time when the river
is at its highest.

Kohl was amazed at the speed with which all the wooden
bridges were removed when gun fire from the fortress announced
the breaking of the ice; only the stone bridges over the small arms
of the Neva remaining. Then communication between the different parts of the city was carried on by boats, or by men daring
enough to leap from one ice-block to another. As soon as the
waters were clear the bridges appeared again with magical swift-
ness.

To Kohl, St Petersburg appeared not only a beautiful but a
cheerful city with its dashing *izvoztchiks*, its crowded market-

7   When high and low mixed together.

places, its frequent fêtes, when high and low mixed together, enjoying, in the winter, the dash down the ice-mountains, in the summer, the swings and roundabouts on the islands. He writes surprisingly:

'There is perhaps no country in the world where all classes are so intimately connected with each other as in this vast empire, or so little divided into castes. Contrary to the prevailing belief, in no country are the extremes of society brought into more frequent contact, and in few are the transitions from one class to another more frequent or more sudden. The peasant becomes a priest on the same day perhaps that an imperial mandate degrades the noble to a peasant or to a Siberian colonist. Hereditary rank is disregarded while public services often lead rapidly to the highest dignities. Even serfs are more nomadic in their habits than our free German peasants.'

Impressive are the common characteristics, customs and speech of Russians over their vast world, whether in St Petersburg, Moscow, Odessa or the confines of China. 'All cling with the same fidelity to the customs of their ancestors. Their food is the same.' Their dress is similar.

At first sight the muzhik may seem dirty and repulsive, but address him in his own language and you will find a good humoured, friendly, harmless and serviceable creature. 'Good day father, what is your pleasure? How can I serve you?' Foreigners think of the Russian peasants as thieves and rogues. Certainly they are great at cheating, 'but they do it with so much adroitness, so much grace, that it is hard to be angry with them'. Kohl found the Russian muzhik so inimitable at story-telling, such an excellent mimic and actor, that he was sad that they did not display their gifts at the fairs, where Italians and Germans played these parts (perhaps they were too cowed by their police). Drunkenness is their vice. As vodka is a government monopoly and the *otkuptchiks* (brandy farmers) grow enormusly rich by this trade, it is encouraged.

'The poor tormented soldier knows no other means of forgetting his condition but brandy; the most fervent prayer of the beggar is for brandy; the servants and peasants thank you for brandy as for God's best gift.'

But drunkenness which makes the German coarse and noisy, the Englishman brutal, makes the Russian humorous and cheerful. In the first stage, Russians gossip and tell stories, sing and fall into each other's arms; at a more advanced stage even enemies embrace.

'The people develop a great elasticity of spirit, freedom from care and cheerfulness in the midst of their humiliation. Their roguery scarcely shows amiss in them; their slavery they bear with as much ease as Atlas bore the weight of the globe.'

Kohl has a whole chapter on the *izvoztchiks*, more necessary in St Petersburg than in any German town. There were at least 8,000 of them. Here no one wants to walk—in the autumn the streets are a bog, in the summer all dust, in the winter nothing is gayer than to dash along the snow in a sleigh. *Izvoztchiks* come from all parts of Russia: German drivers are the most reasonable; the Finns the most gloomy; the Poles the most reckless; the Russians the most cheerful. The Russian *izvoztchik* seldom uses a whip, but keeps up a running conversation with his horse

'seldom giving him harder words than "my brother", "my friend", "my little father", "my sweetheart", "my little white pigeon". "Come my pretty pigeon, make use of thy legs. . . . Take care of that stone there. Now, what art turning thy head aside for? Look out

boldly before thee. Huzza Yukh, Yukh." The *izvoztchiks* lead
a nomadic life among the palaces of the city; many of them encamp
by night as well as by day in their sleighs. They buy hay at shops in
small bundles; peripatetic dealers sell them kvass, tea and bread.
Their plague is the pedestrian. If a horse or carriage touch the
foot of a pedestrian, the driver is liable to be flogged or fined. . . .
The moment the cry is raised that a man is run over, a brace of
budochniks (police who live in booths along the streets to keep order)
rush out from their watch-boxes, and the carriage is carried away
as a police prize. The poor coachman is immediately bound and the
prospect of Siberia is held forth to him, whether the accident was
his fault or no.'

'The world cannot present a more magnificent spectacle than the
display of carriages in the Prospekt on a fine winter's day. There is
something intoxicating in driving up and down amid the wild bound-
ing sea of equipages. The palaces on both sides gleam in the sun-
light: the street, though broad, is filled to overflowing. The carriages
are of all kinds and sizes: here a modest *izvoztchik* dashes along with
a spruce clerk or chambermaid behind him; there a splendid coach
and four, filled with ladies, moves more leisurely along. Coaches and
two show the less ostentatious merchant. Handsome single-horse
vehicles are flying like lightning through the crowd and '*zhivaye,
zhivaye*' (faster, faster) is the cry of the bemedalled magnificoes within them. These are the generals and ministers hurrying to their
appointments, parading their diamonds in such modest equipages,
in imitation of the Tsar. The Tsar himself, wrapped in his cloak,
may pierce the throng, for his affairs are numberless in all parts of
the town. "*Gosudar, Gosudar*" (the lord, the lord) is heard everywhere.'

(It is significant that the Tsars, ever since the time of Peter the
Great, had gone about in this unostentatious way, in a one-horse
vehicle without guards, and helps to explain the popularity among
the common people of even such a harsh and ruthless tyrant as
Nicholas I.)

Kohl has a chapter on the servants in Russia. Serfs are of two
kinds: agricultural labourers who till the lord's fields, and domestic
serfs attached to his household as footmen, gardeners, coachmen,
cooks, etc. They are no better fed than the others, providing their
own bread and kvass, but they have certain privileges and are not
taken for military service, except as a punishment.

'These Russian servants with their shoes of lime bark, and sheep-
skin cloaks, form a strange contrast to the palaces they live in, where

they sleep on the stoves in the kitchen, or the chairs or floors of the rooms. . . . An immense number of servants are recruited from the army. These poor fellows when they are dismissed after twenty or twenty-five years' service have forgotten any craft whereby they might live, have lost their relations and their former masters. On the other hand they have learned to obey to admiration and therefore seek employment to attend on single gentlemen or as porters, watchmen, messengers, etc. If a master desire a being who has no will of his own, who is submissive and patient enough to bear all his whims and ill-humour without a murmur, let him engage an old soldier who, after his fiery ordeal, will find the hardest place easy.

'A fully appointed house of the first class in Russia (without mentioning the numerous resident relations: old aunts, cousins, adopted children, etc., or the educational staff, the German, French and Russian masters and tutors and governesses, the family physician, companions and others who must of course be excluded) has so astounding a number of serving-folk of one kind and another that the like is to be found in no other country in the world. The following may be named as never wanting in the list: the superintendent of accounts, the secretary, the maître-d'hôtel, the valets of the lord and of the lady, the overseer of the children, the footmen, the butler and his adjuncts, the table-setter, the head-groom, the coachman and postilions of the lord and of the lady, the stove-heater, the kvass-brewer, the waiting-maids and wardrobe-keeper of the lady, the waiting-maids of the grown-up daughters and of the governesses, nurses both in service and past it and their under-nurses and, when a private band is maintained, the *kapellmeister* and the musicians. Many of these posts have to be filled on each of the twenty estates that the family may possess; besides the army of stewards, shepherds, gardeners, miners, pensioned servants who have all to be looked after from St Petersburg. For the receipt and payment of money and the correspondence connected with it some of the Russian grandees have almost as much counting-house business as a merchant in a considerable way of business. The head of the financial department often lays an account before his chief of the hundreds of thousands he has received from the gold and platinum mines of the Urals, from the corn-fields of Moscow, the vineyards of the Crimea and the Caucasus, the wool and tallow from the herds of the steppes or salt from the mines of Biarmia; and of the hundreds of thousands he has paid for sturgeon and pineapples, nurses, lackeys and chambermaids. The *dvoretzki* (superintendent of the servants) is usually a Russian who has the full confidence of his lord and lady and can dismiss at his pleasure the domestic serfs. Everyone, even foreigners, pays court to him.'

The wages of the free members of this vast army—the tutors, foreign servants and so on—were extravagantly high. The Russian grandee had most of his services free, from his unpaid serfs, both on his estates and in his household, fortunately for him. Or was it? The idea was growing, even in Russia in the 'thirties, that people worked better for wages.

'It is well known, that a Russian nobleman, in spite of his train of servants, or perhaps because of it, is very badly served. No-one will do what is not his duty. A valet is asked for a glass of water, he tells a footman, who calls a scullion; he is found sleeping somewhere; after a long search for a decanter, he runs to the spring and the water comes when his master is no longer thirsty.'

'Male servants are more numerous than female. The ladies have a chamberlain as well as waiting-maids. These waiting-maids are of all nationalities: Parisian grisettes; Swiss girls pining with home sickness; Swedes come to seek better pay; German Amalias who write sentimental verses; Russian Olgas, furious at the number of foreigners preferred to themselves. Nurses occupy a remarkable position in Russia, often remaining in the family for life: the friend and adviser of her foster-child, always to her house-mates an object of distinguished regard. . . . Long after her period of service is over, she receives innumerable presents from the family. Something of superstition is mingled with this kindness, for Russians ascribe to the nurse all manner of mysterious influences over the nursling.'

Every spring, when the ice melts in the Gulf of Cronstadt, ship-loads of foreigners arrive in Petersburg, along with the parrots, macaws and other exotic rarities.

'Exhausted by sea-sickness and home-sickness, frightened by the bearded Russians, pierced through by the chill of a St Petersburg May they issue from their cabins, despair in their eyes. . . . Their entrance into a rich and distinguished house is a new stage of suffering; and if the rude voices, long beards and filthy clothing of the barbarous population of the harbour frightened them, here the glitter of unwonted luxury alarms them. The loud tumultuous life of a great house in Russia, where no one understands their feelings, over-whelms them; and, quartered in an apartment with the tribe of children entrusted to their care, they have scarcely a corner to themselves to weep out their grief.'

The Russians, though warm-hearted, have no use for sentimentality. Not only the English and Germans, all Westerners seem sentimental to them.

'Some manage to accommodate themselves so thoroughly to the Russian element as to exchange their own national peculiarities for those of Russia and to remain for life in their new home. Superannuated English nurses, Frenchwomen and Germans, enjoying all the privileges of adoption, can be found in many Russian families.'

The majority of tutors came from France and Germany, the governesses from French-speaking Switzerland. Many came from the Baltic provinces, Germanized Esthonians and Letts. Russians paid their teachers highly: three to four thousand roubles yearly was usual, but sometimes six or ten thousand was offered to lure a tutor to Siberia. By a ukase of 1834 they were granted all sorts of privileges: the right, as servants of the state, to wear uniforms; those in noble families, after two years' service, to enter the fourteenth rank of the nobility. It is interesting to note that, at this stage of Russian history, the Germans had to a large extent replaced the French as torch-bearers of culture and civilization. Schiller and Goethe, Hegel and Kant were admired by the intelligentsia as Voltaire, Diderot and Rousseau had been in the eighteenth century. Because of this and also because of the proximity of Germany, the majority of tutors were German. St Petersburg kept the most highly qualified but

'it is wonderful, as in the provinces, what a cry of astonishment is raised at very moderate endowments. . . . The tutor in a provincial house is always an oracle, the governess a prophetess. If at table anything crops up relative to any science, all eyes turn to the oracle. "You must know, sir. If you do not, why do you call yourself a learned man? You, as a German and a qualified teacher ought to know everything. The Devil take you else, why do we pay you *Nyemtzi* (Germans) so much money?" . . . Learning and science help the teacher but little in Russia; the appearance of them is the one thing needful. Musical talent, piano-playing and singing are of great value and will win him many a heart; but the most valuable qualifications are elegant dancing and address at cards. There are a multitude of foreigners in Russia, who through accomplishments like these, have won the highest influence in families, which they guide as the Jesuits are said to have done formerly. This is easy, as the Russians have more confidence in foreigners than in their own people.'

(In another part of his book Kohl deplores the fact that the Russian considers every Western product superior to his own. The marketeer pretends that his own hand-made leather or wooden goods, even his delicious fruits, are German or French. The Slavophil movement, in which everything native was best, had not yet got under way.)

It was not only in private families that Germans obtained so much influence. They adapted themselves so well that they obtained the highest offices in the state and in the army and were to be found everywhere. The Imperial family, after all, had a great deal of Teutonic blood. Not till a United Germany had been achieved by Bismarck, after the Franco-Prussian War of 1870, did that country become a threat to Russia and the hatred of Germans, which Curzon noted in the 1880s, become widespread. One can, of course, notice at an earlier date than this, Russian dislike of the arrogance and pedantry of the German—in Tolstoy's portrait of German officers, for instance, and in some of Turgenev's German characters. (Yet often they are represented as lovable people, such a Karl, Tolstoy's childhood tutor.)

Kohl noted the Russian frenzy for improvement and education, which had seized her ever since Peter the Great had launched her on the ocean of European civilization, a frenzy unknown since the Renaissance in Italy. Academies, universities, national schools, gymnasiums, started forth as at the stroke of a conjuror's wand within the wide limits of the empire. Multitudes of French and Germans had wandered over the land for the last century, scattering the seed of Western culture. The Tsar and Tsarina spent a great part of their time in the inspection and improvement of the public institutions.[1]

Kohl, used to the pedantic thoroughness of German scholarship, thought Russian learning superficial.

'The Russians, of all European nations, place most value on outward show. They touch only the surface of justice, truth or science This makes itself felt in their tribunals, where the whole hierarchy of presidents, judges, etc. are in the best order, but there is no justice; in their army, where rank and uniform are rigidly exact and manoeuvres executed with military precision, but tactics and military science are wanting. It is the same in their schools where no lesson can be given except in uniform. There is a constant anxiety about outward appearance, continual reproofs and punishments for trifling faults of dress, walk, speech, etc.'

[1] It is true that, in the eighteenth century and the time of Alexander I, there was a great increase in educational institutions, but Kohl did not realize that Nicholas I, terrified that enlightenment might spread liberal ideas, had cut down the numbers who might enter the gymnasiums and universities and did not encourage the founding of primary schools. Ignorance kept the people more submissive to tyranny.

Kohl is critical of the curriculum in Russian gymnasiums but, compared with the curriculum of English public schools of the nineteenth century, it was enlightened. Much stress was laid on mathematics, geography and Russian history and on languages, taught four or five at a time, mostly by the direct method. The weakest point was in natural science. Kohl heard boys translating out of Greek into Latin, out of Latin into French, German and Russian 'which they did very readily. Questions were put in Latin and German and answered in the same tongue'.

It is significant that in 1832, when all Polish schools were suppressed after the 'rebellion', the Tsar founded the Pedagogical Institute in Petersburg, as a supply of teachers able to 'Russify' the Poles was seen to be necessary. It was under the direction of a learned German.

'Girls' schools are scarcely less numerous in St Petersburg than boys'. The most famous is the Smolny Institute. The greater part of the eight hundred girls brought up there are nobles. Those of plebeian birth are in a separate building, have another dress, other attendance and another table. This institution and similar ones in other cities are for the daughters of impoverished nobility what the corps of cadets is for their sons. If they do not know what to do with their sons, they put them into the cadet corps; if they cannot educate their daughters at home, they send them to one of these institutions. . . . The examinations in these establishments are the most showy spectacles imaginable. Mothers, sisters and aunts go in coaches and four. The scholastic part of the examination is followed by a concert at which the pupils perform; and then a ballet, in which they display their skill in dance. The whole concludes with a supper and ball.'

(The régime at the Smolny, with its music and dance, appears more animated, less stuffy, than that prevailing in Becky Sharp's school in the early nineteenth century.)

Kohl did not think much of the training of the priests in the seminaries. Instruction was given in Latin and Russian and sometimes in Greek. He gives an account of a public examination. On these occasions the students drew questions out of a box. The first student drew '*Quid est angelus?*' and replied, 'A holy spirit serving God in Heaven.' He was then asked how many angels there were and replied that the number could not be precisely given, whereupon another pupil chipped in with, 'Twelve legions.' 'How many are there in a legion?' asked the priest. 'Four thousand five hundred, at the time the Bible was written,' was the prompt reply. The first pupil was then told to take a piece of chalk and work out on the board how many there were altogether and came out with the conclusion, satisfying to his examiner, that there were exactly 54,000.

At the same time, although as a good Protestant he thought that there was too much form and ceremony and too little teaching in the Russian cult, he realized that it meant a great deal at least to the common people. He describes in detail the ritual of the Passion Week. On Holy Thursday the occurrences of the Day are read out from the four Evangelists, after mass. The churches are thronged. Every member of the congregation holds a taper in his hand. They are burnt throughout Thursday evening, extinguished on Good Friday and not lit again till midnight on Easter Eve. On Good Friday a box is laid in the church covered with a cloth on which the body of the Redeemer is painted or embroidered. The people go in and out, and kiss the simulated wounds.

'Many, I am certain, are keenly impressed with the sorrows that the Saviour bore for them and feel the deepest grief for His death. . . . In the last days of the fast, expectation is strained to the highest pitch. The devout are exhausted with the kneeling and listening to the long readings. Many have eaten nothing for the three last days. The churches are dark as the grave. It is customary for one of the congregation to take upon himself the office of reading; one of the lower classes will advance, light his taper and read the Old Slavonic till someone else releases him. Except the beautiful singing, no custom of the Russian church seemed to me so touching and edifying as this public reading. . . . A feeling of brotherhood is infused in the congregation. Towards midnight the throng increases. The priests begin a mass which is but languidly performed till, all at once, at the hour of midnight, the whole scene changes. The golden door of the ikonostasis (the middle door of the painted screen that separates the Holy of Holies from the rest of the Church) flies open and the cry goes forth *"Christos vaskrezi"* (Christ is risen), *"Christos vaskresi iz mertvui"* (Christ is risen from the dead). At the same moment the whole church is illuminated not only with the lamps and chandeliers but by the countless tapers of the congregation, who now cry out *"Vai istina vaskresi"* (He is risen indeed). Some priests remove the pall from the corpse and two others in their richest dress pass through the church with censers in their hands repeating the joyful words.'

The whole ceremony, Kohl said, brought before his eyes the wonder and excitement experienced by the first Christians two thousand years ago. After this, the priests bless the special foods which the humble people have brought to the church—the *kulitches* or cakes, the *paska* or towers of white cream-cheese, and the brightly painted eggs, and go happily home to their feast. (The rich arrange for the consecration to be done in their houses.)

On the Monday after Easter, people go to the cemeteries to remember their dead, bringing food, which some distribute to beggars and others eat sitting boldly on the tombs. Kohl was touched by the cries of an old woman whose married daughter had recently died.

> 'Ah, my dearest daughter, why have you left your old mother with her seventy years? Could you not wait till she had gone? Ah, my daughter, is it not against nature that the child should leave the mother untended? And your little son, your Feodor, he too is left. Alas, alas, my daughter! Son and mother are left alone.'

The priests then came with burning tapers and crucifixes and performed a special service over her grave.

Of the Russian clergy Kohl felt much as the Russians did themselves.

> 'If you invite a Russian, who has dined, to eat again he will answer, "Am I a priest that I should dine twice over?" This refers to the running about of the popes from one funeral feast or christening banquet to another. A Russian driving out and meeting a pope, holds it for so bad an omen, that he will rather turn back, if he has not, by spitting, warded off the evil influence.'

But, ignorant and venial as they were, they had one great merit: 'They are, not less than other Russians, distinguished for their tolerance in religious matters.' They had very good relations with Lutherans and this was important in a country which, besides the many German residents in the towns, had at least a quarter of a million German colonists. Invited originally to teach the Russians better methods of cultivating the land, they were reproached by many for their stand-offish ways, but Kohl, hearing many Russians say, 'That's the way the Germans do it,' felt that they had considerable influence. Certainly the country owed much to them. They could boast that they were the first to cultivate the steppe, to extirpate snakes, to take measures against locusts, that they always paid their taxes and that it was to them that the improvident Russians looked in time of famine.

Kohl returned to Germany in 1838 and published his impressions of Russia soon after. They were so enthusiastically received that Kohl decided to give his life to writing travel books. He wrote on Hungary, Ireland and Scotland, but nothing proved as lasting as his *Russia*. This was translated into English and published in 1842. It is still quoted by foreigners who write books on the USSR. He was an acute observer and much of the Russia of the 1830s which he described is true of the Russia of today.

BARON AUGUST VON HAXTHAUSEN

Studies of Russia[1]

IN THREE VOLUMES	Hanover 1847–53

BARON HAXTHAUSEN undertook his journey of discovery in 1843. He had studied rural institutions in his homeland of Prussia and wanted to see for himself how they compared with the Russian. He was encouraged to do this by his own government and, travelling under the auspices of the Tsar, he was able to study in detail the workings of the *mir* or village commune. His enthusiasm for that institution was an undoubted encouragement to the Slavophils; indeed, Haxthausen claims that it was he and some other Germans who were inspiring in Russian youth their new love for their national institutions and were inducing them to explore their origin. Western civilization, the Baron wrote, had left untouched the basis of Russian life, the peasantry that were the bulk of its people. That basis was patriarchal, an extension of the family still found among the Slavs, whether Balkan or Russian, and unique in Europe. The *mir* provided complete equality for its members and what was later called grassroots democracy. The Tsar was the father of a vast family and it seemed natural and right to the peasants that he should have absolute power, as the father did in old patriarchal society; or so says Haxthausen.

Haxthausen, naïve in his enthusiasm for the primitive, contributed richly to the myth of the 'Russian soul', although by the time this myth surfaced in Western Europe the composition of the Russian soul had become noticeably more complex.

[1] *Études sur la situation intérieure, la vie nationale et les institutions rurales de la Russie.* The extracts are translated by the Editor.

The benevolent baron, full of curiosity, travelling all over European Russian with his interpreters, described many things besides the village *mir*.

Haxthausen had read his Custine and refutes the Marquis on many occasions. Custine had said that if there were a crowd there would be revolution, so they were not permitted. Haxthausen had seen many crowds enjoying themselves in Petersburg and Moscow, and gaiety among simple people.

'The lightness and physical grace of the Great Russian peasant make him delight in dancing. When women dance by themselves, or with men, their movements are slow and serious but the men, dancing on their own, especially the Cossacks, give themselves up to the dance with a passion, a vicacity of gesture and mimicry which are very characteristic. The men's voices, when they sing, are of a range, a timbre and a sweetness truly remarkable. Whatever the volume, it is never harsh.'

Haxthausen thought that the Russian peasant was deeply religious. In communal life the word *mir* had something holy in it, meaning at the same time the commune and the universe. He quotes the proverbs: 'God alone is judge of the *mir*'; 'Throw all upon the *mir*, it will bear all'; 'The sigh of the *mir* breaks down rocks'; 'All that the *mir* decides must be done.'

They had a special feeling about their ancient cities, and spoke of Mother Novgorod and Mother Moscow. The simple people want to see their holy city at least once in their lives and cross themselves when they first catch a glimpse of it. Napoleon should have occupied St Petersburg and not Moscow. Haxthausen first saw the rebuilt city from the Sparrow Hills where Napoleon, on horseback, surrounded by his Old Guard, waited for the boyars and the city authorities to lay at his feet the keys of the ancient residence of their Tsars—and no-one came. From here

'the view of Moscow is truly grandiose. Four hundred churches with their innumerable green and golden cupulas stand out from a sea of red roofs. In the middle, crowning the whole scene, standing on its high hill, rises the Kremlin, surrounded by thirty-two churches and two hundred towers and campaniles.'

Yet Moscow was changed. The nobles were no longer so rich after all they had sacrificed in the war to free their country from the French. Before this time, the nobles and their serfs made up the greater part of the Muscovite population of a quarter of a million.

'In our days [i.e. in 1840s] it is the factory-owner, with his thousand workmen, who replaces the opulent grandee with the myriad servants of former times. . . . There are only a few old boyars, great lords of the *ancien régime* like Prince Galitzin, who are still surrounded with numerous domestic serfs.'

Haxthausen noticed that about a third of the Moscow houses belonged to women. This was because men lost their fortunes so quickly in Russia; often their wealth was confiscated for some misconduct in the public service, or it was lost in some risky speculation to which merchants were all too prone. By putting their real property in the name of their wives, they salvaged part of their fortune.

But it was the magnificent new boulevards, the parks and gar-

8 'With no other tools than the axe and the chisel.'

dens full of trees and flowers, that added so much to the beauty of Moscow and its immediate surroundings.

Like most foreigners, Haxthausen is full of admiration for the *izvoztchik*, but carpenters, 'the most characteristic Russian type', won special praise.

'He knows no other tools than the axe and the chisel. With them he travels over the whole empire, finding work everywhere If you look at the delicate carvings that adorn the peasant's cottages, it seems impossible that they have been made with such heavy and inadequate tools. The carpenter in the country despises even the saw. In the north where wood is superabundant, the peasant who needs a plank, cuts down a tree and moulds the wood with his axe to the desired thickness.'

Haxthausen, very set on being favourable, stresses the splendid opportunities which Siberia gave to convicts when their years of forced labour were over.

'They are free and independent; for, in Siberia, serfdom is forbidden and has never existed. The only authority which they acknowledge is that of the commune. Nowhere are they exposed to the vexations and arbitrary decisions of petty clerks, who are few in number there. With a little energy they can in two or three years have an assured future.

'Siberia is still a patriarchal country, simple in manners. It is old Russia, with its frank hospitality and its spirit of compassionate charity.'

Unfortunately the recent discovery of gold has had a demoralizing effect.

'A crowd of adventurers looking for gold have streamed over the country. . . . Instead of cultivating the fields, workers rush to the goldfields. . . So far this has remained a free industry. Let us hope that soon the government will take it in hand and subject it to a stricter supervision.'

Haxthausen, who saw convicts arriving in chains at a staging-post on the Volga, goes so far as to admit that in former times their sufferings were great. Scarcely a third used to arrive at their destination. Once down the mines they never again saw the light of day. Now there are fewer convicts and their lot is not so hard. Their journey as far as Kazan is not very painful because of the charity and kindness of the Russian people. Later, perhaps, it could be-

come more arduous. 'At every halt they are overwhelmed with
gifts; one sees crowds of women waiting their arrival with all
kinds of provisions.' In a prison near Moscow, Haxthausen
watched his compatriot Dr Haase working with the convicts—
a task to which he had devoted his life.

'If there are sick among them, he has them examined, and if they
cannot walk they are transported in carts, or released if they are
incurable. He asks them if they have special requests. These can
sometimes be gratified. A barber may be given razors so that he can
ply his trade, a convict can say goodbye to a friend. Haase also
distributes alms and gives New Testaments in their own language to
Germans, and prayer-books in Hebrew to Jews. Wives may
accompany their husbands (otherwise their marriage is dissolved)
and the children may go too, except in the case of serfs, if their lords
oppose it, and Jews.'

Rather curiously, Haxthausen found conditions in the newly
established factories in Moscow very tolerable—in fact, workers
there were much better off than in Western Europe.

'As they are nearly all born in the country, they spend only part of
their time in industry. . . . Twice a year their employers are obliged to
give their workers several weeks' leave to go back to their families,
especially at Easter and at harvest time. This explains their healthy
looks and gaiety!'

Haxthausen was fascinated by the dissenters of Russia, and was
the first foreigner to make a serious effort to find out something
about their various doctrines. The difficulties were almost insur-
mountable 'as the sectarians take great pains to hide their beliefs'.

He writes first about the most fanatical sects, those who nowadays interest psychologists more than theologians. In North Russia and Siberia there were some people who every year burned
themselves alive, taking literally the words of Christ about the
baptism by fire. The *Skoptzi* (eunuchs) who castrated themselves,
numbered about 30,000. 'Many of them were dealers in gold and
silver.' Some married and had a child before they mutilated themselves. The *Chlisti* (flagellants) considered the *Skoptzi* their
brothers, but Haxthausen could not find out their beliefs.

With the Razkolniks he did not have this difficulty. He found
them eager to talk

'for the true Russian is sociable, gay, expansive and confiding, above all to a foreigner. Moreover the Old Believers have more confidence than other peasants. Most of them have a certain education and in this are superior. Nearly all can read and write, although only Old Slavonic. They all know their Bibles and can quote them by heart from one end to the other. Used to theological discussions, they acquire a certain eloquence.'

Haxthausen cites a dialogue between an Old Believer and an Orthodox Christian. The Razkolnik (an old man with a long white beard) supported his beliefs either with a quotation from the Bible or from tradition. In defence of the beard, for instance, he appeals to a saying of Moses and to the sacred pictures representing God the Father and Jesus Christ.

'The principal seats of the Razkolniks are in Siberia, in the Urals, in the province of Saratov and among the Cossacks, whose ranks are continually supplied from deserters, fugitive convicts from Siberia, unfrocked priests and monks expelled from their monasteries. The Razkolniks are found mainly in the country and among merchants and industrialists who were originally peasants. There are no gentry amongst them.

'One of the splinter groups of the Razkolniks, small in number, have all their goods in common. They do not acknowledge the rights of the family, nor of inheritance or private property. Our followers of Saint-Simon, socialists, communists, etc., would do well to go to school with these simple peasants.'

Haxthausen got close enough to be able to distinguish between the Molokani and the Doukhobors. He was told that both had their origin in the eighteenth century; many thought that they had the same doctrines, for both sects, like the Quakers, had given up the forms and ceremonies of the Church: the priesthood, the sacraments of baptism and the mass and the adoration of saints. But, while the Molokani believed in the inspiration of Holy Writ and the divinity of Christ, the Doukhobors said that belief in the historic Christ was not necessary to salvation. 'The Holy Scriptures are of divine origin but they have a mysterious and symbolic sense which it is given to the Doukhobors alone to understand. Christ is a spirit and in the souls of the faithful.'

Haxthausen was deeply impressed by the account of their doctrines given in writing to the governor of Ekaterinoslav in 1791. The Doukhobors did not believe in a personal God superior to and independent of the world. The Trinity of the Godhead they

saw reproduced in the spiritual capacities of man—God the
Father is the memory, God the Son is the reason, God the Spirit
is the Will. The Deity dwells in the souls of men. 'How could
simple, illiterate Russian peasants', Haxthausen writes, 'evolve
such profound speculative ideas?' The governor's reply was far
inferior to their statement both in intelligence and style. Their
beliefs recalled those of Jacob Boehme and other mystics.

> 'Hitherto,' he writes, 'none of the educated classes have been found
> among the sects. . . . The more wonderful therefore, is the acuteness of
> intellect and force of imagination which they manifest, and which
> testify to the great intellectual gifts that still lie dormant in the
> Russian common people.'

He was impressed too, because family ties among the Doukhobors were based on mutual affection, never on the obedience due
to a father.

> 'There is only one father, God, who dwells in each individual; and
> one mother, universal matter or nature, the earth. The Doukhobors
> never call their parents "father" or "mother", but only "old man"
> or "old woman". A father calls his children not "mine" but "ours"
> (the commune's). The men call their wives "sisters". But natural
> sympathies and instincts are stronger than dogmas. Thus we have
> both heard and seen, with the Doukhobors, the same affectionate
> veneration of children for their parents, and tender love of parents
> for their children universal among other Russians.'

Alexander I who, passing through a Doukhobor village, was
surprised by its prosperity, had allowed some families to settle on
the River Malotschna in the government of Ekaterinoslav. In
1841 Count Vorontzov, the governor of the province, expelled
them to the Transcaucusus. He accused them of hideous cruelties
and crimes. Haxthausen lists these accusations without comment.
(In 1867 a Mrs Filiber proved, by researches she made on the
spot, that the denunciations were false.)[2]

---

[2] The later nineteenth-century story of the Doukhobors may be briefly told.
In the spring of 1895, those in the Caucasus who had been accustomed to carry
arms to defend themselves against marauding hillsmen, decided to destroy
them and to proclaim publicly their refusal to serve in the army. On the night
of June 28, the Doukhobors gathered round the bonfire in which their arms
were melting. While peacefully praying and singing hymns, they were attacked
by Cossacks, sent to restore order, and many were killed or wounded. After this,
their lands were confiscated, 4,000 of them exiled to mountain villages, and
their leaders put in prison. Tolstoy was appalled when he heard of this. Their
doctrines resembled his own: like him they advocated chastity, vegetarianism,

To Haxthausen it was a relief to leave Russian sectarians and go among people of his own language and origin. In the Mennonite colonies of the River Dnieper he could imagine himself in Western Prussia. Unlike the Russian peasants near by, they went in for dairy farming, producing excellent butter, cheese and meat. Their sheep, vegetables and orchards were famous. Their Bible-Christian way of life impressed Haxthausen. He listened to a sermon given by a lay member of the community which he found simple, touching, without any false rhetoric.

'When we left the church we made the acquaintance of one of the most remarkable and interesting Germans who live in Russia, Johann Kornies.' He had all the qualities of leadership but 'his religion forbids him to accept rank or title. All he wants is to fulfil the promise that every Mennonite makes at his baptism; not to try to rule over others and to refuse military service.' (It was because of their pacifist principles that they had left Prussia when Frederick the Great had brought in conscription.)

Haxthausen was amazed when Kornies showed him a large Tartar village built in the German style.

'The solidly built houses all had chimneys, an enclosed court-yard, poplars on both sides of their front door, and flower beds and orchards with a large number of fine fruit-trees. In the courtyard there were carts and piles of bricks made of dung, for winter heating.'

In one of the houses they were received by

'a Tartar, remarkable for his strength and good looks, who was mayor of the village and who received Kornies with respectful cordiality. Our host consented to show us his women in their national costume, a remarkable favour on the part of a Mussulman. He left us and returned in a quarter of an hour with three women dressed in the

---

abstinence from tobacco and alcohol, pooling of property and non-resistance to evil. Like him they believed in the ethical teaching of Christ rather than his divinity, and rejected the ritual of the Orthodox Church. When Tolstoy found that his protests to Nicholas II went unheeded, he published a letter in *The Times* of London about the atrocities, and got his son to interest the Quakers in the fate of the Doukhobors. In 1898, the government, irritated by the international scandal created by their persecution of an innocent people, gave permission to the Doukhobors to emigrate. Canada assigned them large tracts of uncleared land and nearly 7,000 Doukhobors were resettled there. Tolstoy, by his appeals, helped to raise the large sums needed for transport and resettlement. He had by this time given away his property, but he assigned to the cause the royalties of *Resurrection*.

For recent research on the Doukhobors see G. Woodcock and I. Avakamovic, *The Doukhobors* (Faber & Faber, London, 1969).

Tartar manner, with a veil over their mouths. They were young, petite and fat, but not beautiful according to our ideas.'

'The more one lives with the Mennonites, the more one understands that their lives are ruled by neighbourly love. Their courtesy is different from the ceremonious courtesy of the Russian peasants who, under the influence of vodka, become excessively tender. The Germans are somewhat awkward and stiff, reminding one in this of their mother country, but they are always ready to help each other ... in a word to practise the doctrine of the gospel in its purest and most lofty form. That is why there is perfect equality amongst the members of the community. As agriculture is for them a religious duty, they must all of them remain peasants. . . . The relations between masters and servants are like those between fathers and sons. . . . There are, of course, with the Mennonites, as everywhere, inequalities of fortune and position, pride due to wealth, and other weaknesses inherent in frail humanity. But they are the exceptions.'

Haxthausen then remarked on the exceptional conditions given to the German colonists by the government: land, free of taxation for ten years and free from military service in perpetuity. This land they cultivated in common, but the industrious colonists bought or rented additional fields from their neighbours and some earned money as day labourers and as artisans, for they had skills, such as watch-making, weaving, shoe-making, carpentering and so on. 'The Mennonites are always introducing improvements in every branch of agrarian economy.' Although, at first, they had used manure for heating, they had subsequently planted so many trees for fuel that they could now use the manure more profitably in fertilizing the soil. The government and nation should learn from these Germans that the clearing and cultivation of the steppes is possible, 'and then what will Southern Russia become?'

Haxthausen was amazed that the government did nothing about the great scourge of its people, drunkenness. On the contrary, they encouraged it, for in most provinces vodka was a government monopoly and brought enormous sums to the Treasury. Moreover, in the *kabaks* (taverns) it was often shockingly adulterated. The worst drunkards were the White Russians and they were the most degenerate. The government had no monopoly in the Ukraine and here the vodka was better. Great Russians tried to smuggle it in to their country and were punished with Siberia or enforced military service, if they were discovered.

Haxthausen has nothing to say against serfdom (perhaps he did not want to offend his official sponsors) but he admits that the *kabak* was the only refuge for the poor peasant, the only place where he could spend his leisure and drown his griefs.

Haxthausen's voluminous work was translated into several languages and counterbalanced the effect of Custine's book. He encouraged the Slavophils in their idealization of the Russian peasant community. He was quoted by all later students of the subject (notably Mackenzie Wallace, Stepniak and Sir John Maynard). These writers, while realizing Haxthausen's inaccuracies and absurdities, give him due credit for breaking into a new field of research and for finding something more in the rural life of Russia than just drunkenness and barbarism.

AN ENGLISH LADY
(M. A. P. SMITH)

Six Years' Travels in Russia

London 1859

THIS English lady lived in Russia during the six years that preceded the Crimean War. She ends her book with a description of the last illness and death of Nicholas I (which she heard from her Russian friends) and with hopes that they will forgive us for the injuries inflicted on them (an attitude to the war which scandalised her Tory friends, though we can sympathize with it now). For, unlike other English visitors of the time, Marie Edwardovna, as they called her, had fallen in love with Russia and saw everything there in the most favourable light. She even dared to say that there was much we might learn from them: that some of their ways of life were superior to ours. It is true that all her views were coloured by the upper-class families with whom she lived and travelled. She was almost as untroubled as they were by political questions; she was as unaware as they of the ferments below the surface of what appeared a stable society or, if aware, thought of them as due to a few misguided agitators. Her book is of interest because she describes with lively detail a vanished way of life, not with the usual condescension of the foreign visitor but with affection and admiration.

On her arrival in Russia she was straight away enchanted by St Petersburg, by 'its domes and clustering cupolas covered with gold, or silver, or blue, or green, spangled with stars'. She even found the muzhiks on the quay 'well-conditioned and happy-looking and comfortably clad in sheep-skin coats', and the tradesmen 'placid and dignified with flowing beards and long-skirted kaftan'.

Passing the Customs without difficulty she spent her first days in a hotel but was soon sharing the life of her upper-class Russian friends.

It was November, but how warm Russian houses were compared to the English! Joyous fires blazed in the Dutch stoves, fed by birch logs. Looking out of the window you see white spirals of smoke that leave 'no murky streak' on the pure blue of the sky. 'What a contrast to our dear, dirty, foggy, soot-begrimed old London!' In England what resolution you need to leave the warm sitting-room to mount the draughty stairs and go to your ice-cold bedroom. Here, with the double-windows and stoves, you live as in an Italian climate, wearing your summer dresses all the winter through. Most important in every Russian house is the vestibule or entrance-hall for the heavy outdoor clothes; the furs, caps, galoshes, fur-lined boots, without which it is impossible to put your nose out of doors. Here also the footman sits to help guests to disrobe when they enter the house.

Russian houses are differently arranged from ours. Rooms communicate with each other, often by sliding doors. They are larger than ours, for space is not such a problem. Yet—a curious feature—in St Petersburg, as so often in Germany and France, there are no separate bedrooms. 'The bed-chamber appurtenances are hidden by a screen, while the other portion is arranged as a sitting-room.'

'Marie Edwardovna' watched a house being prepared for the reception of its owners on their return from their annual visit to their country estate. She saw four stalwart young men polishing the parquet floors. A hard brush is strapped to their right foot 'and all in a row they undulate to and fro with a precise, monotonous step, as in a polka-mazurka, leaving a clean, polished surface behind them.' In the *gostinaya* (parlour) two bearded men are hanging the curtains, in the drawing-room girls are arranging the flowers. In every sitting-room there are plants: heliotrope, jasmine, roses and hanging-plants. Before the family can settle in, there is an essential ceremony: the pope, after reading a passage from the Gospels and saying a prayer, passes through all the rooms, sprinkling them with holy water, 'looking like a sorcerer, in his dark flowing robes and long lank locks, repeating as he goes some appropriate prayer supposed to exorcise the house from all malignities, from *domovois*, hobgoblins, demons, evil-eyes and all such hyperphysical influences'.

9 'Flowers and plants are an expensive item of household expenditure.'

'Flowers and plants are an expensive item of household expenditure. These are arranged on broad sills, niches, pillarettes or in vases. An evergreen creeper called the Dutch vine flourishes most luxuriantly indoors, continually throwing out glossy, serrated leaves of rich light green, contrasting with the darker shades of the growth of former years. Sometimes it may be seen making the circuit of a room, climbing round the doorways and windows, enframing pictures, embracing marble nymphs.'

Our English ivy, which refuses to grow out of doors, is here a pampered indoor plant.

It is odd to find in Russian homes of the mid-nineteenth century so many features that our architects have recently adopted: open-plan, central heating, smokeless fires, even the bed-sitter or, as it is called in this book, 'semi-bedroom', the cloak-room in the entrance-hall and the hanging-plants. It is true that the vast servants' quarters at the back of the house are no longer necessary and that a garage is a neat substitute for the stables in every courtyard, large enough for the horses and carriages which even modest families needed, with rooms next door to them for the coachmen and postilions. There are other differences: there was no piped water-supply in Russian cities. In St Petersburg water was brought, in great vats, from the Neva. Not that Russians went in for less washing than our Victorian ancestors; the opposite was true. The weekly bath was a sacred duty (it had been introduced into Russia by St Andrew, so it was said) but it took place in the wooden bath-house in the courtyard and in boiling steam. To wallow in your own soapy water, as our great-grandparents did in their hip baths and as we do still, seemed unspeakably unclean to Russians. For their daily ablutions, maids and valets poured water over the heads and hands of their masters and mistresses.

Rents in St Petersburg were almost as high as in London, but they included water, light in the hall and on the stairs, and fuel for heating and cooking. Many of the modern houses in St Petersburg were divided into flats, rare at that time in London. These were sumptuous on the lower floors, but unspeakably squalid in the attics. Here

'the air is laden with the odours of sour cabbage, coffee, soup, Russian leather and pitch. The sounds are as diversified; boorish-sounding German, loquacious French, laughter and screams of children, twang of guitars, singing of canaries, snarling of dogs, mewing of cats, crowing of cocks, cackling of hens and cooing of doves. Here live (besides indigent foreigners) cooks, laundresses, poor students, tailors, custom-house officials, chorus-girls and young priests. The grandees below them live in a different world and know nothing of their neighbours. Every house has, as in France, its *dvornik* or concierge.'

Necessities of life were cheap but luxuries dearer than in England. Tea was dearer but, imported from China, was superior to ours. It was taken with lemon or rum and a necessity of life for all ranks. Sugar, extracted from beetroot and melons, was the only kind used, as the Tsar did not allow slave-grown sugar.[1]

Mrs Smith's special friends were relatively modest. The head of the family had the rank of a colonel. The entire family consisted of five ladies and two gentlemen. Their servants were all serfs, except for a German maid and a soldier's daughter. The German maid attended entirely to her mistress, dressing her hair, making her gowns and tidying her semi-bedroom. Russian maids did the same for the young ladies, making not only their dresses but their bonnets and corsets, even knitting socks, making lace for them and weaving cloth.

The cook, as in all similar families, was male and did all the catering: he was given a fixed sum and provided what he liked, selling left-overs to inns or the tenants of the attics. The serfs had their black bread, their cabbage-soup and raw herrings. The main duty of the eldest daughter of the house was to look after the storeroom. She went there every morning with the cook to see what needed replenishing. Here shelves were packed with jars containing preserved fruits and pickles, boxes of raisins and almonds, cases of sardines, flasks of sunflower oil, candles and soap. There were strings of dried mushrooms and of biscuits, for fasts. Under the shelves there were drawers where spices were kept and cereals native to Russia, like buckwheat and millet, also sago, tapioca, rice and macaroni. On the floor there were sacks of flour, kegs of butter for cooking, green coffee beans (which the cook roasted every week, grinding it fresh every day) Gruyère cheese (Russia made scarcely any of its own), honeycombs, sugar, salt and lamp oil.

There follows a succulent account of a typical dinner, in this case given to a party of twenty, though not much more elaborate than the usual family meal.

First came the *zakuski* (hors d'œuvres of sardines, radishes,

[1] This was one of the material results of the Quaker influence on Alexander I.

III

Right: Molokani women (p. 277).

Below: The drab monotony of the villages of
Great Russia (p. 287).

XIV

Above: Horses with the whirlwind in their manes (p. 12).

Below: 'Wolves howling round the troika' (p. 282).

10   'A brace of *budochniks*' (p. 233)

caviare, bread and butter washed down with vodka) served as an appetizer and taken before sitting down to the table. The main meal began with **borsch**, an excellent soup made with several kinds of meat boiled together with white cabbage (and sometimes with beetroot) to which sour cream was added. (The **borsch** was accompanied by patties filled with mincemeat). Next *blini*, pancakes spread with caviare or butter, then a native fish in white sauce with truffles and capers, followed by boiled fowls in white sauce, preserved peas and French beans, tongues cut in slices, sauté potatoes, grouse roasted in sour cream with cranberry sauce and salted cucumber, and finally iced pudding. Wines were principally French and Rhenish, but there was also sherry and port (the so-called English wines) and even porter. Each dish, even the potatoes, was served separately. 'A Russian dinner is inimitable, its various dishes light, nutritious and cooked to perfection. It is served quietly, expeditiously and, however large the party, without the least trouble to the host or hostess, who are thus enabled to give their guests their undivided attention.' Compare the poor English hostess, carving the joint at her table or watching her husband struggling with it and facing, as she does, a curtain lecture when the party is over, 'The saddle of mutton was raw, the peafowl done to rags.' This after worrying for days about arrangements! 'The English might learn a few lessons in comfort, economy and elegance from the Russian cooks and waiters.' And the dinner would cost less. ('Marie Edwardovna' omits to note that in England the servants would be paid, the hostess not having the advantage of serf-labour.) Even in the provinces, dinners were much the same, 'one dish handed at a time and its composition equally good.' Because in Russia cellars were filled with blocks of ice, even in the hot summers food was kept fresh. The plentiful use of sour cream in cooking was another noteworthy feature of the Russian cuisine, also yoghurt, eaten as a sweet with sugar, a valuable 'anti-scorbutic' and at that time unknown in the West.

Marie continues her criticism of her compatriots. The Americans are much better liked than we are. 'They are the people for us,' a nobleman remarked. 'They possess all that we admire in the English, without that unapproachable *hauteur*, that impenetrable barrier with which you surround yourselves.' Americans, like the Russians, are extravagant in tastes and habits. Their country is as vast and as undeveloped and, like the Russians, they do not look backwards, while we 'brood over the relics of time'.

Even governesses are better treated in Russia than in England. They are paid more and not so much is demanded of them. In old age they are pensioned off, not turned penniless into the street, or they spend the rest of their days in the family they have served.

'Marie Edwardovna' admires the ceremonies of the Orthodox Church; she does not complain even of the long Lenten fast. The fare is wholesome; cabbage soup with mushrooms, patties made with flour and raw, shredded onion, fish with lemon juice, salmon and green peas, and vegetarian cutlets, made of mushrooms, flour and potatoes fried in vegetable oil. For sweets, tapioca boiled in red wine, or arrowroot with cranberry juice. She admits that the poor often take nothing but black bread and salted cucumber but many do have herrings and tea. But Marie was not concerned with the poor in Russia any more than she was in England. In Lent, as there are no amusements, more time is given to study, and there are often lectures in private homes by learned Germans who discourse on electricity or galvanism. About the great national festival of Russia, the Easter midnight mass, Marie is unreservedly enthusiastic. There are no seats in the churches because Russians say they cannot sit down in the presence of the King of Kings, before whom even the Tsar bows his knee. She describes the ceremony in detail: the brilliance of the midnight rejoicing, the divine singing of the choir, and finds in it sincerity and Christian love. Reflecting that, in Russia alone, 50 million Christians were at the same moment 'celebrating the Blessed One's triumph over death and the grave', she thinks sadly of her own church 'cut up into fragments by dissent'.

Marie was present when her friends prepared for their annual visit to the family estate, a journey of a thousand versts or more. Preparations went on for a month, for everything must be taken with them, every pin and needle, every piece of soap or yard of muslin. There was no town near the estate, where such things could be bought. Villages in Russia had no shops.

Marie's second volume describes her journey far and wide in European Russia. She started it in winter in a sleigh, lent her by friends, and with Eudoxia, a Russian friend, as her companion. As, with Eudoxia, she was translating an abridgement of Karamzin's *History of Russia*, she interlards descriptions of the towns and monasteries they visit with historical notes, of less interest to us now.

In her wanderings round the country Marie experienced the traditional hospitality of Russians and has little but good to say of her hosts and hostesses. She regrets that agriculture should have improved so little since the Middle Ages and that, although cattle are plentiful, almost no butter or cheese is made. She is surprised at the peasants' hatred of potatoes, and that, although we import their excellent rhubarb from the Volga, the Russians never cook it, although they sometimes eat it raw. Buckwheat, which they use in their *kasha*, is easy to grow and nutritious and tasty, and she thinks we ought to adopt it. The peasants drink great quantities of water. As this is often foul it explains the prevalence of cholera.

Altogether Marie's second volume is less interesting than her first. Her descriptions of Moscow, the Volga, the steppes, the black earth district, etc., are much like other peoples'. She ends with a moving account of the last days and last words of Nicholas I, who died in 1855. In common with her upper-class Russian friends, she loved the Tsar and did not share the spiteful glee of her compatriots over the *Punch* cartoon which showed him, on his death-bed, killed by that very 'Général Février' he had hoped would fight on his side against the perfidious English and French in the Crimean War. Although we know too much from the writings of Herzen, Turgenev and Tolstoy to share Marie's enthusiasm for this harsh, obscurantist tyrant, we can feel with her that England needed his forgiveness for one of the most indefensible wars in our history.

To do Marie justice, although blind to the sins of the Tsar, she was shrewd enough in her assessment of the evil effects of slavery on the Russian peasant. To it she put down their besetting sins: lying, drinking, cunning. Reflecting on the possibility of a future peasant revolution she wrote: 'They seem happy and contented enough as we see them now, but doubtless each could tell of some act of oppression and violence which weighs heavily on his heart and which will inevitably be avenged, one day or other, by him or his children's children.' All the same, she believes their revolt is a long way off. Seeing a serf thanking his master for a beating, she says, 'It will certainly take . . . centuries for such a people to be in a condition to appreciate the blessings of freedom and perhaps they are too Asiatic ever properly to do so.'

Whether capable of appreciating freedom or not, Marie ends by hailing the advent of Alexander II who was committed to restore it to them. She hopes that Britain, the champion of liberty, will 'honour the hero of her favourite cause'.[1]

[1] It is interesting to compare this English lady's impressions of Russia in the 'fifties with Don Juan Valera's. Valera, poet, novelist and man of the world was, from 1856 to 1857, Secretary in the Spanish Embassy in St Petersburg and was dazzled by its splendours and lavish hospitality. He especially admires Russian women. Many of them speak six or seven languages. Their conversation is brilliant; they discuss not only novels and poetry but religion, metaphysics, hygiene and education. Even their games are scientific and literary. (In the one most in vogue, the company is divided into Sphinxes and Oedipus's. The Sphinxes write down questions and riddles, the other side the solutions.) Whole nights are spent in these 'mental gymnastics' or in improvising verse or drawing-room comedies. Valera is as enchanted as the English lady with Russian cooking (culinary art at its highest peak) and the tea direct from China, but he is less tolerant of their fasts and the terrible, long drawn-out Lent when theatres are shut and there are no banquets or balls. So many of the nobles are Voltairian; their religion is a pretence and merely a demonstration of national pride. But the Easter Eve ceremonies sweep away Valera's criticisms. No foreigner has described these so eloquently and with such understanding of their symbolism. When the resurrection is celebrated at midnight and the Russians kiss each other, 'they all truly believe themselves brothers, rich and poor, servants and lords. The three Easter days are a universal *agape*'. Valera realized that Russia had begun to have a literature (Turgenev was coming into fashion) and to contribute to the arts and sciences. He was impressed by their splendid Library of Asiatic languages. He believes that they have a civilizing mission in Asia and hopes that they will triumph there over the hated English with whom they are bound to have a clash. Before he left Russia, Valera talked with some intellectuals, enthusiastic for the new Tsar, Alexander II, and full of hopes for a future of liberal reforms, even of freedom of speech. He wondered if their hopes were justified.

See Juan Valera, *Obras Completas* (Madrid, 1942), Vol. I.

ALEXANDRE DUMAS

Adventures in the Caucasus[1]

TO travel through the Caucasus in the middle of a fierce war suited Dumas' romantic, exuberant nature more than any other of his journeys. Everything came as grist to his mill: the fearful discomforts, the physical difficulties, above all the danger. 'At first one fears it; then faces it; then longs for it.' He had the same advantages that he had had in the rest of his travels in Russia. Everyone, especially women, wanted to meet the author of so many best-selling novels. He was advised to wear an order, before starting on the Caucasus, as this won great respect in Russia. He put on the order of Charles III of Spain, given him in 1846, and was, with these trappings and the loyal Kalino's affirmations, everywhere 'treated as a general'.[2] Above all he wanted not only to write adventure stories but to live them himself and prove himself as brave and as hardy as one of his own musketeers. Later on in Paris, at the Princesse Mathilde's weekly dinners, he often recounted his Russian adventures. This is how the Goncourts described him:

'A giant figure, with hair turned pepper and salt and the tiny, clear, sly eyes of a hippopotamus, ever observant even when lowered. . . . With Dumas there is an indefinable something of both a side-showman's hawking wonders, and a travelling salesman from the Arabian Nights.'

Dumas hoped to visit Shamyl: 'Shamyl the Titan, who struggles from his lair against the Tsar of all the Russias. Will he know our

[1] *Impressions de Voyage. Le Caucase.* The extracts are translated by the Editor.
[2] Kalino was a student of Moscow University and was Dumas' guide and interpreter.

name? Will he allow us to sleep a night in his tents?' But the Titan
did not invite him.

Dumas knew something of Lermontov who, for attacking the
Tsar's tyranny and writing of lost liberties in his poems, was
exiled to the Army of the South and became the poet of the Caucasus. He lived, fought and died there, losing his life, like Pushkin
before him, in an infamous duel in which, though he shot into the
air, his opponent shot to kill. Dumas probably did not know that
Count Leo Tolstoy, disgusted with the inanities of Moscow life,
had gone there in 1851 and was changed for ever by the impact
of the mountains, of the rugged mountain people, of life and death
in the Caucasian campaigns. In the *Cossacks* he is writing of himself when he describes his hero Olyenin's first sight of the mountains: 'From that moment, all that he had seen or thought or felt
assumed for him the new, sternly majestic character of the mountains. All his recollections of Moscow, his shame and repentance...
all disappeared and never returned again.' (Turgenev considered
Tolstoy's *Cossacks* the most perfect writing in the Russian language.)

To understand the impact of the Caucasian campaigns on the
Russian gentry who took part in them, one must remember the
emptiness and frivolity of their lives under the tyranny of Nicholas I—frivolity which rightly shocked the Marquis de Custine.
The Caucasus was an escape from futility: gave them activity,
danger, comradeship, contact with nature of an extraordinarily
exhilarating kind. To some of these gentry the war was, as to so
many of the more primitive Cossacks, a crusade, the Cross against
the Crescent, a Holy War, as it was to Shamyl and his puritanic
Muslim adherents. (It is illuminating to compare these campaigns
with those of our men in India, fighting the Pathans on the North-
West Frontier or conquering the Sikhs in Scinde: campaigns that
inspired a few tales and songs by Kipling, but no great lyrical
poetry. Far away from our bustling, self-absorbed island, the
Indian saga had far less effect on our lives and minds than the
Caucasian campaigns—fought on what they considered their own
soil—had on the Russians.)

Although Dumas could not know all that the Caucasian drama
meant to Russia, he sensed something of its romance and its
savagery and he gives a racy account of his Caucasian experiences.
His writing, indeed, is what one wants in a book of travel—full
of exciting adventures, of exact detail of sights, sounds and tastes,

with vignettes of the people he meets and records of the conversations he had with them. It compares favourably with our other travellers' accounts. Gautier gives exquisite descriptions of cities and landscape but does not introduce us to a single Russian, nor record a single conversation. As for our Englishmen, they too often feel hostility and contempt. 'All Frenchmen', wrote Dumas, 'have an innate sympathy with the Russians.' A good way to begin contact with a new country.

To follow the whole of Dumas' adventurous journey would be to quote the whole book. A few extracts may give its flavour.

Nothing excited Dumas more than his first sight of the whole Caucasian range from the Shalbuz to the Elbruz, with the snow-covered peak of the Kasbek towering up in the midst of it.

'For a moment we stood silent before this splendid panorama. This was not the Alps nor the Pyrenees; this was nothing that we had ever seen nor even imagined. This was the Caucasus, the stage chosen by the first tragedian of the ancient world for his first drama,

11 'This was the Caucasus.'

a drama whose hero was a Titan and whose actors were gods! Alas! I had not brought my Aeschylus with me. Had I done so, I should have sat down and reread *Prometheus* from the first line to the last. It is easy to understand why the Greeks made these magnificent peaks into the cradle of the world.'

In Dumas' time, the Elbruz had not yet been climbed. 'To do that, the mountaineers say, one would need a special dispensation from God Himself. It was on the crest of this mountain, according to tradition, that Noah's dove rested when it flew out of the ark.'

Everywhere he went, Dumas found the imprint of the ancient world and, with his classical education, it enhanced his delight. Later, sailing home on the Black Sea, he thought of Jason seeking the Golden Fleece in the Argo, 'a ship such as no man in Colchis had ever seen'.

Dumas' journey involved much discomfort but he welcomed it.

'When a man spends the night on a plank with his cloak as his only mattress and blanket, getting up in the morning gives little trouble. I jumped up at dawn, washed my face and hands in the copper bowl which I had bought in Kazan (to make sure of having one, for it is one of the rarest objects in Russia) and awoke my companions.'

French gourmet that he was, he was prepared to cook his own dishes and, having discovered, in an Armenian family, the succulent quality of *shashlik*, he cooked bits of marinaded mutton on a metal skewer, which he held over the hot embers of the fires, always made for him wherever he dossed down; 'the nicest thing I had to eat during all my time in Russia'. Dumas was an excellent shot and supplemented his larder with game on all his travels.

Dumas started his journey at Kizlyara, a few miles west of the Caspian Sea, a thriving market town, where Armenians, Tartars, Kalmucks, Nogais and Jews, all in their own picturesque costumes, gathered to trade. His first descriptions are of these people.

'Commerce, apart from the Tartars' enterprising business of kidnapping men, women and children and selling them back to their families, consists mainly of Armenian wine and brandy, silks woven locally, and rice, sesame, saffron and madder grown on near-by farms. . . . As a rule the Armenian has no speciality. Every other race has; the Persian sells silks; the Lesghian, woven cloth; the Tartar, weapons. The Armenian sells everything that is saleable and even the unsaleable. There is a saying here: "If a Tartar gives you a nod, you

can count on him; if a Persian gives you his hand, count on him;
but, if you are dealing with an Armenian, make him sign a paper in
the presence of two witnesses." '

Dumas' admiration of the Tartars was equal to Captain John
Perry's, for whom they worked in the time of Peter the Great.

'What a difference there is between these fierce Tartars and the
humble serfs whom we met between Petersburg and Astrakhan!
Their self-respect, their rugged, independent pride appealed to us.'

He had an equal admiration of the Cossacks of the Line who,
because of his importance and the danger of his journey, were
always assigned to him as escort.

'A Cossack of the Line, born within sight of the enemy he has to
fight, familiar from infancy with danger, is a soldier from the age of
twelve. He spends only three months of the year in his *stanitza*
(village). All the rest of his life, until he is fifty, he spends on horseback
and under arms. He is a splendid soldier. War to him is an art,
danger is a joy. . . . The Cossacks of the Don, on the other hand, are
of agricultural stock, spending their childhood on peaceful plains and
unhappy when facing their enemy ambushed in the ravines and woods
of the mountains.'

Dumas was entertained by the Nijni Novgorod dragoons,
who had served for forty-six years in the Caucasus.

'It was here that I was struck by the difference between the Russian
soldier in Russia and the same soldier in the Caucasus. In Russia,
a soldier is deeply depressed and ashamed of his servitude, humiliated
by the gulf between him and his officers. A Russian in the Caucasus is
gay, lively, happy and high-spirited, proud of his uniform. He has
hopes of promotion, of distinguishing himself, of danger. Danger
ennobles him; it brings him near to his officers. Danger keeps him
cheerful, for it makes him realize the value of life. The French would
be amazed by what a Russian soldier has to endure in this mountain
warfare, living on sodden black bread, sleeping in the snow, dragging
himself and his equipment over trackless wastes of granite rocks,
where no hunter has set foot, over which only the eagle has soared.
And for what a war! A war without quarter or prisoners; where a
wounded man is left for dead, where his mildest enemies collect
their victims' hands, his fiercest, human heads.'

Dumas was often in danger himself. He was several times
attacked by the mountaineers but he was always defended by his
escort. He was treated by the governors of the various districts he

12   'A precipice of seven thousand feet.'

passed through and by the chiefs of police, as someone extremely precious and important. Lavish as was the hospitality he was everywhere shown, it was outdone by Prince Bagration, a Georgian and one of the finest officers in the Russian army. Five hundred men from his regiment accompanied Dumas and his companions to the crest of the Karanai from whence, looking over a precipice of seven thousand feet, they saw the birthplace of the legendary hero, the still unconquered Shamyl, and the convolutions, crests and chasms, the chaotic devastation of the Caucasian range.

'No place in the world has been more tortured by volcanic upheavals than Daghestan, where the mountains, like the people who live in them, seem racked and torn in a fierce, never-ending battle.'

When Dumas came down from the terrifying height he found that he had been made an honorary member of the Regiment of Native Mountaineers. 'After dinner the band played during the entire evening to celebrate my initiation.'

Thereafter, Dumas stayed with Bagration on the Caspian Sea, at Derbent.

13　Hawking on the steppes.

'For four days we had not been separated from Bagration for one hour. He had been our guide, interpreter, our host, our everything. He knew the value of everything and the name of everything. If he saw a dagger he could judge the temper of its steel; if we glanced at a falcon, he at once knew its breeding; if we expressed a desire, he said, "I'll see to it for you", so that we no longer dared to wish for anything in his presence. He was a typical Georgian prince; brave, hospitable, extravagant, romantic and handsome.'

Bagration's care for his guests did not end at Derbent. Dumas discovered that he had arranged for escort, horses and hospitality all the way from the Caspian to Tiflis, where he knew that the French consul would look after him.

After leaving Derbent, Dumas camped on the steppes with a party of Tartars, who were sitting round a bonfire making themselves griddle-cakes from the flour they were carrying from Baku to army headquarters in the Caucasus.

'There was something peculiarly romantic about eating supper on the steppes beside the Caspian Sea with the descendants of Genghis Khan and Tamerlane. On the one side lay the mountains of

Daghestan, whence at any moment a troop of brigands might sweep down upon us and force us to fight for our lives; on the other this great lake, almost as unknown today, in spite of Klaproth, as it was in Greece in spite of Herodotus. All around us we could hear the bells of fifty camels as they cropped the withered grass, or see them with their necks stretched out on the sand'.

Dumas' next host was Prince Tarkanov, or rather his son, a boy of twelve, who knew French and did the honours. He shocked Dumas, who liked hunting game but not human beings, by regretting that brigands were getting scarce, as so many had surrendered to the Tsar. At the same time, he was sure that he would kill at least three. They were expecting an attack that night and Dumas asked the boy if they would kill him.

' "Oh no," he laughed, "they wouldn't be such fools as to cut off my head. They'd prefer a high ransom and they know that, if they take me, my father would sell everything, even to the last button of his uniform, to get me back. He loves me so much." '

This kidnapping racket interested Dumas immensely. Women in one area, he discovered, were not often carried away, as so many had perished when dragged through the icy Terek. The brigands preferred tougher game who would survive.[3] (Later on, on his journey, Dumas was to hear the sensational story of the abduction of two Georgian princesses, their children and their French governess, Madame Drancy. They were kidnapped in 1854 and exchanged for Shamyl's son in 1856. Madame Drancy published their experiences when she returned to Paris and they have been brilliantly retold by Lesley Blanch in *The Sabres of Paradise*. Dumas met one of the princesses in Tiflis. He was struck by her look of profound sorrow which he understood when she told him that her two youngest children had been torn from

[3] Captain Richard Wilbraham, travelling in Transcaucasia in 1837 heard harrowing tales, wherever he went, of people carried off by brigands and held for ransom. Often large sums were demanded, which the relatives had great difficulty in raising. The government refused to contribute, for fear of encouraging the traffic. Wilbraham talked to a German who, with several others, had been carried off by Circassians and kept for months near the foot of Elburz. They had suffered from hunger but were not ill-treated, their duty being to tend the flocks.

See Capt. Richard Wilbraham, *Travels in the Caucasus, Georgia and Persia* (John Murray, London, 1839).

George Ditson, who claimed that he was the first American to travel in the Caucasus, also writes of the traffic. See G. L. Ditson, *Circassia or a Tour in the Caucasus* (New York, 1850).

her arms, when they were passing through the raging Alezan, then in flood.)

Dumas' most moving experience was at Tchervelone, a village famous for its gaiety and beautiful women, descendants of outlawed Muscovite aristocrats, but when they arrived at its gates they saw that it was anything but gay—it was now completely deserted, except for the sentinel on guard. He told them that all its inhabitants had gathered on the far side of the village to witness the execution of a traitor. Two years before, a Cossack of Tchervelone, a married man with two children, had been taken prisoner by the Chechens and held for ransom. While in the mountains, he had fallen in love with the brigand chief's daughter who had returned his affection. He threw in his lot with the Chechens, became a Muslim and married his lovely mistress, as he was now able to have two wives. Soon he was the most daring fighter in the tribe. The Chechens decided to take Tchervelone with his help. He crept in, intending to unbar the gate for them but, on passing his home, he saw through the window his wife and children on their knees, praying before the ikon. The sight so moved him that he went in and embraced them and then gave himself up to the *hetman* (chief) of the *stanitza* (village), warning him of the imminent attack of the enemy. This was beaten off but the renegade Cossack was, in spite of his repentance, condemned to death. The execution was to take place at noon.

'We came at last to the place of execution, a patch of level ground, near the cemetery. The condemned man, who was between thirty and forty years of age, was kneeling beside a newly dug grave, his eyes unbandaged and his hands unbound. A priest stood by him, hearing his confession. A platoon of nine men with loaded rifles was drawn up in line a few yards off. When the priest had given absolution, the *hetman* went up to the condemned man and said: "Gregor Gregorovitch, you have lived as a traitor and a brigand. Die like a Christian and a brave man and God will forgive your sins and your brothers your treachery." The renegade listened humbly, then, raising his head, he said: "My brothers, I have already asked God's forgiveness and He has forgiven me; now I ask yours. Do in your turn forgive me." Then those who had suffered at Gregor's hands came up to him, each in his turn. (He knelt before them as he had knelt before God.) First came an old man, saying: "Gregor Gregorovitch, you killed my only son, the support of my old age but God has forgiven you and now I forgive you. Die in peace." Saying this he kissed him. Next came a young woman. "Gregor Gregorovitch", she said, "you killed my husband, made me a widow, my children orphans, but as God has forgiven you, I must also forgive you. Die in peace." She kissed him and gave place to others, who went up to him in turn with their reproaches. One said that he had killed his brother, another that he had killed his horse or had burned his house. All said: "You are forgiven. Die in peace." Last of all came his wife and children to bid their farewell. But the younger of the two, attracted by the pebbles mixed with the earth thrown up from the newly dug grave, went off to play with them. Finally the *hetman* came forward again. "Gregor Gregorovitch, your time has come." I confess that this was all I saw of the terrible scene. I wheeled my horse round and rode back into the *stanitza*. Ten minutes later I heard shots. Gregor Gregorovitch had ceased to exist. The crowd re-entered their village in silence.'

When Dumas got to Tiflis, the capital of Georgia, he found that his fame had preceded him. The ladies were in great excitement. They all knew his *The Three Musketeers* and his *Count of Monte Cristo*. (His barber who cut his hair so short that he looked like a seal, told him that he had sold his clippings for women to put in their pin-cushions.) They pestered Dumas to tell them of the latest Paris fasions—especially the address of the Paris shop that sold the corset which Princess G. had just brought back and which made waists smaller than wasps'. Beautiful as he found the ladies and gay as he found their city in contrast to Russia, he could not bear to leave Georgia without visiting Vladikavkaz and the Pass of Dariel. He took the route that, so tradition said, Pompey had followed in his campaign against Mithridates. The weather grew worse. In the valley of the Aragva, snow began to fall. Soon it was waist-deep. As they wound up the mountain, several times their *tarantas* stuck fast. They bartered it for a sleigh with five horses and later exchanged the horses for a dozen bullocks

'that ploughed breast-high through the soft snow and dragged us painfully upwards, a yard or two at a time. . . . The country round had a melancholy grandeur, a white, lifeless brilliance. Sky and earth were one, limitless and silent as death. . . . Far below we could see the Aragva, no longer a gleaming silver ribbon as in summer but an ashen-grey band almost black against the snow.'

Warned by the driver of the mail-coach from Russia, which they met on their way, that there was danger of avalanches, Dumas sadly turned back. He found Tiflis in blazing sunshine, although it was already winter.

At the end of January 1859, Dumas, with thirteen crates of the souvenirs he had collected, took ship at Poti on the Black Sea and caught a French ship at Trebizond. 'I cannot tell you what it meant to me to hear again the accents of Brittany and Marseilles. I felt as if I were at home again, the Caucasus a dream.'

He found, however, that he was not quite done with Caucasians. There were in the steerage, three hundred of them, mostly women and children, all destined to be sold as slaves in Istanbul.

DONALD MACKENZIE WALLACE

Russia
(On the Eve of War and Revolution)

London, 1877. Revised editions 1905 and 1912

SIR Donald Mackenzie Wallace was for many years correspondent of *The Times* and, from 1891 to 1899, its Foreign editor. His book is by far the most careful and thorough account of Russian institutions and life written by a foreigner in the nineteenth century. He learned the Russian language and travelled far and wide during six years, gathering information about its principal institutions and about the way of life, the ideals, characteristics, virtues and failings not only of the upper classes, noblesse, and officials but of the merchants and workers in the cities and of the peasants, who in 1877 still formed the bulk of the population.

It is not possible to give a digest of this important book or enough extracts to do justice to it. All that can be done is to reproduce certain scenes to illustrate Wallace's methods of presenting the information which he gathered at first hand.

Much of Wallace's research was on the peasantry, the workings of the *mir*, and the effects of the emancipation of the serfs. Wallace describes first the reasons for the peasants' dissatisfaction with the reform that had given them their freedom. They were granted the communal land, but they considered this theirs already. 'We are yours, but the land is ours', they used to say. Moreover, they had to redeem it from the landlords by payments extending over forty-nine years. They had hoped that their lords would be expropriated and believed that this was the will of the Tsar. Now the peasant was 'free', could marry without his lord's permission, leave his family, build his own house—but what good were these freedoms alone? The *mir* was as strong as ever. It could still force him to pay his various dues, including the immemorial poll-tax that weighed so heavily on every male peasant. It was

14 'The greybeard of the group.'

true that the *mir* was all he knew. Few peasants could imagine liberating themselves from it. Even when he went off to earn money as a craftsman or labourer, in a town or on some other estate, he still belonged to the *mir* and had to pay part of his earnings into its coffers.

Wallace describes a meeting of the *mir*. A crowd is gathered outside the church, men and women in their Sunday best. A woman is explaining to the meeting that her 'old man', who is at present the *starost* (village elder), is ill and cannot fulfil his duties.

' "But he hasn't served a year; he'll get better."

"Who knows?" sobs the woman; "the doctor said that he must be brought to the hospital."

"Why has he not been taken there?"

"Who is to carry him? The hospital is 40 versts off. If you put him on a cart he would die before he had gone a verst. And who knows what they do with people in a hospital?"

"Very well; hold your tongue," says the greybeard of the group. "There is nothing to be done. Whom shall we choose [as new elder]?" Several peasants look down to the ground; no one wants the honour. "There is Alexei Ivanov; he has not served yet," says the greybeard.

"Yes, yes—Alexei Ivanov!" shout the peasants. He protests but is not listened to; he has been duly elected.'

'More important than the elections is the redistribution of the communal lands. In the southern provinces, where the soil is fertile, peasants want to have as much land allotted as possible, but here in the north, where it is poor, and the taxes exceed the normal rent, many peasants strive to receive as little land as possible. A man called Ivan is asked how many shares he will take. "I have two sons and myself. I will take three—or less."

"Less! You talk nonsense. Your two sons may get married and so bring you two new female labourers."

"My eldest son works in Moscow and the other often leaves me in the summer."

"But they both send or bring home money and when they get married the wives will remain with you."

"God knows what will be. Who knows if they will marry?"

"You can easily arrange that."

"That I cannot do," says Ivan. "Times are changed now. The young people do as they wish and when they do get married they all want to have houses of their own. Three shares will be enough for me."

"He is a rich muzhik: lay on him five souls (i.e. five shares of land and burdens)," cries a voice.

"Five souls, I cannot, by God."

"Very well, you shall have four. Shall it be so?"

"Four, four," murmurs the crowd, and it is settled.

'Now comes the turn of a woman who has three little boys, only one old enough for field labour, and an invalid husband. "As the *mir* decides, so be it," she says, with downcast eyes.

"Then you must take three."

"What do you say, little Father? Do you hear that, ye Orthodox? They want to lay upon me three souls! Since St Peter's day my husband has been bedridden—bewitched it seems. He cannot put a foot to the ground."

"He was in the *kabak* (gin-shop) last week," says a neighbour.

"And you," shrieks the woman, "what did you do last parish fête? Was it not you who got drunk and beat your wife till she roused the whole village with her shrieking?"

"Listen," says the old man sternly, "you must take two shares and a half. If you cannot manage it yourself you can get someone to help you."

"Where can I get money to pay a labourer?" wails the woman. "Have pity, ye Orthodox." '

After each householder has been assigned his number of shares, the strips on the arable land and the meadow or hay-field are distributed. They are measured out with great accuracy by the peasants themselves. They are accustomed to work together in this way and to bow unreservedly to the will of the *mir*. 'I know', Wallace adds, 'of many instances where the peasants have set at defiance the authority of the police, of the provincial governor, of the central government itself, but I have never-heard of a single instance where the will of the *mir* was openly opposed by one of its members.' . . . .'Russia', he writes on another page, 'is a land of paradoxes. In the great stronghold of Caesarian despotism and centralized bureaucracy these village communes, containing about four-fifths of the population, are capital specimens of representative constitutional government of the extreme democratic type' (constitutional, Wallace explains, of the English type; unwritten, traditional). It was also supremely egalitarian; every man and woman had equal shares of the communal land.[1]

[1] This scene illustrates some of the unwritten laws of the *mir*. One of these is the marriage customs. Marriages were usually arranged by the parents. In the days of serfdom a wife was an asset because she swelled the patriarchal family and was another pair of hands and in thrall to her mother-in-law. After

Wallaces' research into the beliefs and customs of the numerous religious sects in Russia is especially interesting. He came to the conclusion that there were at least eleven million of the Razkolniki (Old Ritualists) and Bezpopovtzi (Priestless), and five million of the Protestant and 'Fantastical' sects. 'Sectarianism', he writes, 'proves that the Russian people is by no means so docile and pliable as is commonly supposed, and that it is capable of showing a stubborn, passive resistance to authority when it believes great interests at stake.'

The Molokani were of particular interest to him because their religious beliefs appeared to have a beneficial effect on their welfare; they were better housed, better clad and more prosperous than the Orthodox around them. He wanted to discover their beliefs but had to go about it very delicately, as persecution had made them wary.

'When I found a Molokan," he writes, 'I talked for some time about the weather and the crops and led the conversation gradually from weather and crops in Russia to weather and crops in Scotland and then passed slowly to the Scotch Presbyterian Church. When the peasant heard that there was a country where the people interpreted the Scriptures for themselves, had no bishops, and considered the veneration of ikons as idolatry, he invariably listened with profound attention, and when he learned that, in that wonderful country, the parishes annually sent deputies to an assembly in which all matters pertaining to the Church were freely and publicly discussed, I had to answer a whole volley of questions. "Where is that country? Is it to the East or the West? Is it very far away? If our presbyter could only hear all that." '

Many Molokani were exiled to the south-east of Russia, to Samara, the Caucasus and Siberia. 'Their willingness to modify their opinions', Wallace writes, 'in accordance with what seems to them new light, saves them from bigotry and fanaticism but exposes them to evils of another kind.'

---

emancipation, the young couple usually hived off, built themselves a house and formed another unit. They often had to borrow money (mostly from Jews) at exorbitant interest and became paupers. Small units were uneconomic: there was not enough land for them. Moreover, many old privileges were lost—free firewood, free grazing of cattle, free timber to build a new house after a fire. Now everything had to be paid for. Small wonder that emancipation, so passionately desired, so often brought disillusion. On the other hand, hard-working peasants often prospered and Wallace could not get any to admit that they would like to go back to the old days of serfdom.

'False prophets rise among us and lead many away from the faith, ' one of them admitted. There was, for instance, the false Elijah, who said that he had come to proclaim the Second Advent and the start of the millenium. He announced that he would ascend to Heaven on a given day, but when a great crowd gathered to see the miracle and it failed to happen, there was great disillusion. It seemed that Russian peasants of the nineteenth century were as easily carried away by rumours of anti-Christ and millenium as they were in the days of Peter the Great.

Wallace's interest in all the various types of Russians was insatiable. In the country he stayed with land-owners, great and small, reactionary and progressive; in the towns with merchants and *tchinovniks* (civil servants), in St Petersburg and Moscow with princes and intellectuals. He sat in on sessions of the newly created *zemstvos* (local councils). He talked to parish priests, monks and schoolmasters. But he was a nineteenth-century English gentleman and journalist. He was not working with the people, like Captain John Perry or Hume. He saw them from outside and, although he tried to be understanding and impartial, there is often a touch of condescension in his attitude. One can learn infinitely more about old-fashioned landowners from Gogol, the home life of members of the aristocracy and peasant psychology from Tolstoy or of the ordinary people in provincial towns from Chekhov. At the same time the impressions of a conscientious, intelligent outsider like Wallace are of value, and his book rewards study.

VICTOR TISSOT

Russians and Germans

Paris 1881, London 1882

VICTOR TISSOT, a well-known French journalist, published two books on Russia. He wrote the first of these,
Russians and Germans, in order to convince his compatriots that the Russians had lost their admiration of Germans
and that the bulk of the population now hated and feared them
no less than did the French. Russia, he implied, might one day be
a useful ally in the war of revenge that all good patriots hoped
would redeem the humiliation of 1870. Her friendship should be
cultivated.

Tissot tells us in his preface that in his journeys through Russia he wrote notes, 'some in railway carriages, some on board ship,
others on horseback, in *kibitkas* and *tarantasses*, on the Ukrainian
steppes, in the catacombs of Kiev, in the prisons of Moscow, in
the wretched suburbs of St Petersburg, on the miserable sledges
of the Gulf of Finland'. The contempt with which some foreigners
wrote of Russia was unjustified.

> 'It is still a virgin nation. Let us wait until it comes of age before
> we pronounce on its future. . . . If there is barbarity, it is a vigorous
> barbarity which will contribute one day to the development of the
> human race. Besides, this barbarity is less in the manners of the
> country than in the proceedings of the government. There is nothing
> more gentle, more humane than the Russian peasant and murders
> are much less frequent in the Muscovite country districts than in
> the streets of Berlin and Paris.'

Tissot explains that Russia did not fear Germany when she was
divided. The German Reich, created by Bismarck, was a different
matter. After the Congress of Berlin, in which Bismarck had

checked Russian ambitions in the Balkans, fury was added to hatred and fear. He quotes a significant passage from Franz von Loehr's *Russlands Werden und Wollen* (Russia's Development and Ambitions) to show that Russia had a sound basis for her fear. After ridiculing Russia's hopes of defeating an invading army by tactics which had succeeded against Napoleon, von Loehr imagines Germany and Austria invading her frontiers simultaneously, while England (where Disraeli had recently shown such dread of Russia) and, perhaps, France blockaded the Baltic and Black Seas.

'Let us think of the fall of this colossal and barbarous Empire! As soon as European civilization penetrates into these vast wilds, they will be given over to cultivation and colonization. . . . The fall of the Muscovite colossus will stifle every desire of emancipation in the Slavs of Germany and Austria.'

(One wonders if Hitler had read von Loehr when he wrote *Mein Kampf*.)

Of greater general interest is Tissot's chapter on the universities, of which there were seven in Russia, the most important in Moscow and St Petersburg. Nicholas I would have liked to close down the universities, which he thought hotbeds of revolutionary thought, and substitute for them military schools. He did not go so far as this, but he reduced the numbers in each university and forbade the lower orders to enter them. The students were forbidden to have discussion groups. Hundreds were dismissed for some slight offence and swelled the ranks of the intellectual malcontents.

As an illustration of the low level of culture in Russian universities at this period, owing to the Tsar's deliberate policy, Tissot gives the story of a student at St Petersburg in 1855, in his own words.

At his entrance examination he had for companions a Georgian prince and a Karaite Jew, neither of whom knew much Russian but their French gained them admittance, although lectures were in the Russian language. The son of a worker in the Tsar's kitchen, the class expressly excluded by his edict, was admitted as 'the examiners thought that something might be gained if they accepted a young man whose father was near the sovereign'.

'The only subjects to which importance was attached were mathematics and Russian History. The examination in this was conducted by Mr U., panegyrist of Nicholas I, an old pontiff hated by all on account of his pride and obsequiousness to superiors. He had published a manual of history which a candidate was expected to repeat word for word. The direction of the university was in the hands of the Inspector General, an ignorant man who owed his influence to the energy with which he subjected students and professors to the formalities of the rules. No detail of uniform escaped his eye, even to the size of the collar.'

This was the period of the Crimean War. The news that Sebastopol had fallen to the French

'left us utterly indifferent. We had other things to think about than the disaster that had befallen our arms. The scandal of the town, the little events of our student life, our quarrels with the professors, a thousand stories of drink and women, such were our daily thoughts. . . . If by chance the conversation turned on politics, everyone looked round to see that no one was listening. The defeat of the Russian armies caused us no emotion. There was no hatred against the enemy of our country. A few words upon the incapacity of our leaders and the superior organization of the invading armies and that was all. Thus Russia reaped the fruits of the system of repression introduced into the schools. . . . Science and art were as carefully excluded from our conversation as politics. Our only source of knowledge were the old notebooks and manuals handed down from generation to generation. The poor students alone were industrious; the others contented themselves by putting in an occasional appearance to remind the inspectors of their existence.'

Two or three years later there was a dramatic change. The emancipation of the serfs was in the air. The wind of change blew through the universities. The numbers of students doubled, societies proliferated, political discussion was in the order of the day. Russians were allowed to travel to foreign countries. Herzen's *Kolokol* (The Bell), though strictly forbidden, 'had become a power in the state more dreaded than the Third Section (the secret police)'. The chief part in this brilliant renovation belonged to the Academy of Medicine and Surgery in St Petersburg. It was this Academy that nurtured Bazarov, Turgenev's famous Nihilist, the hero of *Fathers and Sons*.

Unfortunately, the new wave of freedom led, as usual, only to reaction. In 1861 rebellions broke out in the universities of St Petersburg and Moscow, and lectures were suspended for several months. Many distinguished professors resigned.

'Year by year [Tissot wrote in 1881] hundreds of students are expelled and are thrown into the streets of the large towns, where they make capital out of the pity they inspire or of the deep-seated hatred which is stirring up the people. They organize conspiracies, make themselves the intermediaries between the revolutionaries and the Nihilists who have taken refuge in Switzerland, or they go among the people, as their expression is.'

Tissot was one of the first Western observers to attempt an analysis of what had become known as Nihilism since Turgenev coined the word in his *Fathers and Sons*. Tissot's book was published when, because of the assassination of Alexander II (the Tsar Liberator), Nihilism had become a household word and made the great and powerful in Europe tremble if they had to visit Russia. A new detail was added to the popular image of Russia. Now there were not only wolves howling round the troikas driven by wild muzhiks over the endless snow of the steppes, not only cruel landlords thrashing their peasants with the knout or driving them in chains to Siberia, but, even worse, there were Russian citizens concealing bombs in their fur coats, sworn to murder their rulers and tear down the foundations of society. Lord Dufferin, the British ambassador, was obliged to represent his Queen at the obsequies of the murdered Alexander in the cathedral of St Petersburg, a ceremony that lasted four hours and was attended by many foreign potentates. It was widely rumoured that the Nihilists were going to blow it up. Then, as Dufferin observed in his breezy, Irish way, 'the Nihilists might have cleared the whole European chessboard at one go.'[1]

Tissot shared the general horror of the new phenomenon, but he made an attempt to understand it and decried the prevalent exaggerations of the numbers of Nihilists.

'It has been stated that their number is two or three millions. It is in reality two or three thousand, mostly young men of from eighteen to thirty years of age. Their excitement, their proud attitude before their judges in presence of death, their bold and rash proceedings, can only belong to hot-headed youth'.

Tissot realized that the majority of Russian radicals did not believe in terrorism. The Narodniki put their faith in the peasants, and like Marianna in Turgenev's *Virgin Soil* (reviewed by Henry

[1] Quoted in A. Lyall, *The Life of the Marquis of Dufferin and Ava*, Chapter 8 (p. 291 in Nelson popular edition).

James in 1877), went to live amongst them, hoping to educate them in the new ideas. Tissot dedicated a chapter to what he calls (misleadingly) the Fathers of Nihilism: Herzen, Bakunin and Tchernychevski. The two first have become familiar figures and are much better understood than in Tissot's time, but Tchernychevski is less well known. Tchernychevski, in the novel *What Are We to Do?*, which he wrote in prison in the early Sixties, created the type of the new woman, who would be the companion of the new man. Vera, the heroine of the book, tells her fiancé that she will not be dependent on him when they marry; she will earn her own living; they will be equals. Vera set a fashion; many young women wished to learn a trade.

'The most intelligent applied themselves to deep studies; especially the sciences; many went to Zürich to join the schools of medicine at the university. Vera served as the type and model of the female student with short hair, spectacles, and the manners of a boy.'

In 1873 there were scores of Russian girls studying medicine in Zürich. Hundreds of students were crowding into the medical faculty of St Petersburg, hoping to qualify as midwives since they were not yet allowed to practise as doctors. (It is a curious fact that permission for this was to come sooner than in an enlightened country like England, where the struggle for it was just beginning and destined to be prolonged and bitter.) Although Tissot, as a good Frenchman, did not approve of the New Woman he admits that

'women have given to Nihilism and the revolutionary associations a very strong contingent. When courage, passion and self-abnegation have been requisite, they have often surpassed their brethren! It was looked on as a disgrace to take any pleasure in art or needlework, because in the old schools the study of French and music, and lessons in dancing and embroidery, had taken the place of more serious occupations.'

(The initial change in girls' education had been made when, in 1858, a ukase had ordered the creation of 'gymnasiums' or grammar schools for their higher education.)

Meanwhile Tchernychevski, the creator of the 'new woman', after two years in the Fortress of Peter and Paul, had been condemned in 1864 to fourteen years' hard labour in the mines of Siberia but, although he disappeared from the scene in person, he remained a potent force, especially amongst Russian youth, who gave him a martyr's crown and organized protests to obtain his pardon. It was said of him that 'imprisoned in Siberia, isolated, powerless, he had done more harm to Russian autocracy than ever Herzen and Bakunin did during their exile in Europe'.

Obsessed as Tissot was by hatred and fear of Germany, he wanted Russia to be strong, and was worried about the state of her armed forces. She spent nearly half her budget on them, two-thirds contributed by the peasants, but he considered them in a deplorable state. This had been shown up in Russia's recent war with Turkey. In 1877 she sent an army into the Balkans to free the Bulgarian Christians. The war was represented as a crusade, but what horrible disillusionment came to those who fought it!

'At the beginning of the winter of 1877 when the army had to cross the snowy chain of the Balkans, the soldiers had no boots. The contractors had sold boots with cardboard soles. The siege of Plevna was held up for want of spades and pick-axes. . . . The contractors supplied worm-eaten flour, bad bread, worthless forage. . . . The unlucky peasants who undertook to transport provisions across Rumania and Bulgaria were not only not paid but also pillaged and ill-treated; some died of hunger; others returned as beggars to their villages, which they had quitted at the head of their carts and horses, proud of the contract which had given them their mission. . . . The hospital and ambulance service broke down. At Simbiza, the hospital, which had been built for 630 wounded, had to receive 3,000. The disorder and dirt were indescribable.[2]

The Russian soldier is intelligent, distinguished by his great force of will; fatigues and privations are of slight importance to him. He pushes the spirit of discipline to a heroic extent. But are not these individual qualities lost in the movement of the whole body? No strategy; no real action; no capable officers; no good generals; and administration and an ordinance corps stuck in the old ruts.'

Not a very reassuring picture if France was looking for an ally against her old enemy.

---

[2] The scandals, the mismanagement of the whole campaign, the shocking sufferings of the soldiers who fought it, remind us of the English mismanagement of the Crimean War—of the boots all for one foot supplied by contractors, of the ghastly state of the hospitals at Scutari. We could not crow over the Russians. The difference was that we had a free press which Russia had not. Russell, *The Times* correspondent, the first ever sent by a newspaper to report on a war, did give a truthful account of what was happening and, owing largely to Florence Nightingale and Sidney Herbert, genuine attempts at reform were made, both in the army and in the hospitals.

Like most foreigners, whether Protestant, Catholic or atheist, Tissot disliked the Orthodox Church which,

'entirely subject to the Tsar, helps to keep the people in darkness and fosters the grossest superstitions. The muzhik believes firmly that nothing ever happens without the consent of the saints. This saint can cure madness, another can discover robbers for you. There is a saint who helps the hen to lay eggs and the peasant women to see them; this one finds wives for the boys, that other husbands for the girls. In the towns the clergy go in State carriages with an ikon of the Virgin to visit the sick, and make fine revenues out of their rounds. A robber who prepares to open the poor-box in a chapel promises a taper to his patron saint if he will aid him.'

Tissot was interested in the numerous sects in Russia—especially in the Old Believers. One of the reasons for their indignation at Nikon's reforms was because he made the year begin in January instead of September. How could the world have been created in January? There are no apples on the trees then. How could Eve have got one? (Surely a reasonable question.)

The Western world is surprised that Alexander II's reforms have done so little to improve life in Russia. They forget that

'all the Russians of the second half of the nineteenth century are sons and grandsons of serfs or of nobles who treated their serfs with savage cruelty. All the Russian shopkeepers had for fathers serfs who had bought from their masters the right to leave the manor and settle in a town.'

Tissot realized the sad fact that many peasants were worse off after emancipation than before.

Victor Tissot penetrated beneath the surface of Russian life. His book is desultory and ill-arranged and he had not the benefit of hindsight that we have now but, besides travelling far and wide in Russia, he had studied Herzen whose writings, although not his politics, he admired, and he knew and often quoted the Turgenev novels. Thoughtful Frenchmen of his day must have learned much about the real Russia from his book, but the general public certainly found the second book he published easier reading and enjoyed it as a picture-book, at a time before there were cinemas or TV.

VICTOR TISSOT

Russia and the Russians. Kiev and Moscow[1]

Paris 1884

THIS was the second of Tissot's books on Russia. It was more picturesque than the first. It was less of a polemic. There was not so much about the German menace. It was lavishly illustrated with 240 line drawings (those of the artist Praniaschnikov are excellent). Tissot was a romantic and his descriptions are often highly coloured, but the records of the talks he had with all types of Russians have an authentic ring. Moreover, he was one of the few to make a study of the Ukrainians, to undertstand their special characteristics and see how they differed from the Great Russians.

They seemed much gayer. Tissot watched them at hay-making. The women and girls, following the men and gathering the hay into cocks, were a brilliant sight in their many coloured skirts, their white shirts rich with embroideries and red kerchiefs round their heads. In the evenings the harvesters gathered round a bonfire, the old men smoking their pipes, the young ones singing to their flutes. On Sundays they danced and the girls sang old ballads of love and war or else they improvised songs.

' "Talk to a Ukrainian, [Tissot's guide told him] you will be surprised at his vivacity, his sensibility, his passionate love of freedom. Deeply attached to his country he leaves it only with the hope of returning. The Great Russian, on the other hand, is a nomad, a vagabond, a wanderer. He likes adventures, journeys, pilgrimages, commerce, fairs, everything that fulfils his desire for movement, his longing for change. The Little Russian (as the Ukrainian is called), a farmer at heart, hates cities and is only happy when lost in the

[1] *La Russie et les Russes. Kiew et Mouscou.*

immensity of his meadows. . . . . The difference between the north and south of Russia is not only in its climate, soil, architecture and costume but also in its manners, customs and language. . . . Women here have a different status. A young girl is never married without her consent. And once married she counts for something in her husband's house. Her advice is listened to. . . . And her dress has more originality and colour. The Little Russian is more supple, more agile than the Great Russian. You see in him the fearless horseman of the steppe, the descendant of an ancient warrior race." '

Tissot's guide was not unnaturally prejudiced in favour of his countrymen. Five years before Tissot's visit, the Tsar had issued a ukase forbidding the use of the Ukrainian language. This persecution had increased their sense of difference from the Great Russian and their loyalty to their own people. That there was a difference Tissot saw with his own eyes. Accustomed as he was to the drab monotony and colourlessness of the villages throughout Great Russia, he was enchanted by the cottages he found in the Ukraine, 'with their porcelain stoves ornamented with strange designs, their holy pictures above which hung towels embroidered with cornflowers and marigolds'. More astonishing still there were gardens full of sunflowers in front of the cottages and often an orchard at the back.[1]

The emancipation of the serfs, Tissot was told, had brought great benefits to the Ukrainians: 'Before this he was a brute, hiding himself away in a hovel, now he lives in his own house.' Often he sends his son away to be educated, even to attend Kiev university. In this again there was a contrast between the south and the north, where because of the harsher climate and poorer soil peasants had often been better off under serfdom when a good landlord would give him help if his crops failed, as they so often did.[2]

[1] The Editor came across a Ukrainian village in the famine area of Buzuluk. Its inhabitants had been settled there during the disturbances of 1905 because, though it was also Black Earth country, it was so far east that it was less populous than the Ukraine and there was more free land. Cottages here were better built, sprucer and cleaner. They had gardens and there were trees in the streets. Inside there was well-made furniture, even beds. Whether through better husbandry or greater cunning in hiding their grain from the requisitions of the Red Army, the inhabitants had not been so decimated by famine as in the Great Russian villages. It was only in this village that we found women skilled in embroidery. In that part of Great Russia (which may possibly have not been typical) Ukrainians belonged to a higher level of peasant culture.

[2] Xavier Hommaire de Hell, passing through the Ukraine in 1838, was appalled by the sub-human, brutalized state of the peasantry there. Girls,

Tissot heard much about the superstitions of the Ukrainians.

'With their childish credulity, they love fantastic stories. They believe in the existence of spirits, fairies, undines and sorcerers. Good spirits protect in particular the daughter of the house, the cattle and horses; evil spirits are rowdy at night, preventing sleep. Vampires, sons of a devil and a witch, escape from cemeteries at their death, for their bodies are incorruptible, and come at night to suck the blood of sleepers. The *rousalkas*, undines who live in rivers, long for Christian baptism, for they are the souls of the drowned or of infants who died without the sacraments. If, after seven years, they have not met anyone who will redeem them by making the sign of the cross over them, they will remain undines for ever.'

Tissot quotes Schevchenko, the great Ukrainian poet, who wrote in his native language and recounted in his verse many of the legends and stories of his countrymen. He had been forbidden to write and condemned to go as a common soldier to Orenburg. After an exile of ten years, he was allowed to return, not to the Ukraine, but to St Petersburg, where he died in 1861.

Tissot noticed, as all travellers did, the coarseness and ignorance of the popes. He asked a Russian friend whether they were usually drunkards.

' "How can you expect them to be anything else? [was the reply]. Only their cloth differentiates them from the peasant. Like the peasant the pope earns his bread by the sweat of his brow. He ploughs the field, pastures his beasts. His wife works like a peasant, with her hands. Some sell vodka. Poor, burdened with large families, insufficiently supported by the state or commune, they are obliged, for bare subsistence, to resort to all sorts of devices: to charge heavily for baptisms and weddings, even to bargain with the dying for the price

---

married at fifteen and accustomed to the harsh labour of the fields, were old women at thirty. The only relaxation for them, as for the men, was in sleep or drunkenness. They 'work only because they are forced to'. On the other hand Haxthausen noted (in 1843) that, in contrast to those of the north, the Ukrainian villages were pretty, the houses well built and clean. The peasants suffered from their servile state (they had been free till the time of Catherine II) but their spirit was not entirely crushed. Having before their eyes the free Cossacks, they resisted all unusually oppressive measures and threatened the landlords who made extra demands on them. Their love of dance and bright clothes showed that they had retained some gaiety of spirit.

See Adele and Xavier Hommaire de Hell, *Travels in the Steppes of the Caspian Sea, the Crimea, the Caucasus, etc.* (London, 1847); and Haxthausen, *Russian Empire,* 2 vols. (London, 1856).

Left: 'The last sounds I heard were the jingling of chains' (p. 299).

Below: Even the police are very tolerant of them (p. 310).

of absolution. I knew a pope who refused extreme unction to a dying child until the father had promised him his best goose or pig"[3]

"Does not this conduct bring religion into disrepute?" [asked Tissot].

"Not in the least. The priest with us is not God's representative—he is only a kind of valet or servant." '

Tissot's guide went on to explain that in former times priestly office was practically hereditary. There was an ecclesiastical caste, attached to the church like the serf to the soil. It was difficult for a priest's son to become anything else 'but now, when the universities are open to them, they crowd in and, finding no jobs at the end of their studies, become Nihilists'.

Tissot, who was always hearing about Nihilists, as a conscientious journalist, longed to meet some real live ones. He hurried to Kiev. For a time, he could think only of its beauty. It was 'a fairytale city, a city of pink houses with green roofs, of golden domes and silver bell-towers, of red palaces, of gardens of an Asiatic magnificence'. At the monastery of Lavra, he saw what was then one of the most characteristic sights of Russia—an immense crowd of pilgrims.[4] 'Some came from the Urals, others from Georgia and the wild regions of Kamchatka, from the Crimea and the Gulf

---

[3] The Editor was told by her cook (in the Buzuluk area) that the pope had left her aunt's coffin in the snow and refused to read the burial service until they had paid him their last kopeck.

[4] Xavier Hommaire de Hell and his wife travelled from Istanbul to Odessa on a boat overflowing with pilgrims returning from Jerusalem.

'It is impossible to express the filth and disorder. . . . The deck which was already heaped from end to end with goods and provisions, was crowded besides with a disgusting mob of pilgrims, mendicant monks, Jews and Russians or Cossack women, all squatting or lying about at their ease without regard to the convenience of the other passengers. . . . The Russian people are possessed in the highest degree with the mania for pilgrimages. All these beggars set off barefoot, with their wallets on their back and their rosaries in their hands, to seek Heaven's pardon for their sins; appealing on their way to the charity of men, to enable them to continue that vagabond and miserable life which they prefer to the fulfilment of homely duties.' (Compare Stephen Graham's attitude to the pilgrims whom, seventy years later, after the 'Slav soul' had been discovered, he accompanied to Jerusalem. See Stephen Graham, *With Russian Pilgrims to Jerusalem*.)

Even the Hommaire de Hells felt more lenient to the hundreds of women pilgrims they encountered near the remote capital of the Don Cossacks, 'like a swarm of locusts suddenly dropped from the sky, most of them barefoot, carrying their shoes in their hand. They had been to the catacombs of Kiev.' There is much more pious fervour in this nation than in the Muscovites, they remarked; a natural integrity and no hypocrisy. Like all good Raskolniks, they abjured tobacco and alcohol. (The Don Cossacks were mostly Raskolniks.)

K

of Finland.' Some of them came in bands marching in single file, chanting their sad songs and might have been years *en route*. Some were cripples, some blind, but many came to fulfil a vow. The monks they believed were miracle workers 'but the passion for a nomadic life, inherent in the Russian character, is the real reason of their love of pilgrimages'.

The monks gave meals to all the indigent and even put up for the whole winter those who were too far from home to struggle back through the snow.

Used to Catholic monasteries, Tissot was surprised that the monks did not teach or become missionaries. At Lavra, besides their devotions, they all did manual work. There were blacksmiths, carpenters, spinners, weavers and painters of ikons; others looked after the cows and made butter and cheese. Many became bishops.

In spite of having a guide who seemed an initiate of secret societies and to be intimate with dangerous revolutionaries, Tissot was thwarted in his hope of conversing with 'real, live' Nihilists, but his experience was illuminating. His guide took him one dark night to the home of a lady of his acquaintance who let rooms to girl students. The house had no light in it. The hostess told them simply that the girls had fled. They had left a note.

' "We don't know when we'll come back. Sell our possessions to pay our debts." Yet they were such good girls, worked so hard, never went out at night. One of them wanted to be a doctor. They talked too much—they were always discussing religion, politics, the immortality of the soul, the unity of mankind. When the police came and ransacked their rooms they didn't find anything incriminating and I could not tell them anything against them.'

There were no bombs. The revolutionary tracts had probably been burned. Tissot revised his opinion of what Nihilists were really like. He had been appalled by the poverty in which most of the students lived, a poverty unknown even in the most squalid haunts of the Left Bank in Paris. He decided that it was not strange that Russian students should dream of the transformation of a society that gave most of the population such a raw deal.

The French, who took Tissot as their travel guide through a country that few of them knew, could find in his books something besides picturesque descriptions and amusing anecdotes.

GEORGE KENNAN

Siberia and the Exile System

London and New York 1891

THE publication of George Kennan's description of the life of exiles in Siberia did more than anything else to bring to an end the century-long love affair between the United States and Russia. It had been a strange friendship. That the Tsars of All the Russias, the most powerful and tyrannous autocrats of Europe, should have flirted with a republic founded on all the democratic principles which they so studiously flouted—Habeas Corpus, equality before the law, free speech, religious toleration, and all the other rights of man—is one of the curiosities of the modern world. Little is said about it in English history books. Perhaps we have chosen to ignore it because it was based so largely on hatred of our own country. Not even love unites people so strongly as an intense, well-directed hate.

A few words must be said about this Russo-American friendship, before the impact of Kennan's revelations can be properly assessed.

France, in American mythology, is her oldest friend. The nineteen-year old Lafayette, fighting (entirely on his own initiative) on the side of the oppressed American colonists, has never been forgotten.

'Our next oldest traditional friend [writes Thomas Bailey] is Russia. She was on our side, or appeared to be, not only during the war of Independence but also during the hardly less critical years of the War of 1812 [with England] and the great Civil War. Little wonder that the legend of the Tsarist affection for the new republic took such a deep hold.'

When Catherine the Great refused, politely but firmly, George III's request for 20,000 of her fierce Cossacks to subdue his rebellious colonists, it was assumed that the Tsarina was sympathizing with a valiant people struggling for their freedom. Did she not correspond with Voltaire and dabble with liberal ideas? The reasons she gave—exhausting war with the Turks and so on—could not have been the real ones. The outcome, at any rate, was on the whole a happy one. Instead of Cossacks, highly skilled in rapid warfare as well as in rape, loot and murder, America received the somewhat less practised Germans and their gratitude to the Tsarina was undying. (As late as 1920, voices were raised in America protesting against the sending of her doughboys to fight the Bolsheviks in their civil war, on the grounds that Catherine had refused to intervene with her Cossacks in the War of Independence.)

An even more tangible bond between Russia and America was their fury at the British interference with the freedom of the seas and the rights of neutrals to trade with her enemies. Catherine's image was darkened when she seized a large slice of poor, little Poland, but there was nothing that besmirched Alexander I's reputation for Americans—not even Tilsit, for to many of them (although not to the New Englanders) it seemed right that he should side with their oldest friend, the French, against the hated English in the Napoleonic War. In 1809, the United States sent their first ambassador to St Petersburg, John Quincy Adams. He found a warm welcome. The Tsar hoped that the new republic over the ocean would become the commercial rival of Great Britain, which was so arrogantly seizing neutral ships and crippling trade.

Adams, a Puritan from New England who read the Bible from cover to cover every year and felt guilty at the time he had to waste attending banquets and balls in St Petersburg, salved his conscience by cementing the friendship between his country and Russia, so passionately at one about the freedom of the seas and the wickedness of the British intereference with it. America needed a friend, especially in 1812, when anger about the seizure of her ships had led her into war with England. As scant notice of this little war is taken in our school textbooks (because, perhaps of the ignominious part in it played by our glorious navy, and the valiant feats of the American 'fir-built frigates'), it is not generally known, over here, that Alexander offered to mediate between us and our rebellious ex-colonists and, although nothing came of the offer and peace was concluded without his intervention, America felt grateful for his kind intentions and chalked up another good mark for Russia. They were pleased, too, that that great country had noticed their exploits. 'You are constantly beating at sea the English, who beat all the rest of the world,' the Russian Chancellor remarked to Quincy Adams.

Between this time and their Civil War, there were ups and downs in the friendship between Russia and the United States. During the Crimean War, American sympathy was with Russia, and a number of American doctors worked for their wounded. On the other hand, American sympathies were with the Poles in their savagely repressed risings of 1830 and 1863, and with the Hungarians in 1848, whose revolution Nicholas I helped his brother-Emperor of Austria to put down. This was not only because of the black accounts their ambassadors in St Petersburg gave of Tsarist tyranny and obscurantism, but also because of the flood of Polish and Hungarian refugees who sought freedom in their country. All these things were forgotten when, at the darkest moment for the North in their fight to preserve their Union against the South, a Russian fleet arrived in New York. At a time when the British and French were favouring the South and it seemed as though they might intervene in its favour, this friendly gesture was received with a tremendous burst of enthusiasm. Everywhere, from Boston to Washington, the Russian sailors were banqueted and fêted, and toasts were drunk to Lincoln the Emancipator (of slaves) and Alexander the Liberator (of serfs). That the Russians wanted to remove their fleet from the Baltic, in case the British and French intervened over Poland, was noted only by a few very astute Americans and had no impact on the public mind.

When, in 1867, Russia sold Alaska to the United States for the ridiculous sum of $7,200,000, it was hailed as another friendly gesture on the part of the Tsar Alexander II. It would have been ungracious to stress that, as the Russians were vastly extending their Empire across Asia, Alaska seemed not worth the expense and trouble of exploitation. Not even the Russian extension of its power in the Balkans in the late 1870s alarmed America, for were they not fighting to free their Christian brethren from the 'unspeakable Turk'? In 1881 Alexander II was assassinated by Nihilists. He had been America's one true friend in the Civil War and had sold them Alaska (which was proving very profitable). American grief at his death was widespread and sincere. After the disappearance of the Tsar Liberator, things were never the same between the two countries. The long love-affair began to show signs of wear. Moreover, American engineers and technicians employed in the building of Russian railways and its expanding industry were maddened by the inefficiency and corruption that hampered their activities and their consuls were burdened by their complaints and claims. Alexander III had none of the liberal impulses of his father. He was cruel and despotic. Scapegoats were needed for the murder of Alexander and for the growth of Nihilism, and the Jews filled the bill. The shocking pogroms of the 1880s resulted in the flight of Russian and Polish Jews into the eastern states of America. Unlike the quarter of a million Jews, mostly of German origin, already in the States, these were not a prosperous, hardworking people but a ragged, terror-stricken horde. America saw her land becoming a dumping ground for the victims of Tsarist tyranny and it displeased her.[1] Then, in 1891, when pogroms were easing off, another bombshell exploded: the publication by George Kennan of his two-volumed book, *Siberia and the Exile System*. No book since *Uncle Tom's Cabin* had had such an impact on public opinion.

In 1885, George Kennan was commissioned by the *Century Magazine* to write a series of articles on the prisons of Siberia. He had already spent two years there. When only twenty years of age he had been part of an expedition organized by the Western Union Telegraph Company to survey a possible telegraph route across Siberia to Alaska. This came to an end when, in 1866, a cable was laid across the Atlantic, but it had given Kennan first-hand experience of a region almost unknown to the West.

[1] Isabel Hapgood, who spent two years in Russia at the close of the 1880s and learned the language, tried to combat the growing hostility to Russia of her countrymen. In her book *Russian Rambles* (1895) she writes, 'I am told that I must abuse Russia if I wish to be popular in America! . . . I am sure that the Russia of Ivan the Terrible's time would precisely meet its views. . . . In spite of all that has been written about Russia, the common incidents of everyday life are not known. . . . Russians of all classes, from the peasant up, possess a naturally simple, sympathetic disposition and manner, as a rule, tinged with a friendly warmth whose influence is felt as soon as one crosses the frontier. Shall I be believed if I say that I found it in custom-house offices and gendarmes? For the rest, characters vary quite as much as they do elsewhere.' She wrote many articles for the *Atlantic Monthly*. She gave an interesting account of a visit to Tolstoy in Yasnaya Polyana, in which she quoted the Countess's opinion of her husband's disciples: all 'small, blond, sickly and homely, as like to one another as a pair of old boots'. Isabel Hapgood helped in the knowledge of Russian literature in America by her *Survey of Russian Literature, with Selections* (1902).

He had become fluent in Russian and interested in the Russian people, but he had had no opportunity to visit prisons and was convinced that the reports on them by political exiles in England, notably Stepniak and Prince Kropotkin, were exaggerated. On the whole he sympathized with the Russian government in its efforts to get rid of its terrorists and revolutionaries. As his attitude was well known, he was given official help by the Russians to make his investigations. Actually the conditions in which he found the exiles were horrible beyond belief and he did not spare his readers in describing them. At the same time, he wrote in a factual way, giving (as far as was possible without bringing his informants into danger) chapter and verse for his findings so that their authenticity could not be doubted.

Kennan's first articles were dramatically illustrated by George A. Frost, who had accompanied him. These illustrations spoke even more forcibly than Kennan's narrative: endless lines of convicts with chains between their legs, trudging through the snow, guarded by soldiers armed with guns and whips; the forwarding prisons, filled to the roof with men and women; men shot as they broke from the line in a bid for freedom. In 1891 these articles and pictures were published in book form.

Kennan begins peaceably enough with a short description of his journey through Russia. He was amazed in Nijni Novgorod at what seemed to him a vast city, with 'churches, mosques, theatres, markets, banks, hotels' entirely empty of life, with grass growing in its streets. This was 'the caravanserai' for half a million traders and only occupied during the period of the fair for two or three months every year. He was surprised too that the great extension of the railways hadn't as yet killed the most famous fair of Russia. Kennan and Frost sailed up the Kama to Perm, 125 miles from Ekaterinburg to which they travelled by the new railway. This town had become prosperous because of the recently exploited minerals, fabulous in variety and value, of the Ural Mountains. The most important of these were iron, copper and coal but there were also gold and precious stones.

Ekaterinburg was similar to other Russian towns:

'The same wide, unpaved streets, the same square log houses with ornamented window casings and flatly pyramidal, tin roofs, the same high board fences between the scattered dwellings. the same white-walled churches with coloured or gilded domes, the same *gostinoi dvor* or city bazaar.'

where one could find everything that the Empire produced and many things it didn't. Kennan was especially delighted to find American peanuts and instructed the shop-keeper how to roast them and make them eatable. He was impressed that Ekaterinburg had some pretensions to 'self-culture' with a Ural Society of Friends of Natural Science, two newspapers (unfortunately heavily censored in Moscow) and an occasional opera season.

Kennan and Frost were entertained in the lavish Russian manner by the superintendent of the Berozeu gold-mines and immensely impressed by his tasteful home and exquisite garden, with its flowers, fountains, cherry-trees and conservatory filled with oranges, lemons and pineapples. After supper they played croquet on the lawn. It all seemed very civilized. They were less impressed, however, at seeing women in the gold-mines working eleven hours a day for a dollar two cents a week and felt that it was worse than penal servitude. As yet they little knew what this was like. They were soon to see.

From Ekaterinburg to the Siberian border, a distance of two hundred miles, Kennan and Frost went by 'horse express service' along the great Siberian road which stretched 3,000 miles from the Urals to the head-waters of the Amur River. They passed a caravan of freight waggons—the careful Kennan counted 1,450 of them on the first day—and commented on the riches of Siberia, which daily sent so many tons of its products to Russia. When they passed the post at the entrance to Siberia, Kennan thought of the heartrending scenes the pillar had witnessed in past centuries, for it was here that the convicts had said good-bye to their beloved country, many of them kissing the ground and taking a little Russian earth to accompany them in their exile.

Siberia was not the entire icy waste which the Americans had imagined.

> 'To the traveller who crosses the Urals for the first time in June, nothing is more suprising than the fervent heat of Siberian sunshine and the extraordinary beauty and profusion of Siberian flowers. There were long stretches of wheat and rye and great expanses of prairie. The roadside was bright with wild-roses, violets, honeysuckle, iris and the golden trollius and there were seas of forget-me-not.'

But Kennan was surprised that there were no scattered farmhouses. The peasants, nearly all on Crown land, did not own their property, and lived in villages which looked poor and neglected, their wide streets often a sea of liquid mud where a few pigs wandered. There were no trees or gardens but the *izba* windows were brightened with fuchsias, oleanders, pinks, geraniums, tea-roses and cactus.

Tiumen was the first Siberian town they came to. They arrived exhausted after forty hours without sleep, jolted almost to pieces in their cramped *tarantas* (carriage). The next day they presented their letters of introduction to the chief police officer and at once got permission to visit the forwarding prison through which all exiles had to pass.

Transportation to Siberia, Kennan explains, had begun soon after its conquest in the seventeenth century, but at first it was disabled criminals, mutilated by the barbarous punishments then in vogue, who had been sent there. At the end of the century, mutilation as a punishment had been forbidden and banishment to Siberia substituted. As well as for crimes of violence, men were exiled for minor offences such as fortune-telling, prize-fighting, snuff-taking, driving with reins (considered a Western innovation: Russian peasants were supposed to ride the horse or run by its side), begging, and setting fire to property accidentally. In the eighteenth century, when the mineral and agricultural resources of Siberia were discovered, the government realized that convicts could be useful and many were condemned to hard labour in the silver mines of Daurski and the mines of Transbaikal. When in 1753, the Tsarina Elizabeth abolished capital punishment (and it should be remembered that Russia was the first country to do this), murderers were condemned to hard labour and perpetual exile in Siberia, but at least had their lives. In the reign of Catherine II, when the demand for labour increased because of the exploitation of the mines, the list of offences, punishable by exile trebled. Jews were exiled for non-payment of taxes, serfs for cutting down trees without leave, non-commissioned officers for various misdeeds, and the number of political offenders and nobles who had fallen from favour increased greatly. Up to the close of the eighteenth century it was an unorganized system. Exiles were driven like cattle, often begging their way, because there was no provision for feeding them, but in the early nineteenth century this was remedied. They were given identity cards showing who they were and where they were bound for and exile station-houses were erected along the most important routes. The first of these was at Tiumen.

L

It was at Tiumen that records were kept of all exiles to Siberia and the categories to which they belonged. The records started in 1823 and Kennan was allowed to copy them. Exiles, he found, were divided into four categories: hard-labour convicts, penal colonists, persons simply banished', and *dobrovolni*, women and children who voluntarily accompanied their relatives. The first two lots, supposed to be criminals, were deprived of all civil rights and condemned to spend their lives in Siberia. Their heads were half shaven and they wore leg-fetters. As those 'simply banished' were not necessarily criminals, they wore no fetters and might hope to return home when the term of their banishment had expired. Analysing the figures for 1885, Kennan found that the largest single class (5,536 out of 15,766) was composed of the women and children who went voluntarily, and that more than half of the supposed criminals and the 'simply banished' had had no trial but were sent by a mere order from the Minister of the Interior or of some official.

These cool facts showed Kennan's careful avoidance of sensationalism and made his description of the terrible conditions in the prison the more convincing to his readers. But it was the prison hospital that roused the greatest horror and compassion.

'The most common disorders seemed to be scurvy, typhus, typhoid fever, acute bronchitis, rheumatism and syphilis. . . . Never before in my life had I seen faces so white, haggard and ghastly as those that lay on the gray pillows in those hospital cells. As I breathed that heavy stifling atmosphere, poisoned with the breaths of syphilitic and fever-stricken patients, loaded and saturated with the odour of excrement, disease germs, exhalations from unclean human bodies and foulness inconceivable, it seemed to me that over the hospital doors should be written "All hope abandon, ye who enter here".'

(Florence Nightingale had thought the same when she entered the hospital at Scutari, but that was thirty years earlier.)

It was not surprising that the annual death rate in the Tiumen prison ranged from 23 per cent to 44 per cent—a death rate, Kennan thought, exceeding that of any pestilence in Europe in the Middle Ages. He noted that the prison wardens and the colonel-inspector of transportation were themselves incensed at conditions. The colonel had often reported them to Petersburg, but his complaints were unanswered.

The day after visiting the prison, Kennan witnessed the departure of one of the marching parties.

'There was a jingling of chains as some of the prisoners who had been lying on the ground sprang to their feet; the soldiers of the guard shouldered their rifles; the exiles crossed themselves devoutly, bowing in the direction of the prison chapel; and at the word "March." the whole column was instantly in motion. Three or four Cossacks in dark-green uniforms and with rifles over their shoulders, took the lead; a dense but disorderly throng of men and women followed, marching between thin, broken lines of soldiers; next came the *telegas* (waggons) with the old, the sick and the small children; then a rearguard of half a dozen Cossacks; and finally four or five wagons piled high with gray bags. The last sounds I heard were the jingling of chains, and the shouts of the Cossacks to the children to keep within the lines.'

The next day Kennan witnessed the embarkation of 700 exiles on convict barges taking them to Tomsk—a voyage that lasted at least seven days. Here the overcrowding was as shocking as in the Tiumen prison.[2] Kennan was struck by the diversity of types

[2] Robert Ker Porter visited a prison in Moscow, where conditions were as horrible as in Siberia. Here the prisoners 'dragged on a dying life, or rather a tortured one; miserable fare, miserable sleep, and an atmosphere fraught with every calamity which foulness can inflict'. But this was in 1806 and at that date prisons in England were not exactly convalescent homes, as we know from John Howard. The interesting discovery Ker Porter made on his visit was of seven men in a less gloomy room. They were officers guilty of forgery, and soon to be transported for life to the mines of Siberia.
Here Ker Porter draws a comparison between the Russian and English penal systems, much to our disadvantage. Here, he says, we hang a man not only for treason, murder and forgery but for stealing half-a-crown. A short while ago a woman, left destitute with two children because her husband had been pressed into the Navy, had stolen some coarse linen from a shop. She was hanged at Tyburn, to the joy of shopkeepers, though there was a baby still sucking at her breast. Being a practical fellow for an artist, Ker Porter considered death a wasteful punishment. These seven forgers working for the rest of their lives in the mines of Siberia would be doing something useful for the State, the government would benefit from their labour and at the same time their fate would be a salutary warning to other would-be-forgers. But, although he gave his cold approval to the condemnation of the seven poor Russians, Ker Porter did add what he called 'a few pleadings' for the miserable inmates of our own dungeons, stressing that the Mosaic law had not required death for theft but only restitution—this was all that God required. Although he approved Russia's abolition of capital punishment he did not fail to note that the condemnation of a man to two hundred lashes with the knout meant executing him in a particularly terrible way. Was it something sadistic in his nature that made him insist on witnessing this punishment and describing it in horrifying detail? (There are no statistics to show how often the Russians circumvented the Tsarina Elizabeth's humane law in this manner, but Tolstoy, in *Hadji Murad*, describes Nicholas I hypocritically praising the abolition of capital punishment in his enlightened country and condemning refractory students and heretics to what would be certain death after running the gauntlet of soldiers.)
See Robert Ker Porter, *Travelling Sketches in Russia and Sweden* (London, 1813).

among the prisoners, more than three-quarters of whom were wearing leg-fetters:

'There were fierce wild-looking mountaineers from Daghestan and Circassia, condemned to penal servitude for murders of blood revenge; there were Tartars from the lower Volga, Turks from the Crimea, whose scarlet fezzes contrasted strangely with their gray convict overcoats; crafty-looking Jews from Podolia, going into exile for smuggling; and finally common peasants in great numbers from all parts of Europe and Russia. The faces of the prisoners generally were not as hard, vicious and depraved as the faces of criminals in America. Many of them were pleasant and good-humoured.'

Frost made sketches of the different convict types. This caused them extreme amusement. They laughed and joked like schoolboys off for a picnic.

In Tiumen, Kennan bought a *tarantas* (a covered, four-wheeled carriage) and he and Frost started on their journey across Siberia to the mines of the Transbaikal. With their *podorozhnaya* (order for horses) they were able to hire, at a small price, either post-horses or 'free horses' all along the route. Whenever they stopped at an *étape* (halting station for convicts) or at an assembly place like Semipalatinsk, Omsk, or Tomsk, Kennan visited the chief officials and received permission to see all he wanted. Afterwards, when he lectured in America, he was always asked how this was possible and why he was never arrested. He admitted that he was fearing arrest the whole time. This had never happened, he supposed, because he had always presented himself to the highest authorities with his letter from the Minister of the Interior and received their permission.

We cannot accompany Kennan to all the stations of the cross which he visited on his self-imposed pilgrimage. At Omsk he found they had demolished the prison where Dostoievky had spent four years of penal servitude. (His *From the House of the Dead* had been translated into English in 1881 and to Kennan it was a bible.) The forwarding prison at Tomsk affected him even more actuely than the Tiumen prison, because the exiles, after so much more of their journey, were in a much worse condition. There were 3,000 in huts designed for 1,400. The sheds for family parties, packed to the ceiling with 'weary-eyed men, haggard women and wailing children' harrowed him most. Why should women and children guilty of nothing but devotion to husbands or fathers have to undergo such intolerable suffering? Why should so many babies have to die? It was little wonder that typhus epidemics broke out, In the hospital Kennan found young nurses with strong, intelligent faces, obviously medical students, banished for 'untrustworthiness.'

It was not the statistics that Kennan collected so conscientiously that affected Americans so deeply; it was his human stories. Before his investigations they had thought that the political prisoners sent to Siberia were all Nihilists who cared for neither God nor man and went about throwing bombs and plotting the overthrow of the State. They had believed that these wretches had been condemned in a court of justice to a deserved punishment. Kennan revealed to them that from the beginning of the exile system, hundreds of thousands had been sent to Siberia by what was called 'administrative process', that is, without trial, and often without reason given. That the Minister of the Interior or one of twenty different classes of Russian officials could, by the scrawl of a pen, condemn innocent people to the intolerable sufferings of banishment, blackened the name of Russia, for so long hailed as America's friend and ally. In the reigns of Nicholas I and of the 'liberal' Alexander II, thousands of men and women were exiled to Siberia, not only by order of the Tsar but also by order of mere officials, even of the elders of the village communes and private landowners. Was not every human being entitled to a trial, to know of what he was accused, to call witnesses in his defence? Kennan mentioned the case of two brothers exiled because of mistaken identity and of a woman exiled because she dared to write to Alexander III, telling him of the case and asking for redress. A doctor was banished for coaching two medical students exiled from St Petersburg to central Russia because of 'untrustworthiness'. He was sent to the Arctic regions of Siberia. His young wife, after the birth of their baby, tried to follow him. She left the baby with friends and started the 6,000 mile journey, joining a band of convicts as she could then travel at government expense. When she reached Irkutsk, she was still nearly 3,000 miles away from her husband. She 'had endured without complaint the jolting, the suffocating dust, the scorching heat and cold autumnal rains on the road, the bad food, the plank sleeping-benches, the vermin and the pestilential air of the *étapes*', but at Irkutsk, her health gave way. She discovered that she would have to travel for weeks, on dog or reindeer sledges, through the Arctic solitudes of north-east Asia. She died insane in the Irkutsk prison hospital. Kennan heard her story from exiles who had travelled with her, one of them a well-known member of a provincial *zemstvo*.

In the course of his travels Kennan met more than 500 political exiles, the first ones in Western Siberia, where they were living in comparative freedom. They were introduced to him by the official in charge, who told him that many of them were young men and women of high attainments. (One thinks of Lenin and Krupskaya translating the Webbs' *History of Trade Unionism* and doing a little quiet fishing in the rivers.) One of them was making anthropological researches among the Kirghiz. A woman impressed him because she told her experiences without bitterness or exaggeration. After a year's solitary confinement in Moscow, she had been banished to a dreary settlement in Siberia and only recently been brought to the comparative civilization of Semipalatinsk. They talked cheerfully of literature, art and American politics. In his country they would have been thought of as the mildest liberals.

In Tomsk, Kennan had long talks with Prince Alexander Kropotkin. He was not a revolutionary, like his famous brother Peter, but had been too outspoken in his criticisms of the corruption and spying in the government office where he worked. He was exiled, without trial, to a town on the Yenesei River in Eastern Siberia. (As a student he had been imprisoned for having a copy of Emerson's *Self Reliance* and refusing to say who had given it to him.) Here he had lived with his wife for four years, making botanical and geological collections and founding a museum. He was an accomplished astronomer but had not had the instruments necessary to carry on his researches. When he was transferred to Tomsk he had had more books, but was constantly harried by the police, who suspected him of communicating with his brother. (A year after this meeting with Kennan, Kropotkin, on the eve of his release and return to Russia, committed suicide.) The writer Felix Volkhovski was an exile with whom Kennan struck up a warm friendship. His health and been shattered by long imprisonment in the Fortress of Peter and Paul. He knew American history and literature and Kennan managed by secret means to correspond with him after he had left Russia, hearing in this way of the suicide of his wife and the death of his little daughter. The sequel to this friendship was sensational. In 1889 Volkhovski knocked at Kennan's door in Albany. Assuming the character of a retired army officer he had travelled 2,800 miles from Irkutsk to Vladivostok where he was hidden on a British coal steamer, and taken to Japan. From there, on another British ship, he sailed to Vancouver, the passengers paying his fare, so that he should not have to go steerage. This adventure is worth recording for escapes were extremely rare from Siberia.[4] Attempts were often made. Escapers were known as *brodyags*. Kennan talked to several *brodyags*, marching in fetters from Tomsk to Irkutsk. Some of them had escaped half a dozen times from the mines. They had always been captured or had given themselves up from hunger and despair. 'I know *brodyags*', the captain told Kennan, 'who have been over this road sixteen times in leg-fetters. God only knows how they live through it.' When they broke from the marching line, they were of course shot at by the guards but these were not always good marksmen.

About *brodyags*, such a feature of the Siberian landscape, Kennan heard many tales when he reached the gold mines of Kara. Here half the hard-labour convicts lived in 'free commands' outside the prison walls.

'Every year when the weather becomes warm, the free command begins to over-flow into the forests; and for two or three months a narrow but almost continuous stream of escaping convicts runs from the Kara penal settlements in the direction of Lake Baikal. The signal for this annual movement is given by the cuckoo. The cry of the bird is taken as evidence that an escaped convict can once more live in the forests, and to run away, in convict slang, it to go to General Kukushka for orders. In Siberia, as a whole, the number of runaway exiles and convicts who take the field in response to the summons of this popular officer exceeds 30,000. Most of the Kara convicts who "go to General Kukushka for orders" in the early summer come back to the mines under new names and in leg-fetters next winter; but they have had their outing, and have breathed for three whole months the fresh, free air of the woods, the mountains and the steppes. . . . They do not expect to escape altogether; they knew that they must live for months the lives of hunted fugitives, subsisting upon berries and roots, sleeping on the cold and often water-soaked ground and facing death at almost every step. But, in spite of all this, they cannot hear in early summer the first soft notes of the cuckoo without feeling a passionate longing for the adventures and excitements that attend the life of a *brodyag*.

A prison official told Kennan of a convict servant who begged

[4] Nabokov in a spirited defence of the old régime of Russia asserts that escapes were easy and cites 'St Leo Trotsky, pulled merrily through the snow by reindeers, bringing like a new Santa Klaus, his gifts to the West'. See his autobiography, *Speak Memory*.

him to lock him up in the summer for, he said: 'I am old and grey-headed now, I can't stand life in the woods as I could once, but if I hear General Kukushka (cuckoo) calling me, I must go.'

Many prison officials winked at escapes because they could continue to draw the rations and clothes of the runaways and sell them on the black market, but to the peaceable burghers of Siberia the *brodyags* were a great menace. In order to survive they had perforce to steal and in Siberia there were many times the number of crimes of violence recorded in European Russia. In fact, the strong protests against the whole exile system that came out of Siberia was less out of sympathy for the politicals than out of outrage that their country was a dumping ground for common criminals, half of whom were not tidily locked up in prisons but living in colonies in remote areas or in free commands from which it was not hard to escape, even though only temporarily.

Incidentally, the oddest exile Kennan met in Siberia, also the oldest, was not a *brodyag* nor a convict—it was the bell of Uglich, banished to Tobolsk, in 1593, by order of Boris Goudunov for having rung the signal for insurrection at the time of the murder of the Tsarevitch Dimitri. The bell had been consecrated and purged of its sins. Uglich was demanding it back, saying that it had been punished enough by three centuries of exile, but Tobolsk would not let it go.

Kennan discovered something profoundly illustrative of Russian psychology: the convicts organized themselves into secret unions called *artels*, and as in their village *mirs*, they chose their own headman or *starosta*, made their own rules, had their own standards of honour and their own penal code. The *artel* bribed executioners to flog lightly, soldiers to smuggle vodka, tobacco and playing cards. They levied taxes, distributed privileges, and the punishment for disloyalty was always death.

To Kennan the most physically exhausting part of his journey was from Tomsk to the Transbaikal, through Eastern Siberia. The autumn had begun and continual rain had turned the roads into seas of mud.

'The jolting of our heavy *tarantas* through deep ruts gave us violent headaches and prevented sleep; . . . we suffered from cold and were tormented by predatory insects from the road-side prisons and *étapes*! To be forced to live for weeks at a time in clothing infested with fleas, lice or bedbugs gave me a humiliating sense of physical defilement.'

But even greater than the physical exhaustion was the nervous strain. Kennan was a warm-hearted, imaginative man. Day after day he witnessed suffering that he thought unparalleled in the civilized world and he could do nothing to alleviate it. In the second volume of his book Kennan gives a picturesque sketch of Catherine Breshkovsky, the 'Grandmother of the Russian Revolution'. An aristocrat who spoke French, German and English fluently and was a gifted musician, she had twice served out penal terms in the mines of Kara.

'The unshaken courage with which this unfortunate woman contemplated her dreary future and the faith that she manifested in the ultimate triumph of liberty in her native country, were as touching as they were heroic. Almost the last words which she said to me were: "Mr Kennan, we may die in exile, and our children may die in exile, and our children's children may die in exile, but something will come of it at last.". . . . I cannot recall her last words to me without feeling conscious that all my standards of courage, of fortitude, and of heroic self-sacrifice have been raised for all time, and raised by the hand of a woman. Interviews with such political exiles—and I met many in the Transbaikal—were to me a more bracing tonic than medicine.'

When Kennan reached Transbaikal, his health broke down and he made haste to return to his country. He was, in any case, anxious to tell his story. With the optimism characteristic of good Americans, he hoped that his revelations might induce the Tsar to reform the whole system. A petition was drawn up in Philadelphia, after one of Kennan's lectures, asking Alexander III to do something about his prisons. It cited the Civil War friendship when his father had sent his fleet to New York; it received thousands of signatures. Alexander turned a blind eye. Copies of the *Century Magazine* that reached Russia were severely censored, whole pages being blacked out. Yet many read it in secret and Kennan's admirers credited him with inflaming the Russian masses against their master and thus inciting them to revolt in 1917.

Kennan was no revolutionary, nor was he a prophet. He had some inkling of the hidden riches of Siberia, but nothing told him that a city of scientists dedicated to explore them would sprout up there sixty years after he had seen its exiles trudging through the mud nor that, in the 1960s, the Albert Hall in London would be listening to a choir of young men and maidens from Omsk,

Dostoievsky's 'House of the Dead', and watching their mild yet disciplined dancing, triumphant with health and high spirits.

Kennan had not done what he had set out to do. He had sympathized with the Russian government's treatment of what he thought of as Nihilists; he had gone to Siberia to vindicate it. An honest man, when he saw what the truth was he told it. Notwithstanding all Russian denials, America and England now knew for certain what Tsarist tyranny was and what Siberia stood for.

GEORGE HUME

Thirty-five Years in Russia

London 1914

EORGE HUME's Scots grandfather moved to the south of England to take up a partnership in a brewery. His son, also a brewer, settled in Feltham in Middlesex and brought up his children with Spartan discipline. George was apprenticed at eighteen to a firm in Ipswich 'to learn the whole art and mystery of mechanical engineering'. He finished his apprenticeship with flying colours and started his career as engineer in the navy installing engines in several of our men-of-war. The last vessel on which he was engaged was the *Mithridates*, ordered for the Russian Navy, and it was in this ship that he sailed to Russia, arriving there in 1857, a year after the end of the Crimea War. He had made several voyages on Russian ships, even taking ship-loads of pilgrims: Christians bound for Palestine and Moslems on their way to Mecca. It was a rough and arduous life. The career of ship's engineer did not satisfy him. He was an enterprising man. Somehow the idea came to him that he might be the first man to introduce the reaping machine to the steppes of Russia. There was no reason for him to doubt of success. He was expert in his trade and was, besides, fluent in German and French which he had learned in Ipswich, and was quickly picking up Russian.

George Hume's account of his thirty-five years in Russia is exceptionally interesting. He was shrewd, optimistic, energetic, determined to overcome all obstacles. He was also kindly, exuberant, responsive to what was best in the warm-hearted, hospitable though backward people with whom and for whom he was working. Moreover, he came to Russia at what he believed to be a turning-point in its history. The death of the tyrannical, obscurantist Nicholas I (in 1855), the ascension to the throne of the more liberal Alexander II, gave him hopes (which in the end proved exaggerated) that Russia had started on the path which would lead to a Western kind of parliamentary democracy. Certainly she had started on a path of great ferment and change.

What Hume writes about the Crimean War strikes an odd note.

'The Crimean War is now generally considered to have been a great mistake on the part of England. To Russia, however, it was a great boon; it had certainly left her temporarily humiliated, but her unexpectedly gallant defence had gained for her the respect and sympathy, not only of late enemies but of all civilised communities. This paved the way for the introduction of those great reforms which have raised her in so short a time from a state of semi-barbarism to a co-equal voice with the other Great Powers in the destinies of Europe. It was the boom of the allies' cannon that aroused her from her long sleep of apathetic indolence and made possible the great reforms of Alexander the Liberator.'

Good Anglo-Saxon Protestant that he was, it was fortunate that Hume's first attempts to introduce his reaping and threshing machines were made in the German Colonies to the north of the Crimea, bordering the Sea of Azov. These were largely inhabited by the Mennonites we have already met with Haxthausen.

'The villages of this section of the colonies embraced the whole district from Berdiansk to the River Malotchnaya. They are models of arrangement and construction, each farm being provided with barn and stables, the dwelling-houses all substantially built, tiled with Dutch tiles and white-washed. Another pleasant feature is the large number of storks, whose nests are perched on the ridges of the houses.'

Hume received ungrudging hospitality from these German villages and was invited to all their social gatherings. When in 1861 the first trial of one of his machines was carried out,

'the Russian peasants following it were simply astounded at seeing the corn come rolling off in a long continuous swathe, ready for the binder. At last they took off their caps and crossed themselves, praying devoutly that they might not have been present at some invention of the devil. On another occasion, when our steam thresher was at work, a deputation came begging our man in charge to call out the unclean spirit that was at work.'

Hume found that the Mennonites were much esteemed for their hard work and honesty. Like Haxthausen he was astounded that they had found asylum, liberty of worship and the rights of citizens in the most tyrannical of countries. Unfortunately their Russian converts did not fare so well. At harvest time there was a great immigration of labourers from the interior and many of these attended the evening meditations of the Mennonites, called *Gebetstunden* (Prayer Hours). They became missionaries of the new doctrines when they returned to their villages and were known from the name of their meeting as Stundists. As they tried to live according to the Gospels they refused the rites of the Church and the priests losing their fees for marriage, christenings and funerals, got the authorities to take action. There was much persecution.

Hume, writing his book thirty-five years later, tells the subsequent history of the Mennonites. When, in 1870, Russia introduced universal military conscription, vast numbers of Mennonites emigrated to Canada, the USA and Holland. At length the Tsar, regretting the loss of such good farmers, sent General Totleben (the hero of Sevastopol) to propose a compromise. Mennonites were offered alternative service in the Red Cross or in the Forestry Department and many stayed.

As the corn fields were often fifteen or twenty miles from the villages, Hume kept his threshing machines in them and bivouacked on the steppes during the time with the peasants, sharing their lives for seven weeks.

'Our machines required, for carting and working, about seventy men, and being always with the men I learned to know them thoroughly and respect them. I found many of them endowed with a very fair amount of common sense, who, had they been educated, would have made for themselves careers in life. Many of the proprietors of villages had selected from among their serfs youths to be educated as doctors or trained in first aid. To me the peasantry as a class became very attractive. Many of them had trudged on foot some two or three hundred miles, returning in October with the money they had earned. Some of their wives accompanied them to do the cooking. By nature these uneducated men are, with very few exceptions, polite yet not subservient. They are hospitable to a degree unknown to any workmen in our own land.'

The Crimean district where Hume was living was in Little Russia amongst the Ukrainians, while the harvesters came from Great Russia. He was amused at the violent language they hurled at each other. Although often drunk, he found them, as so many foreigners did, good-natured and jolly in their cups, and passers-by, even the police, very tolerant of them.

In 1861 Alexander II issued the ukase emancipating the serfs. Hume had made friends with a certain Popov, the son of General Popov, a Crimean hero, from whom he he had inherited 7,000 serfs.

> 'It was from the balcony of M. Popov's house', he writes 'that I heard him read out to his 7,000 serfs, drawn up before his house, according to their village, the Emperor's ukase granting them their freedom. There they stood in serried ranks, as fine a body of men as you might wish to see. Standing without a smile, they listened with reverence to their Emperor's message. Yet on the close of the ceremony there was no responsive cheer. It was evident from their silence that they felt keen disappointment at no mention having been made that, together with their freedom, the whole land of the proprietors was to become their property.'

They were convinced that the Tsar's orders had not been fulfilled.

In Hume's district each male serf received about eight acres of land, for which he had to pay rent. There were many cases where the peasant was materially worse off than when he had been a serf.

Living as he did amongst the peasants, farming with them the black earth of southern Russia, Hume became intimately aware of the precariousness of their lives. Drought is the greatest menace. One year out of three, he writes, some parts of Russia are in a state of semi-starvation. In 1862 lack of snow and spring rain meant complete failure of the harvest in his district.

> 'When one considers that in a vast empire like Russia 90 per cent of its population are dependent for their living on the soil and that throughout a whole year all their hopes, all their capital and energies are centred on an abundant yield, it is a pathetic thought that a single hailstorm or even the winds of heaven may destroy in one short hour the labours of a whole year.'

Hume enumerates the other menaces to their crops which the peasants face: the Hungarian beetle which appeared in the 1860s and devoured the wheat; the *souslik*, a kind of rat, which devastated large tracts of land; and, occasionally, the locust. Five times Hume was caught in the middle of a locust storm. In Berdiansk the sky was darkened by their passage, and the country devastated thirty miles distant from that town. On the fifth occasion he was travelling in a train to Baku. 'The sky became darkened, the windows rattled and the wheels of the train became clogged and it was brought to a standstill.'

Good Scotsman that he was, Hume was appalled by the wastage of land. The steppe beyond the Sea of Azov to the east was part of the vast, black earth region where 'no pebble the size of a thumb-nail is to be found' which yet, for lack of water, remained in his day a vast semi-desert where the nomads from Asia, Kalmucks, Kirghiz, Bashkirs and Tartars herded their flocks. But already geologists had discovered an underground water-supply and a Scottish firm had made an oasis by boring an artesian well. If the government were to take the initiative and irrigate these steppes, the region would become fertile. Hume was indignant that 'the negligence of man should allow the winter snows and spring rains to run to waste, carrying with them large deposits of the rich black earth, which can never be replaced' and clog the rivers. Yet Hume, unlike most of our travellers, enjoyed riding or driving over these lonely steppes, gazing in a pleasant wonder at their vast skies, their burning sunsets and their strange mirages.

He admired the grass-root democracy of the *mir* or village commune. Every male adult had voting power and freely expressed his opinion at their meetings. The flaw was that most of them were illiterate and so under the domination of the clerk of the commune who, having some education, could impose on the rest. In fact the greatest need of Russia was for schools. In cases Hume knew of, the *zemstvos* (a sort of county council which Alexander II had introduced) had opened schools, but the government, fearing the growth of subversive ideas if the poor were educated, had forbidden them. Hume as a stout bourgeois, was alarmed by the growth of Nihilism, but did not think that this was the right way to combat it. He felt that lack of schooling was at the root of many of Russia's troubles. The *tchinovniks* were corrupt and oppressive but they were often ignorant and shockingly underpaid. Students oppressed by the authorities were in a 'chronic state of passionate anger'.

Hume, in 1867, moved to Kharkov, where he continued his business enterprises. Trial by jury had just been introduced by the liberal Tsar, and in this town Hume witnessed a trial of which his account reads like a Chekhov story. A poor young *tchinovnik* had been dismissed from a government office for 'calling out an offensive remark at a theatre'. Unable to get work even as a coachman or doorman, because he was so shabbily dressed, he had stolen some clothes from his landlord. The judge told the jury that they must decide whether the accused had only taken the clothes or if he also forced entry. The jury returned a verdict of guilty of theft but as for 'forcible entry' they said: 'God only knows, we don't.' The judge told them that speaking in this way they were guilty of contempt of court and might incur a year's imprisonment. They were sent back, duly humbled, and returned a verdict of 'not guilty of forcible entry' to the annoyance of the judge. The prisoner was sentenced to lose his civil rights and nobility.

Hume tells us of the violent repercussions in Kharkov of the Russo-Turkish war of 1877–8. This brought all the export–import business of his firm to a stop for two years. The war was a popular one. The Turks were massacring their Christian subjects in Bulgaria and the cry went up, 'They are murdering our brethren'. A vast army poured over the Danube and besieged the Turks in Plevna.

> 'All private transport by rail was prohibited, the Government having attached every railway van in the south for the transport of the army and stores to the seat of war. Kharkov being a great strategic point for both Europe and Asia could not give the private merchant any transport facilities for over two years.'

Hume decided to accept corn from his customers instead of money. The price of corn was very low as it could not be exported, so that this was advantageous except for the great difficulty of storing it and preventing loss by rats, theft and damp. 'We were landed with thousands of bushels of wheat on uncovered wayside railway stations, open to the air and subject to the inclemency of the seasons.' But the peasants and landlords were glad to pay in kind (money was scarce) for the steam reapers and threshers, which by this time had become very popular.

> 'Day and night [he writes] the trains rushed on bearing relays of men and stores. These on their return journey brought the thousands of sick and wounded from the battle-fields of Bulgaria and later the thousands of the gallant defenders of Plevna, the real heroes of the war. Of these Turkish prisoners there were interned in Kharkov about ten thousand men . . . their fine physique being in sharp contrast to that of their Russian escort.'

The Russians admired the bravery of their enemies and on the whole treated them kindly. Hume was, in general, deeply impressed by the generosity and warm-heartedness of the Russian peasants and their great tolerance. He believed that their exceptional hatred of the Jews was due to economic and not religious reasons.

'The Jew, compelled to live by his wits, and debarred by repressive measures from the employment of his undoubted talents for the benefit of the State, preys upon the community. He enriches himself by impoverishing the people, and more especially the peasant'.

Hume explains that the peasant who could only count on one good harvest out of three, was often forced to borrow money and even mortgage his land to the Jew. In the Jew he saw all the iniquities and cruelties of capitalist exploitation. As for religion the muzhik was singularly tolerant.

'He uncovers his head and crosses himself before the funeral procession of a Jew or Christian with the same devout reverence, and not even when incited by the Holy Synod has he risen against the ever-recurring dissenting forms of worship.'

Hume found a large variety of these dissenters in Vladikavkaz, formerly a place of banishment for all sects in opposition to the Orthodox Church. Here he found Molokani; Sabbatarians who belong to the Orthodox Church but keep Saturday instead of Sunday as their holy day; Jews practising polygamy and the seclusion of their women; Chlisti, or self-torturers; and Doukhobors.

Hume, though shocked by the repressive measures of Alexander III after the assassination of his predecessor, was even more shocked by the growth of Nihilism. He did not, like Custine in 1839, believe that revolution was inevitable or at least highly probable. He was distressed by the sufferings of the Poles. After the abortive revolution of 1863

'fifty thousand of the youth of their nation were hurried off in chain gangs to Siberia. I can yet vividly recall the long line of prisoners, fettered from waist to ankles with connecting chains and joined up into a gang by one long chain passing down the line; I can feel once more the indignation aroused at seeing the main body as they clanged their weary march ten versts daily to the northern Siberian desolation. Still more do I remember the peasants' carts, laden with delicately-nurtured women, the whole guarded by brutal soldiery. The almost daily passage of these chain gangs worked so much on my wife's feelings that her health suffered. It seems quite certain that the rule by autocracy has been a failure.'

Hume remained an optimist. It was so self-evident to him that England was the best country in the world, with the best government and constitution, that he never troubles to say it. (The only criticism he makes of his country is that it is always losing excellent markets because of its slowness in fulfilling orders. 'Owing to the lack of adaptability of our business men we have long been out-rivalled by Germany.' German salesmen visited him weekly—English never.) He assumes that other countries will copy ours and that Russia would gradually develop a sound, constitutional democratic government, avoiding both reaction and revolution. Russia had so many different nationalities, so many different climates and customs, he observed, that centralization was an anachronism. It should become a United States of Russia, on the analogy of America. For his own part he, felt he had done something for this country he loved by making two blades of grass grow where one had grown before.

LIST OF TSARS AND TSARINAS IN THE
PERIOD 1553–1900

Ivan IV (the Terrible) 1533–84.
Feodor 1584–98
Boris Goudunov 1598–1605
Time of Troubles (the two False Dimitris) 1605–13
Michael (the first Romanov) 1613–45
Alexis 1645–76
Feodor II 1676–82
Ivan V and Peter I, joint rulers 1682–89
Peter I (the Great) 1689–1725
Catherine I 1725–27
Peter II 1727–30
Anne 1730–40
Ivan VI 1740–41
Elizabeth 1741–61
Peter III 1761–62
Catherine II (the Great) 1762–96
Paul 1796–1801
Alexander I 1801–25
Nicholas I 1825–55
Alexander II 1855–81
Alexander III 1881–94
Nicholas II 1894–1917

GENERAL BIBLIOGRAPHY

BABEY, Anne. *Americans in Russia 1776–1917*, New York, 1938.
BAILEY, T. A. *America Faces Russia*, Cornell University Press, 1950.
BLANCH, Lesley. *Sabres of Paradise*, London, 1960.
BREWSTER, Dorothy. *East West Passage*, London, 1954.
COX, E. G. *A Reference Guide to the Literature of Travel*, Seattle, 1949.
CRANKSHAW, E. *Russia and Britain*, London, 1944.
KONOVALOV, S. *Oxford and Russia. An Inaugural Lecture*, Oxford, 1947.
KONOVALOV, S. *Oxford Slavonic Papers*, Vol. I, Oxford, 1950.
KONOVALOV, S. *Oxford Slavonic Papers*, Vol. X, Oxford, 1962.
LASERSON, M. M. *American Impact on Russia*, New York, 1950.
PUTNAM, P. *Seven Britons in Imperial Russia, 1698–1812*, Princeton University Press, 1952.
VERNADSKY, G. *Kievan Russia*, Oxford, 1948.

Part I

HAKLUYT, Richard. *The principal navigations, voiages and discoveries of the English nation*. 1st edition, London, 1589. Enlarged to 3 vols., 1598–1600. Modernized text, Everyman Library, London, 1907–9. (Hakluyt contains Chancellor, Jenkinson, Burrough and some Fletcher and Horsey.)
FLETCHER, Giles. *The English Works of Giles Fletcher the Elder* (ed. L. A. Berry), Wisconsin, 1964.
FLETCHER, Giles. *Of the Russe Commonwealth* (ed. R. Pipes and J. V. A. Fine), Harvard, 1966. (This edition includes documents such as the protest of the Muscovy Company.)
HERBERSTEIN, Sigismund von. *Rerum Muscoviticarum Commentarii*, 3 vols, Vienna, 1549.
HERBERSTEIN, Sigismund von. *Notes upon Russia* (trans R. A. Major), Hakluyt Soc. London, 1851.
HORSEY, Jerome. In Samuel Purchas: *Purchas his Pilgrimage*, 4th edition, London, 1626; Modern edition, *Hakluytus Posthumus or Purchas his Pilgrimes*, 20 vols, Glasgow, 1905–17.

Part II

COLLINS, Samuel. *The Present State of Russia in a Letter to a Friend in London*, London, 1671.
GORDON, Patrick, *Passages from the Diary of General Patrick Gordon of Auchleuchries*, (Spalding Club), Aberdeen, 1859.
MIÈGE, Guy. *A Relation of Three Embassies . . . in 1663 and 1664*, London, 1669.

OLEARIUS, Adam. *Voyages and Travels of the Ambassadors from the Duke of Holstein to the Great Duke of Muscovy, etc.* (trans. J. Davies, London, 1662. Modern Edition, *Travels of Olearius in Seventeenth Century Russia* (trans. S. H. Baron), Stanford University Press, 1967.

PAUL OF ALEPPO. *The Travels of Macarius* (ed. L. Ridding), London, 1936.

STRUYS, Jean. *Voyagien door Moscovien, etc.* (*Voyages in Muscovy*), Dutch edition, Amsterdam, 1677; French edition, Amsterdam, 1718.

Part III

CASANOVA, Jacques. *Histoire de ma vie*, Wiesabden, 1960–62.

CHAPPE D'AUTEROCHE, L'Abbé. *A Journey into Siberia* (trans. from French) London, 1770.

COOK, John. *Voyages and Travels through the Russian Empire, Tartary, etc.*, 2 vols, Edinburgh, 1770.

COX, William. *Travels into Poland, Russia and Sweden*, London, 1792.

HANWAY, Jonas. *Travels from England through Russia into Persia*, London, 1753.

HELBIG, G. A. W. *Russische Günstlinge*, Tübingen, 1809.

KORB, J. G. *Diary of an Austrian Secretary of Legation at the Court of Peter* (trans. from Latin by Count MacDonnel, 2 vols), London, 1863.

MACARTNEY, George. *An Account of Russia in 1767*, London, 1768. also in BARROW, John: *Some Account of the Public Life of the Earl of Macartney*, Vol. II, London, 1807.

MASSON, C. F. P. *Mémoires Secrets sur la Russie*, 2 vols, Paris, 1800, and Paris, 1804.

PERRY, John. *The State of Russia under the Present Tsar*, London, 1716.

RICHARDSON, William. *Anecdotes of the Russian Empire*, London, 1784.

DE SÉGUR, Comte. *Mémoires*, Paris, 1827.

SWINTON, A. *Travels into Norway, Denmark and Russia in 1788, 1789, 1790, and 1791*, London, 1792.

VIGOR, Mrs. *Letters from a Lady in Russia*, London, 1775.

Part IV

ADAMS, John Quincy. *Memoirs* (ed. C. F. Adams), 12 vols., Philadelphia, 1874–77, Vol. II.

ATKINSON, J. A. and WALKER, J. *A Picturesque Representation of the Manners, Customs and Amusements of the Russians*, London, 1803–04.

CARR, John. *A Northern Summer or Travels round the Baltic*, London, 1805.

CLARKE, E. D. *Travels in Various Countries of Europe and Africa*, London, 1811, Vol. I.

JAMES, J. T. *Journal of a Tour in Russia*, London, 1816.

JOHNSTONE, R. *Travels through Part of the Russian Empire*, London, 1815.

PORTER, R. Ker. *Travelling Sketches in Russia and Sweden*, London, 1813.

KLAPROTH, Jules. *Voyage au Mont Caucase et en Géorgie*, 2 vols., Paris, 1833.

LYALL, Robert. *The Character of the Russians and a Detailed History of Moscow*, London, 1825.

DE MAISTRE, Joseph. *Les Soirées de St. Petersburg* (ed. de Saint-Victor.) Paris, 1888.

DE MAISTRE, Xavier. *Oeuvres*, 3 vols. Paris, 1877.

DE STAËL, Madame. *Dix Anneés d'Exil*, Paris, 1821.

WHEELER, Daniel, *Memoirs*, London, 1842.

WILMOT, Martha and Catherine. *Russian Journals* (ed. Marchioness of Londonderry and H. M. Hyde), London, 1934.

WILSON, Robert. *Private Diary of Travels in the Campaigns of 1812–14*, London, 1860. Also ed. A Brett-James, London, 1964

Part V

BRANDES, Georg. *Impressions of Russia*, Copenhagen, 1888, English Version, London, 1889.

BREMNER, Robert. *Excursions in the Interior of Russia*, London, 1839.

CURZON, G. N. *Russia in Central Asia in 1889, etc.*, London, 1889.

CUSTINE, Marquis de. *La Russia en 1839*, Paris, 1843.

DUMAS, Alexandre. *Impressions de Voyage. Le Caucase*, Paris, 1859; reprinted, Paris, 1900.

GAUTIER, Théophile. *Voyage en Russie*, Paris, 1866.

HAPGOOD, Isabel. *Russian Rambles*, London, and Cambridge (U.S.A.), 1895.

HAXTHAUSEN, Augustus von. *The Russian Empire, its People, Institutions and Resources*, 3 vols., Hanover, 1847–52.

HOMMAIRE DE HELL, Adèle et Xavier, *Travels in the Steppes of the Caspian Sea, the Crimea, Caucasus, etc.*, 3 vols, Paris, 1844.

HUME, George. *Thirty-five Years in Russia*, London, 1914.

KENNAN, George, *Siberia and the Exile System*, London, 1891.

KOHL, J. G. *Russia*, London, 1842.

LABENSKY, F. K. *A Russian Reply to the Marquis de Custine* (trans. from French and ed. by H. J. Bradfield, London), 1844.

MORLEY, Henry. *Sketches of Russian Life*, London, 1866.

NOBLE, Edward. *The Russian Revolt*, London, 1866.

OLIPHANT, Laurence. *The Russian Shores of the Black Sea*, London, 1854.

SALA, G. A. *Journey due North*, London, 1858.

SCOTT, C. H. *The Baltic, the Black Sea and the Crimea*, London, 1854.

[SMITH, M. A. P.] *Six Year's Travels in Russia*, London, 1859.

TISSOT, Victor. *Russians and Germans*, Paris, 1881; English translation, London, 1882.

TISSOT, Victor. *Russians and the Russians*, Paris, 1884.

VALERA, Juan. *Obras Completas*, 2nd edition, Madrid, 1942, Vol. I.

WILBRAHAM, R. *Travels in the Transcaucasian Provinces of Russia*, London, 1839.

GENERAL INDEX

INDEX OF PERSONS